BEYOND
BLUFFS

ALSO BY JAMES A. MCKENNA

Beyond Tells: Power Poker Psychology

BEYOND BLUFFS

MASTER THE MYSTERIES OF POKER

JAMES A. MCKENNA, PH.D.

LYLE STUART
Kensington Publishing Corp.
www.kensingtonbooks.com

LYLE STUART BOOKS are published by

Kensington Publishing Corp.
850 Third Avenue
New York, NY 10022

All Kensington titles, imprints, and distributed lines are available at special quantity discounts for bulk purchases for sales promotions, premiums, fund-raising, educational, or institutional use. Special book excerpts or customized printings can also be created to fit specific needs. For details, write or phone the office of the Kensington special sales manager: Kensington Publishing Corp., 850 Third Avenue, New York, NY 10022, attn: Special Sales Department; phone 1-800-221-2647

Lyle Stuart is a trademark of Kensington Publishing Corp.

First printing: October 2006

10 9 8 7 6 5 4 3 2 1

Printed in the United States of America

ISBN 0-8184-0709-3

To Jan

Who for over forty years continues being

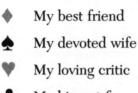

♦   My best friend

♠   My devoted wife

♥   My loving critic

♣   My biggest fan

6. The Mysteries of Poker   124

7. Bluffs That Tell on Themselves   147

CONTENTS

Epilogue   261

Appendices

FOREWORD: POKER AS A MYSTERY

SOME SKILLS THAT poker players develop are obvious. This book will discuss those and will go further into the mysterious skills that some players have and others are lacking. Many poker players will say that they would rather be lucky than good. However, the professionals know that luck is short term and in the long run, poker skills will win. In the long haul, a player must have the discipline to play, fold, and bluff—and at the right times. Some of these skills come from years of experience. Others come from abilities to observe things on a deeper and more mysterious level. This book explores such mysteries as knowing how and when a player is bluffing and the most effective bluffs that fit the person being bluffed.

Ordinary skills on the top of the list include the skills of *patience* and the ability to handle *boredom*. The willingness to wait for the right cards, the right position, and the right odds to come around must be combined with the ability to handle boredom—not an easy task for the many players who are there in search of excitement. Learning to do other things while you are waiting for good cards will help reduce boredom and enhance your game. This book will teach you how to look for clues, how to listen for those clues, and how to track behaviors when a person is bluffing or telling the truth.

Extraordinary skills come to the player who also has advanced people skills. Without people skills, even the most informed player will be wanting. Previously, with my book *Beyond Tells,*° I introduced for the first time a unique way of integrating personality types with reading tells. This book is designed to not only continue to enhance your people skills, but to deepen your awareness of people perceptions that you didn't know you were capable of learning. In addition to the integra-

° Citadel Press, New York: 2005.

tion of personality types, this book will integrate *frames of references.* Knowing how players think and make sense of the world (cards and other players) around them are extraordinary skills that come with advanced people skills.

Patience is a realistic attitude, one in which you expect to win only one or two pots every hour. It means sitting through the garbage hands and not playing out of boredom. Patience is also knowing when to bluff and having the fortitude not to telegraph your hand by betting a good hand too soon. However, a poker player needs a more advanced skill to know when to stop being patient and to act on opportunities to bluff.

Advanced skills require creative contempt for ordinary poker bluffs. I met a successful self-taught artist when I worked as a psychotherapist. He had an expression that I've never forgotten. He said, "Creativity comes from my contempt." I was discussing his rebellious tendencies.

My response was "What?"

"Yeah, contempt is the mother of my creativity."

He explained that he looks at something and will have contempt for it as it is. Then, he will create something better. How does creative contempt fit into poker as a mystery? Most good players will play patiently and wait for high-odds cards to play. Some better players will have contempt for just playing cards that way and wait more for the right opportunity and the right person to bluff. They may have fairly high-odds cards (semi-bluffing) or they may have garbage. The difference is that good players have developed people skills and will play people as well as cards—if not better. We will develop the notion of creative bluffs used with players of all varieties.

A patient player sits back while other players knock each other out in tournaments. Being patient is playing the "waiting game." If you are there to socialize or to get more excitement in your life, patience will slow you down to be satisfied with occasional excitements. This is true of low-limit games. However, when playing pot-limit or no-limit games, excitement occurs more often. In these games it is possible to protect a good hand and not be beaten by someone who impatiently plays bad cards. In lower limit games, more players will tend to chase hands (regardless of odds) since the cost is not too high. Even the skill of patience varies when players are bluffing and when they have what they are representing. We will discuss this difference.

Playing without the patience needed to become a consistent winner is a way to trap one's self. Playing as if each hand is the first hand of the day will be a way to develop needed patience. It's a fact that the cards have no memory and are coming out in random ways. So, the odds of getting two playable cards and having an edge with position are events that seldom happen together. Good fortune is rare in poker. Bad fortune is the norm. Playing aggressively with garbage hands will work for a while; however, in the long run, it will result in misfortune. You will learn when, how, and against whom to bluff with garbage. It is my hope you will learn not to waste bluffs. This includes avoiding bluffing when you don't have to and bluffing more effectively in ways that fit your opponents.

Not playing cards that could trap you into chasing improbable odds is a skill to be patiently sought. It requires avoiding the temptation to play "No Fold 'em Hold 'em" when the game gets boring. Waiting can be replaced with thinking about what other players are doing and how the cards are coming out. Boredom is often the cause of drifting and day dreaming. There are ways to stay centered and to avoid "dreamland."

When you read a good mystery novel, it's not a mystery after you've discovered all the clues and tied together the information —both exposed and hidden. After you discover the clues to look for in poker, you, too, will unravel the mysteries of the game.

—James A. McKenna, Ph.D.
a.k.a. "Jimmy Mac"

ACKNOWLEDGMENTS

WITHOUT THE IDEAS, support, and inspiration of far too many to list, this project would still only be a great idea. When people receive public awards and start naming individuals to whom they are grateful, it never seems to fail that someone very important is forgotten. There are far too many people to thank for their support and encouragement than I can name or remember. I am, however, extremely grateful for the dozens of behind-the-scene assistants. Because of many, I believe together we have produced a lasting reference that defines the life and times of persons at their best and at their worst. Poker brings such extremes out in all of us. The use of deception needed to become a successful poker player has driven us into the realm of magic and advanced communications. For that I am grateful to the pioneers whose contributions to this work are documented throughout and in the Suggested Readings. Without such advances by mental health and communication experts this work could not have been realized. It's the first time that certain ideas have been applied to poker. It's not the first time they have been successfully applied in counseling and hypnotherapies.

During my research, the many players and their frank answers to my probing questions have made this work much more real and valuable. Thanks to those hundreds I have played with and those who answered my questions. Your contributions will be obvious when you read this book. I learned when playing tennis to always compete with better players than me if I wanted to improve my game. I especially want to thank the many better players whom I have studied and learned from. This gratitude includes those whom I've watched bluff and those whom I experimented on with varied bluffing styles. In this book I describe examples that I gathered in my research. I have taken great care to disguise real identities. Sometimes I even changed the sex and ages of people in my stories. Some of you made some money on my research as

I explored the world of bluffing in poker. Some veteran players also discovered that I too could improve. Still, I have remained a poker player trapped in a writer/psychologist's body.

I have been encouraged and motivated to write this book by my editor, Richard Ember. Thanks, Richard, for your patience and wisdom. Through your encouragement and guidance, I have found the book that was waiting in me to play in the big league. I also remain grateful to Stanley R. Sludikoff, publisher of *Poker Player Magazine*. I have been writing for his magazine for more than six years. That opportunity has also helped me to develop into the writer I am today.

Poker room supervisors, dealers, and seasoned poker players were most valuable in the authenticity of the final outcomes of this project. I have used some of their direction in my research. The gaming community has been extremely open and supportive. In particular, I want to express my great appreciation to Station Casino of St. Charles, Missouri, and Harrah's Casino in Maryland Heights, Missouri. The research involved several other casinos in Las Vegas, Reno, Illinois, and Missouri. Some of the photos were taken at Harrah's with the assistance of Vito Casucci, then the casino's poker room manager and one of my models. The Station Casino is where other pictures were taken and where most of my interviews took place. In particular, I want to thank Jack Taylor, director of corporate public relations for Station Casinos. Also, thanks to the late general manager/vice president of Ameristar Casino, St. Charles, Anthony Raymond and his staff.

I am indebted to many volunteers, especially my volunteer models. Each gave of their own time to attend training sessions and to demonstrate the many examples used in this book. Only one model was not acting. That was our dealer-model, David Schmoeller, who is one of the best-liked and efficient professional dealers at the now Ameristar Casino.

Finally, I received so much support from friends and family that I hope all of you will continue to be proud to have been so patient and giving. My daughter Emily and I took the pictures. She helped in many other ways to encourage me when I was tired. My oldest daughter, Terry Wilson, remains one of my biggest fans and I appreciate her encouragement with this work. My other gift from heaven is my wife, Jan. She has been my wife for forty years and knows when to hold me,

The Models

and when to leave me alone. Thanks, Jan, for both. Finally, as God is my co-partner and co-creator, I am forever grateful for the privileges He has extended to me. I pray that this new project does what He intended, whatever that may be.

Here is a list of the volunteer models and their real occupations:

Role Played	Name	Real Occupation
The Dealer	David Lavern Schmoeller	Poker dealer
"Hunch Player"	E. Estelle Schmoeller	Airport security
"High Roller"	Mathew Simpson	Police officer
"Party Hardy"	Marlene Steenberger	Casino security
"Loner"	John G. Baker	Financial advisor
"System Player"	Vito Casucci	Poker room manager

Role Played	Name	Real Occupation
"The Boss"	Lou Lewis	Stockbroker
"Winner"	Normalee S. Baker	Kindergarten teacher
"System Player" and "Party Hardy"	Patti Zimmer	Executive secretary
"Loner"	Robert Long	Computer specialist
"Hunch Player"	Randall L. Windsor	Computer specialist

INTRODUCTION

Use or Abuse of Knowledge

AS A PSYCHOTHERAPIST who has used knowledge about people to help them reach their goals, I have struggled with myself about sharing this knowledge in this type of book. To know how a person is thinking, how they make sense of the problems they are experiencing, and what keeps them stuck in problems and not solutions is knowledge that is a privilege to responsibly use.

It has always been my hope that my writing about poker and poker players would be used to help people to grow and be all that they are capable of being. My struggle has been that sharing this knowledge is also giving players powers to hurt people rather than help them. After all, counselors, psychologists, and other professionals are licensed. Professional mental health workers can be controlled. They can be sanctioned to responsibly and legally use their knowledge about people. Well, there's no such thing as a licensed poker player. So, my dilemma was whether I am sharing privileged information with people who will responsibly use it. Then it occurred to me that I was perhaps being a bit righteous and needed to use both sides of my brain. In fact, as a psychologist who loves to play poker, I have been using this knowledge for years—not just in my clinical practice but to improve my game of poker as well. Is that taking unfair advantage? Is it using knowledge or is it abusing knowledge?

Well, obviously I have resolved my dilemma since you are reading this book. Like anything in creation, the ability to gain knowledge is a God-given gift. What a person does with knowledge only becomes abusive if it is for the purpose of hurting others. The goal of winning at poker is not to hurt people. People can hurt themselves by playing and gambling when they can't afford to lose. The goal of poker players is to be challenged and to get better, to build skills, and to excel as in any other sport. There has been debate as to whether poker is or is not a sport. Maybe it's because people don't want sports to be associated with gambling. Maybe it's the fact that most sports are team oriented. I don't know for sure. All I am sure about is that playing poker is both a skill with numbers and probabilities as well as a skill with people. Poker is a way of communicating with total strangers and making new friends. The conversations of poker players are actions like checking or raising, and calling or folding hands. How a person uses his or her people skills can be for fun and profit or for selfish and evil outcomes. That does not mean that such knowledge is only for the privileged few who could go to college and get degrees in psychology. I hope you agree. Here are some trade secrets applied to the game of poker.

Prologue

As a verb, the dictionary[1] defines "bluff" as *"Confidence of action or speech put on to deceive or mislead others."* Seen as a noun, a bluff is defined as *"when a person lets others think he has more money than he does, that he knows more than he really does, or that he holds better playing cards than he really holds."* As an action, a bluff is *"a bet, especially a large bet, made on a weak hand, to fool players with better hands into believing that they will lose if they stay in the game."* Actually, bluffing involves much more than betting. It's checking, raising, and sometimes even folding (while showing your hole cards).

No discussion of bluffs would be complete without knowing more about the bluffer and the "bluffee." The wisest thing I ever heard about bluffing came from my friend,[2] Doug, who said that it is possible to bluff a player, but that it's next to impossible to bluff a fool. His exact words were, "You can buy one from a player but not from a fool." That's because players may put you on the hand you are misrepresenting. A fool will call because he doesn't know any better or he doesn't care.

The bottom line in bluffing, though, is to know when someone is misrepresenting and when they have the best hand.[3] As I tell you three stories, see if you can spot the bluffers from players who are misrepresenting and who are telling the truth.

---

1. Thatcher, V. and McQueen, A. *The New Webster Encyclopedia Dictionary of the English Language*. New York: Consolidated Book Publishers, 1952.

2. Doug Nitch is a floor supervisor in the poker room at Ameristar Casino, St. Charles. He also trains dealers.

3. Actually, bluffing when you have the best hand is self-defeating, as Mike Caro has observed in his *Poker Player* article on bluffing. See Suggested Readings.

Scene 1–San Diego Subdivision

A car pulls up in the driveway and John stumbles out of the car. With a weave and a few minor stumbles, he makes his was to the front porch. When he gets inside, his wife, Irene, is noticeably upset. She shouts, "You're late! Where have you been?" John slurs his words, glances over her right shoulder, and says, "Oh, I had a flat tire and had to change it. Sorry, I didn't think to call." Now was this a lie, a bluff, or just a drunk who got caught?

Scene 2–Casino Poker Lounge

There's a full table playing Texas Hold 'Em. John's drinking and says, "I'll check." When someone bets in a game of 20/40, John looks up, glances to his left, and raises while saying, "Well, I hate to do this, but we are playing poker!" After a few sighs, everyone folds except the original bettor. He says, "You'll have to show me more than a check/raise to buy this pot! I re-raise!" When he does this re-raise, he glances to his right and then looks John in the eyes. So, do they both have a hand or is one or both of them bluffing?

Scene 3–Downtown Chicago

A handsome young man gets off his motorcycle, wearing his boots and jeans. He goes into a restaurant-bar. He walks up to an attractive young lady and says, "Hi. My name is John and I'd like to buy you a drink."

"Well, I don't even know you," she replies.

For a split second, he glances to his left and says, "I'm new in town, but I moved here to open a new dental practice. I'm Dr. John B. Sheet."

"Well then," she answers as she looks away from him to his left, "isn't it a small world!? I just finished my bar exam and I'm looking for a place to hang my law-practice shingle."

After a few drinks, they leave together but never see each other again after that night. Were they both fibbing, just plain acting like someone they weren't, or what?

In these three stories, how do you know if people are being truthful? Do you just take things at face value and accept everything a person says or does as straightforward? Well, that attitude doesn't work well in life. Not only that, it will get you into deep trouble at a poker table. In fact, it's been said that you can't win in poker unless you know how to bluff. For that matter, one can't survive without also knowing how to read bluffs. It's one thing to believe everything you hear or read; however, it's quite another thing not to know the signs that a person is making up stories.

Here are some answers to see how well you read peoples' bluffs:

In *Scene 1,* everyone can tell that John didn't know how much his drinking was showing. So, he was hard to believe. Actually, though, he was telling the truth. He did have a flat tire and Irene believed him because she knew what to look for. After you finish this book, you will also know what to look for.

In *Scene 2,* it's a mixed bag of truth and lies. John was not bluffing. He set a trap with his check/raise. The original bettor is the bluffer. His re-raise was an attempt to come over John and force him to fold. John, even though he was drinking, didn't buy it. He knew what to look for.

Even though Dr. John B. Sheet in *Scene 3* doesn't look like a dentist and is a bit out of character, he was telling the truth. The attractive young lady was bluffing and pretending to be a lawyer. That's why they never saw each other again. The truth finally came out. It's just that Dr. John didn't know what to look for and got fooled. That also happens a lot in poker.

This book will teach you how to know what to look for, listen for, and get in touch with to tell the truth from a bluff. You will learn how to determine when someone is bluffing and how to not reveal it when you are bluffing. After all, when people read this book, more people will improve their bluffs—in life and in their poker games. Or, will they start telling the truth?

To Bluff or Not to Bluff

I've worked with compulsive liars who avoid the truth, even when they don't have to. In poker, misrepresenting your hand is part of the game. In fact, with the exception of very low-limit games, it's impossible to get ahead in a poker game and *not* bluff. It's knowing when to bluff, how to bluff, and against which players to bluff. Needless bluffing comes when you drive people out of the game whose hands were already worse than yours. That's where slow playing is a solid way to bluff players who don't have much and may keep calling. This technique is dubbed a "Call Station." You can fill up on their calls and chases when you slow-play the best hand. There are certain guidelines to when and when not to bluff. We will get to those later. It's also in knowing who to bluff that makes the difference between success and failure of a bluff.

There are times not to bluff and there are times when the only way you are going to win a particular hand is to bluff. If you bluff at the wrong time, however, against the wrong player, you will find yourself up the proverbial creek without a wild card. Also, the same bluff won't work on all players. Since it is generally thought better to bluff with a few players (as opposed to a multi-way pot), it's important that you read who you are trying to bluff. Second, different personality types will choose different ways to bluff. The playing styles of your opponents (described previously by this author)[1] will give you a head start on both knowing how a player is likely to bluff and how to disguise your own bluffs.

1. McKenna, J. *Beyond Tells*, pp. 137–42. We will review some of this later.

5

Common Bluffs

Most players agree on certain given ideas on bluffing. I mentioned earlier that it is not possible to bluff a "fool," whose play is so loose that he will call a barking dog off a porch. So, why even try? How often have you had a great hand and a loose player sucks out[2] on the river by making an inside straight?[3] Also, it's best to bluff very sparingly in low-limit games. Why? You will find more people willing to chase bad odds in low-limit games but not so in the higher limit games.[4] Incidentally, be sure that the player who appears to be loose really is. That could be his or her bluff.

This reminds me of a statement that I've often said in jest: "When I first started playing Hold 'Em I did a lot better when I didn't know how to play." I was staying with garbage and calling raises that would take miracles to win. Some of my early opponents can sadly remember those miracles that did come and how I sucked out on the river. I also recall how surprised I was when other players folded. As a matter of fact, I was bluffing when I bet and didn't know it. I'd bet on cards with poor odds of improving and more experienced players would fold, thinking I had more than I actually had. Of course, they got me more than I got them in the long run. So, I guess it's good that I finally learned how to play the game. Except, sometimes part of the game is acting like I don't know what I am doing. It was easier doing that when I really didn't know any better. Is that bluffing?

There's a saying I use that goes, "Good bluffers are hard to find." That means that a bluff is only as successful as to how much your opponent is surprised when you show your hand. Of course, if you succeeded in getting the better hand to lay down their hand, you are not likely to show it—unless, you are setting the table up for the next time you are not bluffing.

Some people will tell you that "You can't bluff a bluffer." Actually,

---

2. "Suck-out" is a common poker term that means a player stayed in longer against poor odds and got lucky to win the hand on the last (river) card.

3. Inside straights usually means drawing one of four cards in the deck. The odds of drawing such a card are 5 to 1 on the flop and 11 to 1 if drawing to the river. Depending on pot odds, it's usually a bad bet.

4. Low limit is where the highest bet is $3 or $6. High-limit games go from $10–$20 or higher.

there may be some truth in this. The fact is, though, bluffers who play a solid game are much easier to bluff than bluffers who play too loose or don't have a clue as to what you might have.

Reading your opponents' hands provides some insurance to "bluffing accidents." For example, I was playing with a young lady who liked to chat on the side (when she was not in a hand) about what she thought people had. She was pretty good and hit the mark on a number of occasions. Her ability to "read" what others had was some insurance against her being bluffed. If she already had the person on a certain hand that wasn't as good as hers, she'd call. If, however, she spotted his or her hand as better than hers, she'd fold. For example, she was head to head with a player who wasn't being aggressive and just called her raise. She had:

His hand was still a mystery to most of us.

She said that she had him on a high card with a small kicker. The flop and the turn came and was this:

Flop   Turn

She checked, thinking that if he bet, he had her beat and she might get a free card on her gut-shot straight draw.[5] He checked too. Was he bluffing or still chasing? The river came and it was (you guessed it):

Of course, she checked and he took some time to bet. He did what I've called "Hocus Focus."[6] She folded her pair of 10s and he showed what? She was right.

His hole cards were:

That gave him Aces over 2s. If she hadn't read his hand earlier, she may have put him on a bluff when he bet the Ace. So, learning to read what opponents have is protection when someone could either be bluffing or could have you beat.

There are times when the only right move is to bluff. So, how do you spot such "stone-cold bluffs?"[7] Sudden changes in action will be one clue. For example, a player limped in and checked twice. Then, in last position, he bets. Everyone folded except the one in front of him who had thought about betting. Neither one had anything but garbage. Only the caller had better garbage and won the pot. How did he know that his garbage was better? Let's take a closer look:

Button Player   Player to button's right

5. With the flop and the turn, her pair of 10s gave her a chance to get a straight if an 8 came. When the card you need is somewhere in the middle of the straight, it's called a "gut-shot" draw.

6. "Hocus Focus," March 8, 2004, *Poker Player Magazine*, California: Gambling Times. When players pause a long time, pretending to have a good hand.

7. "Stone-cold" bluffing is betting with the worst hand.

At the river and after two checks, the board looked like this:

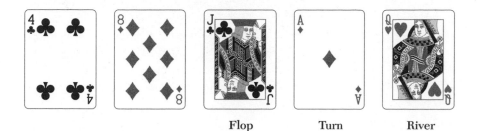

| Flop | Turn | River |

You might ask, "What kept them in this long?" The second player, who called the button's initial bet, had a flush draw with four clubs. Actually, he could have been setting a trap and wasn't proud of his medium-strength cards. The button had position and everyone was checking. Then the Ace came on the turn, and the Queen on the river. So, a bet might get the pot. The one who finally won the pot had a busted flush draw and both checked the turn. Although he didn't make his flush, he called the button's bet on the river. He won because of his 9 of clubs. But, was this just stubbornness or did he know that the button was bluffing? Although he didn't know his garbage was better, he suspected that the button player was betting in a position bluff. He also noticed how the button position placed his bet and how he kept glancing to his right. I will be discussing "Bluff Tells" later in chapter 4 and how to have clues to when a person is bluffing. That's why this garbage call was based on more than intuition.

Betting with the best hand is seldom a bluff and, for that matter, doesn't need to bluff. However, often a person will bet rather than slow play the best hand as a "reverse-bluff." Betting pre-flop with hole cards like a pair of Aces or Kings is not necessarily a reverse-bluff—it's just buying insurance. If you get a call you probably are still out front. Little pairs might fold. In other words, the player is in the other players' heads and thinks, *If I go ahead and bet my three Kings, people with a pair of Aces or two pair will put me on a bluff and call. If I check these trips, they might not bet, fearing a check/raise.* So, most regular players will bet their trip Kings for value and (particularly if there are a lot of people still in) to protect them for giving "free cards" to people chasing to beat trips with a straight or a flush. Therefore, suppose you raised pre-flop, three players called you, and you had the hand shown on the next page:

The Flop comes:

Although you have trips and the best hand, you have three callers who could be chasing a flush, a straight, or have two pair or top pair. You wouldn't want to slow play and give them free draws. Their calls are semi-bluffs, which mean they have something and could improve to beat your three Kings. As it turns out, your trips hold up to the river, but not until someone on the river bets into you. Here's what it looks like when that happens:

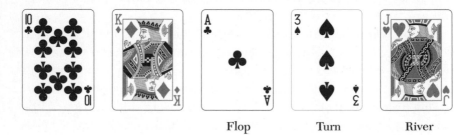

Flop   Turn   River

All the bettor would need is a Queen to beat your trip Kings. Do you call? The player could be bluffing or could have sucked out on you and made a straight. Your call, of course, would depend on how much money is at stake and on your knowledge of the player, including any observed bluff tells.

Finally, for now, there are people who hide their hole cards. Some do this purposefully. That's their bluff to get you to act behind them. This hiding of hole cards might be designed to catch your check and show weakness. Or, they might get you to bet out of turn, so he or she can fold bad cards. Hiding cards can take the form of not playing, feigning being "zoned-out," pretending to have no cards, putting both hands over the hole cards, or hiding your hole cards behind your chips. Either way, it is usually a sign that the player is hiding a good hand. Very much like the "tell" when players bet with their hand over their mouth—not wanting you to know they have good cards.

Trapping is a special brand of bluffing. It's pretending to have a weak hand to induce a bet or a raise. For example, a player with trips starts to bet, stops, and starts to check, then seems to reluctantly bet. Pretending, *Well, I've got a middle pair, but what the heck, I'll bet it anyhow*. This act is a bluff to get the top pair to bet. So, when the top pair bets, the bluff becomes a trap.

The Bluffing Formula

When discussing psychological games in *Beyond Tells*,[8] I created a game formula. This same formula is useful in understanding bluffs. Here, with some modifications, that formula becomes a Bluffing Formula.

There are essential elements in psychological games. Game theorists have created various game formulas.[9] When translated into poker-ese, these formulas become:

Figure 1 Bluffing Formula

$$B + P = PD \longrightarrow T \longrightarrow Payoff$$

B = Bluff   P = Pigeon   PD = Pigeon Drop   T = Trap
Payoff = Win/Lose

It takes a Bluff **[B]** (or a Con) plus a Pigeon **[P]** (or someone with a handle to get hooked into the game) to have a **(PD)** Pigeon Drop. A Pigeon Drop is a con that gets the desired response and anytime after that the **(T)** Trap and Payoff can occur. The Trap corresponds to the surprise and confusion that result when the bluff is revealed. The Payoff usually means that the bluff worked and both the Bluffer and the Pigeon collect their payoffs. The Bluffer may feel one-up and

---

8. McKenna, J. *Beyond Tells*. New York: Citadel, 2005, p. 73.
9. Ernst, F. and Berne, E. See Suggested Readings.

collect the pot. The Pigeon may feel hurt, tricked, sad, angry, whatever. The important thing is that both are taking a feeling payoff. There's sound advice often heard from experienced players when they say, "If you haven't figured out who the pigeon is in the first fifteen minutes, it's probably you."

Here's an example, played in an actual game of Texas Hold 'Em:
The flop comes without any pre-flop raises and there are five players, including the blinds that have called. The flop comes:

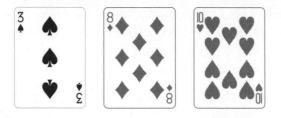

The big blind flops two pair (3s and 8s) and checks. This is a Bluff (Con) and he's looking for a Pigeon, hoping a top pair of 10s takes the bait and bets. A bet by the blind might say, "I've got some of that garbage." So, he hangs back. The other four players call the one who bet with top pair (i.e., a pair of 10s). So, the Bluff caught not one but maybe four potential Pigeon Drops ("fishes"). The turn and river come. On the turn, there's a blank 2 of clubs and then the initial Pigeon Drop with the pair of 10s bets. Then the blind (with two pair) raises the bet to spring his Trap. This switch and sudden aggression is the trap in our formula.[10] That's when the surprised players realize that the blind was slow playing a good hand. That's when everyone else besides the top pair of 10s folds their hands. Top pair reluctantly calls. The river is a Jack of diamonds. The two pair checks at the river, since his 3s and 8s may not now be enough. This is not a check/raise bluff. It's more fear of being outrun. The original bluffer is now facing a possible two higher pair and a possible straight. Also, the pair of 10s checks because his 10s could be beaten by a pair of Jacks. The board now looks like this:

10. It's not unusual in our formula for the bluffer to come out with his Trap after the Pigeon Drops have been duped into believing the slow play and bet.

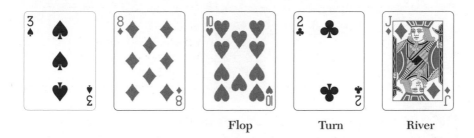

Flop   Turn   River

This may seem complicated and at times it is. However, when you understand the Bluffing Formula you'll not only understand how to improve your bluffs, you will not blindly play into bluffs. Remember, you can't be conned if you don't have a handle or a weakness that makes you vulnerable to bluffs. Again, bluffs only work if they get together with a pigeon (someone with the vulnerability) to create a pigeon drop. Here are some handles that make people vulnerable to being bluffed.

Potential Pigeon Drops

In our formula, a player who has a handle to hook on to is a potential pigeon. Their handles are their weaknesses that make them vulnerable to being bluffed. Often, the expression "It takes one to know one" applies not only to thieves but bluffing poker players as well. That's why it's harder to bluff a bluffer. Following are some things that make some players more vulnerable to being bluffed.

Lack of Playing Experience (New Players)

There's an expression that fits here, "It's hard to beat a beginner or a drunk." I mentioned earlier how much better I did before I knew how to do the right things in a poker game. However, the lack of playing experience makes a new player "pigeon bait" for the experienced bluffer. This bluff wouldn't work on a more experienced player. So, it works like playing with trained pigeons when applied to beginners. Suppose that you are heads-up with a new player. You bet with middle pair (8s) and the other player called.

At this point, the flop looks like what's shown on the next page:

Then comes the turn:

So, when a King comes you check. The other player checks too. You've already decided to bluff on the river, regardless of what comes. When the "Hold 'Em Card"[11] is dealt the new player bets and you re-raise. The new pigeon folds his pocket pair of 2s. Again, don't try this on a more experienced player. That Hold 'Em Card could turn out to be two pair (8s over 2s).

Players with Short Stacks

If you notice a player betting cautiously because he or she is short on chips, you might have a potential pigeon for a bluff. However, that short stack could have been the first bluff. I once asked a friend who came to the table with a short stack whether he was having a bad day or what. Because we knew each other pretty well, he shared with me that the short stack was his bluff.

"What do you mean?" I asked.

"Well, with players who don't know how carefully I play, they might think I'm not doing too well and start betting loosely."

Wow! It already worked on me. I had thought he might be having a bad day. That's exactly what he wanted people to think. That said, players who are not using a short stack to induce a call from you are prob-

11. When the river card is something that can't help any hands it's called a "Hold 'Em Card."

ably vulnerable to a bluff if the opportunity arises. At the same time, a short stack is a potential bluffer who wants to double up and get you to act before you become aggressive. I have had that experience with a short-stack player who checked a pair of Aces. I had Kings, so I bet into him. He doubled my bet and I called. In hindsight, if he would have gone "all-in," I would have folded my Kings. Next, when I checked to him, he went all-in. I called him because the pot odds were good. I got beat. My prayers for another King went unanswered. So, while short stacks are potential pigeons, they (particularly in no-limit games) are dangerously potential bluffers.

If a short stack represents a player who has been losing on a regular basis, he or she is more apt to be pigeon material. For example, I saw this desperation move on a TV tournament. I don't remember who was playing who. I just remember that the player had had some bad luck and was down to his last $350. It was just a matter of time before he would attempt to buy a pot and try to double up. Would he wait until he had good cards or was he going to go all-in with garbage. The other four players had plenty of chips and any all-in bets of $350 would be "chump change" to them. I think that the player knew that. So, he waited for some premium cards. He went all-in with a Queen, King (off-suit). He was head to head with a player who had an Ace, 7 (off-suit). It was a chance for the other player to knock him out and if he lost, it wouldn't hurt him that much. When the show down was over, the all-in player paired his Queen—so did the caller, who won with a pair of Aces.

This was both an example of a short stack attempting a semi-bluff and a caller who knew that he was being bluffed and called with slightly better cards. Short-stack bluffs seldom work in tournaments when opponents will call just because they can afford to take the chance with their larger stacks.

Scared Money

When a player is betting timidly, whether short stacked or not, this is a "tell" that most players will exploit. Players with "Scared Money" are easier to beat and are easier to bluff. Even at times when a player is just betting a good hand and not trying to bluff, a player with scared money might fold after looking at their chips. There's an expression in gambling circles that, "Scared money never wins." It also is a pigeon roost asking to be bluffed. Tight players are easier to control than loose ones. When someone is tight because of their fear of losing money, they play tighter than a bark on a tree. Sometimes such scare is shown by how they show up with chips at the table. I mentioned in the book *Beyond Tells* that how a player buys in will tell something about how they are going to play those chips. For example, let's pretend that a player buys into a no-limit ($2–$1) game with the minimum buy in of $100. He's already saying that all he wants to risk is the minimum. Beware, though, of players like my friend mentioned earlier, who has another stash of chips ready in the pocket and is pretending to be scared or tight. After the smaller buy-in, it's important to watch how the player proceeds. You will discover soon enough whether the player is playing scared money or is bluffing you.

In a $3–$6 hold 'em game, look for players who are being cautious and may be playing with scared money. Often a short stack of chips, like photo 1 shows, will be worth a bluff.

Photo 1 Short Stack

Failure to Read Hands

A lot of players just play cards and only look at their hands to decide whether to bet, call, raise, or fold. This is a mistake and it's actually a weakness. To just play your hand with no idea of what your opponent might have is the proverbial "blind squirrel." A blind squirrel may find the nut, occasionally. Usually, though, you are in for a lot of surprises. Players who fail to read other players' hands are hard to bluff and at times they are easier to bluff. If you know for sure that a player is not even thinking about what other players may have then you've found a pigeon ripe for bluffing. If you fail to assess what other players might have by the way they are betting, calling, checking, or raising actions, then you are vulnerable to be bluffed. If a player makes a move and you have no idea of what he or she is betting on, how can you call that move? If you are simply going by the cards that you have and you are not anticipating what could beat them, you are in the formula—you're the pigeon drop. However, the opposite of players who are not paying attention to what others might have is the player who is good at reading hands. It's been said that, "You can't bluff someone who isn't paying attention."[12]

Sometimes an opponent is paying more attention to how he can be beaten and not to what others might have. For example, I was playing with a pretty tight player. In fact, I jokingly said to him, "You are playing so tight you're going to give yourself a hernia!" I noticed him folding some pretty good hands when his chances of improving were good. He even said, "Wow! I would have had the nut flush if I would have called that raise and saw one more card." It was only a matter of time before we were head to head on another hand. I had flopped middle pair when the flop looked like this:

I was in middle position and everyone checked to me. I went ahead and bet my middle pair of Jacks. Everyone folded except this tight player. He didn't raise my bet. He just called. When the turn was a blank, I bet again. He said, "If I fold, will you show me Aces?" I said, "I'll show you that you did the right thing to lay this one down." He folded a pocket pair of Kings. I was almost ashamed to show him my Jack♦ and Queen♣. I thought that he had a Jack but that I had a better kicker. Was I surprised that he had Kings.

Odds Ignorance

I've heard many players make the statement, "Oh, I just play cards. I don't know how to figure those odds and when I try, it confuses me. So, I just play cards and people." Well, that's a rationalization that's straight from a potential pigeon if I ever heard one. Not knowing how

---

12 Mamet, David. *House of Games.*

to figure odds or not paying any attention to your chances of making hands will make you a prime target for bluffing. Such a statement will put a bulls-eye on your next pot. You can be sure that other players who figure the odds will take you on more or you won't make much on them when you do have the nuts.[13] So, if you don't want to be the object of a pigeon shoot, get some information off the Internet and in books on odds.[14] I say this, even though knowing odds can be overrated. Players who know little about people and a lot about odds don't seem to do all that well. They certainly are at a disadvantage when it comes to bluffing. The only bluffs that work for them are when they have super odds in their favor. You won't find them ever taking "long shots." This leads to the next attribute of potential pigeon drops.

Playing Too Tight

A lot of very solid players who will only play high and suited cards are setting themselves up to be a target. It's much easier to bluff a tight player. That's because of two things: (1) a tight pigeon is predictable, and (2) such players are able to put you on a hand. If that hand is better than theirs or the flop has several over-cards, a tight player will fold in a heartbeat. To bluff a tight player will only work if they think you have them beat. If they put you on a bluff, they can be a "dog with a bone" and won't lay down the better hand. That's why it's so important when bluffing these players to avoid being "caught speeding."[15] You can pay an actual speeding ticket and go on driving. In poker, when you are caught speeding, you will pay for it more than once. Of course, experienced players will use this as a bluff and pretend to be speeding when they have the best hand.

We will discuss the importance of knowing how players are thinking in the next chapter. For now, suffice it to say, you will need to learn the three levels of getting into an opponent's thinking. These are especially important when attempting to bluff a tight player. More about this is coming in the next chapter.

13. The term "nuts" refers to having the best possible hand. Poker legend has it that a player would bet the nut off of his wagon (to bet his wagon) to cover his bet.

14. See Suggested Readings for useful websites.

15. Another poker colloquialism that means being caught trying to bluff or steal a pot.

Playing on Tilt

The three most important skills in avoiding bluffs and being able to pull off successful bluffs are: Focus, Focus, and Focus. That means, as we will see in the next chapter, being aware of how players are thinking, what they think you are thinking, and what they think you think they are thinking. Wow! Try to do even one of those when you are "on tilt."[16] Whenever you get upset in any way about either a bad beat or something someone said, don't play. Go take a break. Sit out a hand or two. When you are on tilt, you are as vulnerable to being bluffed as a baby on a skateboard gliding down the streets of San Francisco. From purely a biological point of view, when you are into a strong emotion, your ability to think is hampered. It's not like the adrenaline rush people experience during emergencies that seems to help them act with precision. Rather, when you are preoccupied with the past, it's next to impossible to notice what's happening in the present.

What you need to do is get centered and let go of the past and the future, for that matter. When you've got one foot in the past and the other in the future, you are playing out of the Jerk Position. One foot's pulled to the past (what happened in the game), the other is pulled into the future (what you're going to do to get even). What's happening in the present goes right between your legs and you will be easy to manipulate into a bluff. That's the reason some less than scrupulous players will do and say things to get players on tilt. In fact, I know one player who could only win a hand if he got others players on tilt. He'd make remarks that bordered on insults and bad manners—all in morbid humor, of course. Not to mention subterfuge.

Before we move into the difference between bluffing as a *poker strategy* and bluffing as a *psychological game*, it's important to make one thing very clear. Namely, no matter how good you are in playing poker, you will be a pigeon and you will get bluffed. That's a given. Even professional players will buy into bluffs. In fact, a player can't play effective poker without bluffing or being bluffed. The sign of a good player is their ability to lay good cards when they figure they are beat. So, it's not whether you bluff or not. It's how blind you are to what you

---

16. When a player goes on "tilt," like a pinball machine, he or she stops operating and makes rash moves.

are doing and whether you can learn and improve your game. As a therapist, I've used a saying: "There's a difference between twenty-five years of marriage and one year twenty-five times over." The same applies to poker players who keep making the same mistakes over and over and don't learn when they step into a bluff or when their bluff doesn't work. That said, let's look at what happens when bluffs are used to play psychological games.

The Verb of Bluffing

When playing poker, it's possible to not bluff and not make moves on other players. Such poker, though, is playing cards and not playing people. Poker is more of a people game. Bluffing is a "pro-active" part of the game. Just as in other sports, there are moves like faking out opponents. At times, a basketball player may jog to the left and then suddenly dribble around a guard to lay up a shot. Then, there's a boxer who will fake a left jab to land a right cross. All sports have this feature. It's part of the action of misleading to gain an advantage. Only it's called bluffing in poker. Watch any baseball game and before you know it the coach is calling for the batter to fake a bunt. This may get players to move in while the batter squares off and takes a full swing. Here are some actions in poker that are designed to get an advantage over other players:

1. Slow-playing good hands
2. Letting weaker hands do the betting
3. Checking to pretend weakness
4. Raising to "play 'em like you've got 'em"
5. Betting aggressively
6. Folding and showing
7. Masquerading

Sometimes these actions will give that advantage. At other times, they may put you at a disadvantage.

Slow playing has the advantage of both misleading opponents into thinking they have a better hand and insuring that more players stay in to build a pot. It happens most often, as we will later describe, with an ordinarily passive player. However, it's also in the aggressive player's arsenal of poker weapons. This type of bluff is still a verb. It's more of a passive-aggressive way to gain an advantage. The disadvantage of this move is not getting as much value as you might from good cards. It depends on the kind of table you are playing (bluffing) at.

Letting others do the betting is another passive way to bluff. It also suggests that other players have better cards and ensures that players stay in. Those players who check or bet can help the full value from your hand. The disadvantage to this bluff is making poor judgments as to the players who follow. If players that follow your check do not bet, the table gets a free card to out-run your hand. It's tough to sometimes have to bet your own hand. If you don't, then be sure that a player behind you is going to bet.

Checking can be both a way to feign weakness and a way to see what others might have. For example, if you have a pair of 10s and you are playing in middle position, a check would be a way to survey the other hands at the table. If someone behind you bets, you know that you have some competition. A re-raise by you on your 10s would tell you how much that threat is. This is actually a semi-bluff, since you could improve your 10s. It's also a way to "take your opponent's temperature." The disadvantage to this checking-bluff is that if nobody acts behind you, it tells you that no one is proud yet. It could also, in a higher limit game, be indicating that someone else is waiting to trap a bettor. For example, a player in middle position checked twice before anyone bet. He had a suited "big slick" (Ace and King). The flop was:

He checked again when the turn showed a blank:

Finally, someone behind him bet (with a pair of 7s and a pair of Aces). Then the slow-playing "big slick," with two top pair, re-raised. He, of course, got re-raised by the player who thought he was the trapper. The trapper got trapped by two higher pair.

Raising a bet (either before or after a check) is making a statement. It's saying that you like what you have and that you think you have the best hand. That's what it's supposed to mean. However, as a bluff, it's a way to intimidate and drive players out. If you are raising with marginal hands or with garbage hands, you want people to fold. If you are raising with quality cards, you may want to narrow the field. Whether you want to narrow the field to just a few players, or if you want to drive all your opponents out, a raise has a lot of potential. It also could backfire on you if someone with a better hand is setting a trap. If so, you just stepped in it with your raise. Suppose, for example, that you flopped top pair and everyone checks. You bet and one of the people who checked before you raises the bet. Your top pair of Aces may have just gotten you trapped by two smaller pairs. Ah, such is poker.

Betting is also an action way to bluff. It may be just a bet to get value out of your hand. If you think that you have the best hand, betting it could be a "paradoxical bluff." This is where getting in the minds of your opponents comes into bluffing. In this instance, others might be thinking, "He wouldn't be betting if his hand was really strong." That's why betting with the best hand works. Poker players are paranoid and on stand-by, ready to be bluffed. By acting like you are bluffing you will get more calls and more value for your hand. Of course, you must know your players. Against a very tight player, a bet might result in a fold. This bluff also works in psychotherapy. There's what is called a "paradoxical injunction," used rarely but very effectively with the right patients. This technique is used to encourage a patient to rebel and do what's good for him or her. For example, I once used this with a rebellious high school student who was acting out and failing his classes. I had developed a whimsical way of kidding him and saying things in jest. I jokingly challenged him by saying something like, "Well, I'm going to wait until next month before I see you again. I know that's okay with you because you really don't want to be here or to change your grades. You might be getting more fun out of upsetting your teachers and parents." And, then in all seriousness, I looked at him and said, "I'd really be surprised if things are any better when I see you again."

Well, as you've guessed (and I wouldn't be telling this story otherwise), he came in the next month and said, "I was kind of looking forward to today." (The first place I was proven wrong. He did want to be here this time.)

I said, "Why? So you could waste some more of my time?"

"No," he said. "I've got a note from my teacher saying how much better I've been doing!"

"Well, there you go. What do I know? I'm just your therapist! Congratulations." His rebellion against authority was beginning to work for him.

Folding your hand and *showing* it is almost always a way to set the table up to call you or to intimidate other players. If you just won a pot and you did it with "garbage," then showing that you won with the worst hand is a way to cause people to go on "tilt" and call you the next time you have the nuts. At the same time, if you had the nuts and won the pot, showing your hole cards would be putting players on notice that you are someone to respect. Unless you are folding and showing to set up a bluff or a threat, it's generally best to not show your hands. If you do, use this bluff only on occasion and not with the same people. Why give opponents free information about you?

Masquerading as someone you are not is probably the most common way of bluffing. Players don't want you to know whether they know what they are doing or not. They want you to figure that out for yourself. So, it's probably a mistake to start talking like you are a poker expert. But, you will hear players talk about what the odds of this or that hand are. That's their way of masquerading that they know more than you do. It's a mistake, because it may work and encourage people to not call when you want them to call you. It also might tell them that you really don't know what you are talking about. Once, a player with a busted straight said, "Well, heck there were eight outs. I could have gotten my gut-shot on the river!" The pot wasn't very big and it cost him a $30 bet with an 11-to-1 shot. There would have to have been at least $330 in the pot to justify this inside-straight chase.[17] So, masquerading as a good player revealed how little he knew about pot odds.

Players masquerade in the way they dress. Once, I noticed a guy dressed up in bib overalls and boots. He looked like a country bumpkin fresh in from the farm. Well, people learned that he was a successful accountant. He stopped his masquerade. He started wearing dark sun-

---

17. "Pot odds" are figured by how much the pot is worth the bet. At 11-to-1 odds, the pot would have to be at least 11 times the bet (11 × 30=$330). See appendix B for figuring odds.

glasses. I mentioned earlier about a player who showed up with a short stack to masquerade at being down on his luck. This bluff was inviting pigeons to take a shot at him. He'd only be in the hand if he had quality cards. When he was not playing the hand, people thought he was being tight because of "scared money." That's the opposite masquerade of another player, who is probably the best stud player in the Midwest. I enjoyed playing $2–$10–$20 with him. He'd always come with much more than he ever needed. He'd stack his "chip towers" high and proudly. If he'd lose a few hands and his towers were shortening, he'd buy more chips. He always liked to have more chips than he needed. I thought that he was just being superstitious or something. So, one day I asked him, "Bill, why do you go back and keep more chips than you need? Everyone knows you are a good player. Are you trying to intimidate players?"

"Not at all," he replied. "I like to give the youngsters a chance to take a shot at me. Lots of chips will push their competitive buttons." So, his large stacks were not a bluff. They were more of a challenge.

Smart and Dumb Moves

Slow playing can be a smart move when you are confident that players behind you will bet. It loses bets if you are wrong. Also, it's usually a mistake to slow play hands that others could easily outrun. By giving free cards, good hands are often lost to flops like this:

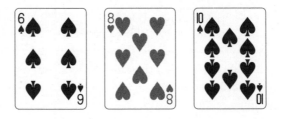

That's because it's too easy to get beat by two small pairs, a flush, or a straight. Slow playing when opponents have draws like this is playing dumb. The smart move would be to make them pay for it if they are going to draw out on you.

Often players will *let weaker hands do the betting*. Again, this can be a smart move or a dumb one, depending on whether you have correctly read your opponents and what the draws are that you are allowing. Generally, it's better to bet or raise your hand than to just call bets. A check with a good hand will invite a bet. In that case, it would be smart to re-raise. Simply, calling can be a dumb move, since again it is inviting players to outrun you without paying for it.

A lot of players will *check to pretend weakness.* If you are already strong, this will be a smart move to set up a trap. Again, re-raise whenever you do this check-raise, otherwise you are encouraging players to cheaply outrun you—unless you have the absolute nuts. Pretending weakness can be dumb when it encourages players with over-cards to yours to bet. Here's an example I witnessed in a game of Texas Hold 'Em:

A player with a pocket pair of Jacks just called and then checked when the flop was:

The pre-flop call, instead of raise, was a dumb move. The check on the flop was a smart move to see if anyone was going to bet the King. Everyone checked behind him. Then the turn showed a blank. The player with the pocket Jacks bet. He had shown weakness before and after the flop, so when he bet he was re-raised by a trapper who had a pair of Kings. The Jacks never did improve. When they showed down their hands, the Kings showed Kings over 10s. In this case, the King, 10 on the flop was pretending weakness (smart) and when he didn't get any action from the guy with the pocket Jacks, he was pretty sure he had the best hand. When the Jacks bet, he re-raised—also, to see if he'd been tricked by a King and a higher kicker. When the Jacks just called, the Kings sighed with some relief. However, when the river showed a 10, this gave the Kings two pair. So, both players were pretending weakness. The Jacks was showing weakness (dumb) before the flop by just calling instead of also raising. When he checked the flop, he was afraid of a possible pair of Kings. When the Kings checked, that was pretending weakness and it paid off in the end.

Raising to "play 'em like you've got 'em" is a useful way to bluff. It can be smart and it can be dumb. It's not really a bluff if you are playing like you've got good cards and you actually do. To play garbage as if you have the best hand is the real bluff. So, this is a smart move when you have a weak hand—as long as you have some other advantages. If you also have position and have been able to read the other players as having weak hands, this is a smart move. However, if any of the players before you calls and is a tight player, you are in trouble with this strategy. If you have one or more loose players in the hand, it's dumb to try this bluff. Although you may be called by a conservative player, this "playing like you've got 'em" only works with players who are paying attention. It won't work with another fool.

Recently, I was giving too much respect to a new player, which turned out to be dumb. I decided that she was calling too many hands. She was to my right and when she called, I would fold if I didn't have much to play with. She was "playing like she had 'em." I decided that she couldn't have had that many good, playable hands in a row. So, I determined that the next time or times that I had decent cards and she limped in I was just going to go over[18] her each time. It turned out that I went from dumb to smart. I decided I would "slap her wrist" for getting me to fold when I thought that she had something worth folding to. I would also make her pay for just limping in. Here are two players who are "playing like they have 'em." It turns out that I was right this time and I won this "pissing contest."

Betting aggressively is only a bluff if it is misrepresenting your hand. It's dumb to bet aggressively with the best hand. However, as I pointed out in *Beyond Tells* betting aggressively is a way of life for some impulsive players. More passive players will bet gently and will never splash the pot. If a normally passive bettor suddenly bets aggressively it's usually a bluff. For the more experienced observer, though, it's a dumb bluff. When a conservative player, who is ordinarily tight, bets aggressively he or she is telling you something. This player is saying, "I dare you to call that!"

---

18. Poker jargon for raising the bet.

When a player is *folding and is showing* his or her hand, it's a setup for something later on. This can only be done once in a while. More than that and it becomes a sideshow rather than a bluffing move. There are several ways to fold and show your hand. Suppose that you have a pair of Queens and the flop has two over-cards. When someone bets, you fold to possible Kings or Aces. By showing your Queens and folding, what is the message? You're teaching others that you are a conservative player who can fold good cards whenever they may be beaten. Why bother teaching anything? Of course, you are setting up for when someone tries to bluff you into doing the same thing in another hand. Either that or you are just dumb enough to think anyone even cares, which means that it's silly to try to teach a pig to sing. It will frustrate the hell out of you and it annoys the pig. In other words, don't even try to show and tell when you are folding to players who are loose and don't care what you had—as long as you got out.

Finally, there are players who like to *masquerade*. Masquerading can also be smart as well as a dumb thing to do. A lot depends on how well you can act and how good a memory your opponents have. When used as a bluff, people will often either masquerade as good players or as bad players. When you get caught speeding,[19] that could be a basis to masquerade as a bad player. Chances are that when you have a good hand, more players will call you the next time you are betting. This strategy works also for tight players who use their reputation and will occasionally bet garbage. That's when their reputation becomes a masquerade. It's a smart one. A dumb masquerade is one that seldom works. For instance, I mentioned how an accountant would come in dressed in bib overalls to pretend he was some country bumpkin. When people know it's an act, it's no longer a masquerade and it's dumb to continue. He was smart enough to know when it was no longer working for him.

Tells Compared to Bluffs

When Mike Caro first published his pioneering work on tells in 1984,[20] many of his twenty-five identified tells were bluffs. In fact, eight of

19. Speeding is poker jargon for being caught trying to steal a hand.
20. Caro, Mike. *The Body Language of Poker*. Hollywood, CA: Gambling Times, 1984.

them actually used the words *bluff* or *bluffing*. Five other tells listed were suggesting bluffs. So, nearly half tells are bluffs. Not all tells are bluffs, yet all bluffs have their own tells. Since those tells were first published, many players have used such tells as bluffs. Here's some suggestions of how Caro's listed tells relate to bluffing:

Tell Description	Tell Used to Bluff
1. "Players often stack chips in a manner directly indicative of their style of play. Conservative means conservative, sloppy means sloppy."	As a bluff, players often buy chips that are the opposite of their play. Some will come in with a "short stack" to pretend that it's scared money.
2. "Players often buy chips in a manner directly indicative of their style of play. Flamboyant means flamboyant; guarded means guarded."	This is only true if the action is not in the player's awareness. Again, as a bluff some players know that you are paying attention to how they buy in.
3. "An unsophisticated player who bets, then shares his hand while awaiting a call, is unlikely to be bluffing."	True—the operational word being "unsophisticated." Beware of players using this to bluff you with garbage.
4. "A trembling hand is a force to be feared."	As a bluff, garbage can get you to shake on purpose.
5. "In the absence of indications to the contrary, call any bettor whose hand covers his mouth."	Also used by actors to pretend they have a bad hand.
6. "A genuine smile means a genuine hand; a forced smile is a bluff."	It's hard to bluff a genuine smile; but, some are good actors.
7. "The friendlier a player is, the more apt he is to be bluffing."	Some players are only friendly when they are bluffing. Know your opponents.
8. "A player glances secretly at his chips only when he's considering a bet—and almost always because he's helped his hand."	Beware of players who read books on poker.
9. "If a player looks and then checks instantly, it's unlikely that he's improved his hand."	Again, make sure it's an unconscious checking.
10. "If a player looks and then bets instantly, it's unlikely that he is bluffing."	Some players will do this intentionally to appear to be strong. They are bluffing (strong means weak).
11. "Disappoint any player who, by acting weak, is seeking your call."	A weak act may be a paradox, hoping you might see weakness as a bluff.

Tell Description	Tell Used to Bluff
12. "Disappoint any player who, by acting strong, is hoping you'll pass."	Some players will act strong with the "nuts." That's their bluff.
13. "Players staring at you are usually less of a threat than players staring away."	Beware of players who are watching your eyes instead of the flop.
14. "Players staring at their cards are usually weak."	Some will hope you think that they are weak—they just may be amazed at how good a hand is.
15. "Players reaching for their chips out of turn are usually weak."	This is only true if the player is not an impulsive-style player. More structured players may use this as a bluff, hoping you read a book on tells.
16. "A player who gathers a pot prematurely is usually bluffing."	Again, doesn't apply to impulsive players. A player who wants a call may do this to pretend he's bluffing.
17. "When a player acts to spread his hand prematurely, it's usually because he's bluffing."	This is true. However, beware of a player who wants you to think he's bluffing.
18. "If a player bets and then looks back at his hand when you reach for your chips, he's probably bluffing."	He could be playing you. It's important to know your players.
19. "A forceful or exaggerated bet usually means weakness."	As a bluff, it's a way to get calls. If the player is impulsive, it's simply his style.
20. "A gentle bet usually means strength."	This is a useful bluff when you have a weak hand. Some players bet this way as a style and could mean nothing other than that.
21. "When in doubt, sit behind the money."	This has nothing to do with bluffing, unless a player is adding to his pile from the cage.
22. "When tells conflict, the player is acting. Determine what he's trying to make you do by his most blatant mannerism. Then generally do the opposite."	When the conflict is purposeful, you've been bluffed into doing the opposite, which is exactly what the bluffer intended.
23. "A misdirected bet is almost always a bluff."	Determine if actually misdirected or fired. The eyes will tell as we will later detail.
24. "Beware of sights and sounds of sorrow."	Some will use sounds to bluff.
25. "Don't call pokerclack."	Same as using sounds to bluff.

The Difference Between a Player and a Fool

Good players are not real tight or real loose. They also seem to have a balance of the ability to change how they play. This includes changing how they bluff depending on who they are playing and what the conditions are at a particular table. When a good player bluffs, it's not just based on his or her hand. He knows that people can be bluffed and cards can't—they play themselves. So, different personality types[21] will require different bluffs. A player knows the difference. A fool doesn't care.

What we are doing in this book (that has never been done before) is showing how good bluffing comes from knowing not only your opponent's personality but also knowing how he or she thinks. Knowing whether the other players are picturing things, taking things in more through their ears, or thinking more in action terms will change the way you choose to bluff.

These are just some of the mysteries of poker that this book will reveal. However, that will have to wait until chapter 4. If you are a reader who likes to jump ahead, I encourage you to resist that urge. To understand the magic of poker, it's important to know how players think, manage cards and people, and from what foundations they are playing. Then, knowing this, you will be better able to fine-tune your knowledge of the ways players (1) think, (2) think you are thinking, and (3) think you are thinking that they are thinking. Poker is fun—it's the players who are complex. So, let's first discuss this in more detail in chapter 2.

---

21. Reference the work of *Beyond Tells*, the first poker book on tells to integrate personality theory.

The Anatomy of Poker Players

The HEAD of a Player

Knowing how to successfully bluff doesn't come so much from knowing what hands and what position works best for bluffing. Successful bluffing comes from knowing how other players are thinking, knowing what they think you are thinking, and finally being good at anticipating what they think you think that they are thinking. Sound confusing? It could be—at first. With practice it will improve your bluffs and keep you from bluffing needlessly. Let's take one at a time.

Knowing How Your Opponents Think

This is not the same as reading minds. A good poker player doesn't have to be a psychic, although it couldn't hurt. Knowing how other players think is more determining whether they are more likely to be very structured (left-brained) or very impulsive (right-brained). Chapter 3 and 5 will give you a menu for determining what personality type your opponents thinks through and how different players make sense of the world around them. Knowing these things is essential to effectively communicating your bluffs and having them understood. That's why it's harder to bluff a fool. A more structured player will figure out what you might have. An impulsively loose player doesn't care.

Knowing What Your Opponents Think That You Are Thinking

This skill comes from paying attention to the body language (tells) that I discussed in *Beyond Tells*. If you have established a tight profile with an opponent, you could use this history to induce a bluff. Suppose your opponent knows that you are a very structured (left-brained) contender. You can cash in on this occasionally by playing garbage the way you would ordinarily play solid cards. Let's suppose that you are in late position and you decide to play: No one raises and three players call besides you. The flop shows this with a Jack♥ and 6♠.

Your Hole Cards

The Flop

One early position player bet? Everyone folds, except you. You've got a runner-runner[1] flush draw, an over-card (Jack), and something more important. You put the bettor on a pair of 9s and he's just as tight a player as you are. You know how he thinks and you called him anyway. What were you thinking!? This is not like you to be as loose as this. What you have already decided to do is bluff if a scare card comes. So, the turn scares both of you:

---

1. "Runner-runner" is poker jargon for needing the next two cards to complete a hand. Like having one heart, flopping two more hearts, and staying to get two more hearts to make a flush.

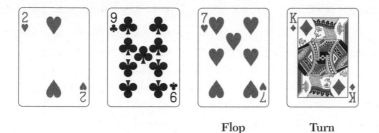

Flop   Turn

That King is no help to either of you. So, you both check again. You could have bluffed with a bet, pretending that you held a King. You wait to bluff on the river, hoping that the board doesn't pair. That would give him two pair and ruin your bluff. So, a bluff at the turn would be some insurance. So, nobody's perfect and you checked. The turn comes and it's a heart and doesn't pair the board. Here's what the board is now:

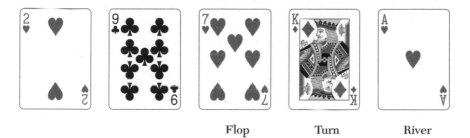

Flop   Turn   River

You know that your opponent is thinking: "He just made a flush or he could have Aces." Since he thinks that he knows you, he probably is thinking that you wouldn't chase with just a flush draw. You probably also had another pair. A bet from you is almost a guaranteed steal.[2] You know how your opponent thinks, you know how he has figured you out, and you have a pretty good idea that he thinks you wouldn't be calling him with the nothing that you have. It's so out of character that it gives you a bluffing advantage. Don't try this on a loose player. It only works because you know how your opponent thinks and had a good read on how he thinks you think.

Trying to figure out how a loose player thinks can be futile. They usually are not thinking—just being aggressive. However, as we will see later, knowing how a loose player thinks and how he or she thinks that

---

2. Poker jargon for bluffing is referred to as a "steal" or "stealing."

you think can be useful. So, you know how little an impulsive, loose player thinks. But, have you figured out how he thinks that you think. Most loose players think that a conservative player is afraid of action and will tuck their tail between their legs as soon as someone starts pushing them around with a raise or a check/raise. For this reason, they will bet into over-cards without a second thought. Their mistake is that they really don't know how a more structured player thinks. Conservative players who have had a lot of experience know that it's the long run and not the short one that makes the money. In other words, they are not afraid of an aggressive loose player. In fact, under the right conditions, they may even be more aggressive than the Party Hardy or the High Roller.[3] For reasons mentioned earlier, an experienced player is afraid to attempt to bluff a loose player—not to play them.

Determining What Your Opponent Thinks That You Think They Are Thinking

This third level of awareness is one of the hardest to master. Yet, it is this skill that will protect you from many bluffs and will help you to know when it is safe to bluff. It is also a way to make what goes around come around. If you can get an opponent to think that you are buying into or that you don't believe them at the right times, you have found the key to survival in bluffs. In other words, suppose that your opponent is on a stone-cold bluff and thinks that you think he or she is strong (when actually you don't). Then, at this third level of deceit, you have convinced the bluffer that you think that they have the best hand. The initial bluffer is totally unaware that he or she is the pigeon. As a matter of fact, this pigeon is convinced that you are the pigeon. Third levels of thinking are what might be called Pigeon Roosts where the bluffers become the "bluffees."

I had the pleasure of testing this out in a $3–$6 Texas Hold 'Em game. I was playing an aggressive player that tried to buy a pot early in a low-limit game. That was his first mistake. He also was in early position, so I said, "Oh, Oh! You're betting from the big blind. You must have quite a hand." I already read him as having a King or an Ace with a small kicker. This was his style and I already knew how he thought. So,

3. See *Beyond Tells* for playing styles and a recap in chapter 5, later in this book.

I wanted him to keep thinking that I thought that he had a strong hand. I was pretty sure he either had garbage or half a strong hand.[4] Actually, knowing this guy, when he has a strong hand, that's the only time he gets quiet and slow-plays. He also wanted to be a trapper when he was a child. Anyhow, to get back to my story, I called his bet; I didn't raise him because I wanted him to think that I was afraid of what he might have. So, I splashed the pot with a call and said, "I hope I'm not donating here!" I was also pretty sure that my pocket Aces would hold up and I didn't want to lose this fish (or, should I say pigeon?). Well, it gets better. The flop comes with an Ace. I already thought he might have a high card with a little kicker. He thinks I've got "squat." He attempts a trap with a check. Turns out he had an Ace and a 2 (off-suit). I bet with my trip Aces and he raises me. Of course, I re-raise and that's when he just called. The rest of the cards (turn and river) were blanks. He stayed, slowed down, though, and just became a "calling station."

By knowing what he was thinking and by manipulating what he thought that I was thinking he was thinking, I was able to get real value out of my pocket Aces. At another time, depending on what I thought people were thinking, I might have raised early to protect my hand. Here's what the showdown looked like:

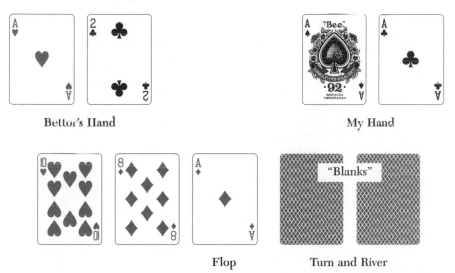

Bettor's Hand   My Hand

Flop   Turn and River

4. This kind of thinking can bite you back on occasion. Such a player does at times, rarely though it may be, have the cards he is representing. If everything was for sure, it wouldn't be poker.

The SHOULDERS of Responsibility and Discipline

Ability to Respond to Bad Times

How a player handles (or shoulders) hard times will test the metal of moving from surviving to thriving in poker. Anyone can play good cards. Some don't get the full value that a more experienced player would. However, the difference between a player and a fool is that a player will take bad times and wait it out or use it as a springboard to success. For example, I once watched a game of seven-card stud. It was head to head and the less experienced, tight player was facing on Fourth Street a possible flush. Here's what you could see:

Tight Player   Better Player

On Third Street, Tight Player (8♦) checked. Since Better Player (7♥) knew his opponent was a cautious player, he bet to see if he could buy it. The 8♦ gets an Ace of spades and the 7♥ gets another heart. This actually gives the first player a pair of Aces. He checks because he wants to see if the hearts will bet into him. The hearts checks as well.

On Fifth Street, the Ace gets a blank and the 2♥ and 7♥ get another heart. The pair of Aces bets, wondering if his opponent made his flush. When the pair of Aces bets the three hearts makes his move.

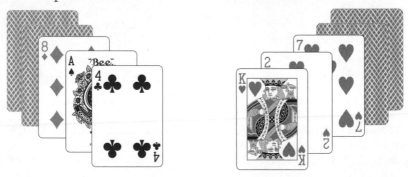

He raises and the pair of Aces just calls. The King and three hearts could've been a source of bluffing the pair of Aces. When the Ace didn't re-raise he said he probably only had one pair. The King could have given the raiser two pair or a flush. The Aces folded on Fifth Street. Under the hearts, Better Player had garbage. The Ace became the pigeon because he was a tight player and the conservative player knew that he could be beaten in several ways. The bluffer knew that with the garbage he had, the only way he could win was to bluff and play like he had made his flush. The pigeon believed him. A looser player wouldn't have. So, this wouldn't have worked with a different player. The bluffer knew his player. This "Rumpelskiltskin" bluffer knew how to take "straw cards" and turned them into gold.

Ability to Manage Time and Money

When players are using their heads they are thinking not only about what's happening at the table, with this hand, or just for the moment.[5] A player has goals and is there to use time as an investment in those goals. I once asked a player who was ahead and then lost it all, "Did you have a win/loss goal?" He didn't even know what I was talking about. Some other players I know would have left when they were ahead. I like to use the formula in limit games of 30 times the big bet. If I am playing $3–$6, and I am ahead by $180, I leave. The same is true of $5–$10 games. When ahead by $300, it's time to leave. That way I won't lose it back.

Baseball and tennis are "goal-time"[6] sports. The goal is for the team or player to reach the highest score at the end of nine innings or a set of six games. Basketball and hockey are "clock-time" sports. The team with the highest score when the clock runs out is the winner. On the other hand, some activities combine goal and clock time. Music entertainment is a combination of both. When the music maestro steps before the orchestra and the orchestra follows the maestro's leads, both create a beautiful symphony. That's both goal time and clock time. Responsible gaming can be a combination of using time to reach goals,

---

5. You might want to compare this to the advance planning needed in a game of chess.

6. Berne, E. *What Do You Say After You Say Hello?* New York: Grove Press, 1972.

to invest time, and to create harmony in one's life. It can also be a way to waste time and create disharmony in a person's life.

Some players approach all gaming as goal time. They come equipped with their win/loss[7] ratios and their strategies. When they reach predetermined goals, they quit. That means for them that gambling is over for that session or that day. Others gamble by clock time. They know what their hourly rate of wins or losses are and they play until that time frame is reached. Responsible gamblers are more like the orchestra leader described above. They use both goal and clock time to determine their final outcomes. And, yes—they must focus on what they are doing and turn their backs to the crowd. They don't let their egos get on tilt and will end up taking their bows for success when the music ends. Every second to a good player is valuable. None are wasted and the rest are invested in what they are there to achieve. It's not how much time players spend gambling that's important. It's how players spend their gaming times. Do they waste it, invest it, or forget it? The average life span consists of less than two and one-half billion seconds. As each second passes away, how time is spent cannot be retrieved. Time can be wasted and the seconds can't be reclaimed. Time can be invested and memories will be cherished. Time spent today can influence the quality of time spent tomorrow. During the billions or millions of seconds we have left, we can learn to spend more seconds feeling good about ourselves. Success will help to make those seconds more positive.

Responsible players spend time setting themselves up to feel good. Whether they win or lose, they're spending time to reach goals and affirm themselves. Of course, when they lose they don't feel good. At the same time, they won't waste time in the "pity pot." Other players will spend their time suffering or endlessly pursuing excitement. Time spent in promoting bad feelings or seeking excitement as a drug of choice is time being wasted. It wastes the seconds ticking away that won't come back.

---

7. McKenna, J. *Beyond Tells*. See p. 10, under Response-Able Players, for examples of some win/loss formulas.

Time Structure and Safety

Earlier we discussed risk taking in how loose or tight people play their cards. There are six ways to spend time while playing cards with others. Some of these ways are riskier than others. Later, in chapter 3, we will discuss psychological games and how they influence bluffing. There are five other ways to spend time with others in a card game. Each is riskier than the other. The least risky way to play is to be withdrawn. The riskiest is to be you and play good cards as an authentic person. Yes, you can be authentic and still bluff. Here's how we spend our time (listed from least to most risky):

1. **Withdrawal**—We can get off to ourselves and have very little to do with others and spend our time being withdrawn. Some sulk. Others just play their cards, silently observing others and preferring to avoid conversations. Slots and video poker machines are ideal for players who prefer to be withdrawn. When these players are bluffing, they are "sneaky" bluffers. That's because they like to hide and then come out firing from behind the proverbial bush.

2. **Rituals**—We can be very ritualistic and routinely repeat whatever casino or playing rituals we prefer. Some players have a ritualistic strategy for every event. Such then become their playing habits. Others have sloppy habits. Rituals can be useful as bluffs, as well as useful habits. For example, most conservative players will ritualistically bluff when they have good position and there has been a round of checking. Also, a player with a middle pair may ritualistically bet after the top card is checked around once.

3. **Pastimes**—We can just pass time with others about how we are playing and about some of the "good old hands." Some just talk about cards and pass time about others things or people. Pastiming is a useful way to scope out opponents to learn how they think. By listening closely, it's possible to know how an opponent makes sense of the cards and the action. We will go into detail about this in chapter 4.

4. **Activities**—We can invest our time wisely and participate in the activity of gaming, paying attention to what we know and being responsible. The activities of poker are watching how you bet, call, fold, and raise. How you talk will also reveal how you can be

bluffed. The activity of poker is one of observing and setting goals
to fit each opponent. Failure to plan such goals will usually mean
planning to fail.

5. **Games**—We can play psychological games and use gaming to be
a victim or to victimize others, as described in chapter 1. Some
like to corner others, while others prefer to be cornered. We will
discuss more about this drama of bluffing in chapter 4 and the
triangle many poker players will web for themselves.

6. **Genuineness**—We can be ourselves, being genuine about our
beliefs and open to the differences in others and their ways of
gaming. Some do this in very charming ways, while others are
quietly pleasant to be themselves. When two or more players are
being genuine, poker can become an intimate life experience. It's
possible to be genuine and to bluff your opponents. The fact that
you have a genuine reputation can work in your favor when you
do decide to bluff. Remember, bluffing is not lying or being disin-
genuous when done in a poker game. That's poker.

We engage all of these ways to spend time. Sometimes we may be
willing to risk and be more open. At other times we'll be withdrawn
and are risking little. A closer look at these ways to structure our time
during gaming can be found in *Beyond Tells*.[8]

The BODY of a Poker Player

A player's body is what pulls all his or her skills together. In the long
run, it's how well a player bets, checks, raises, and folds that mean survival. It's also how well a player can use these same skills to bluff. It's
knowing how to bet and check at the right times. It's the skill of raising
against the right players. And, a successful player even knows how to
sacrifice a hand to set up a steal on a bigger pot. Let's look more closely
at these four modes of bluffing.

8. McKenna, J. *Beyond Tells,* pages 57–66.

Betting Bluffs

Betting at the wrong times can be costly and failure to bet at the right times can limit your profit. Betting is also a way to bluff. Think of betting as a form of communication. What is the bettor saying when he or she makes a bet. All bets are making a statement. The trick is knowing when the statements are true or a way to bluff. A bet is usually saying before the flop in Texas Hold 'Em: "I've got cards good enough to call the big blind bet." Actually, it's really not betting—it's calling. So, a raise here would really be two bets to get the game started. What that bet says is, "I've got good starting cards." However, if it comes in late position after several players just "limped in," it is saying something quite different. It's saying, "Well, I've got a pretty good hand, so let's see if anyone wants to stay when I make it another bet." I call this type of bet a way to "take the table's temperature."

A bet after the flop can be saying, "I've got some of that." If it is coming from an early position, it usually means that the bettor has top pair. However, this bet from an early position could be a bluff, if not a semi-bluff. A player with middle pair may be on a semi-bluff, hoping others will fold or that he or she will improve on the turn. It could be a stone-cold bluff, particularly if the bet is in late position after several checks. I once saw a betting bluffer in a $15–$30 game. A player had a pocket Queen, Ace (unsuited). When the flop came with a high card of King, a player in early position bet $15. He was representing that he had at least the top pair—Kings. The Queen, Ace raised and got re-raised. The Queen, Ace made it four bets and threw in some trash talk, designed to get the bettor on tilt. The original bettor just called. The raiser was saying something and the original bettor was slowing down. The bluffer had nothing but nerve and the skill of wearing down his opponent. When the turn was a blank, the pair of Kings checked so the Queen bet $30. That's when the top pair said, "Man, you must've tripped up!" So, he folded his hand. The Queen high (no pair) couldn't resist (being a player that likes thrills) and showed his Queen, Ace. The other player mourned and said that he laid down an Ace, King. That could have been a fish story. It's was hard to believe that a player would lay down top pair with a top kicker. However, by betting aggressively, the other player was able to bluff and convince the better hand that he didn't have the best hand. That's what bluffing is all about. It's also an example of how expensive bluffing can be. To pull this off it costs the bluffer $105 (five $15 bets and one $30 bet). So, don't leave home to bluff if you are short stacked and remember this only works in limit games. Don't even think about this betting bluff in a no-limit game.

Checking Bluffs

Checking is a way to see if anyone has cards they are proud of. Just calling before the flop is like a check to see if anyone behind you wants to raise the bets. It's a way to also check out other players' styles. An astute player is noticing how people are calling. After the flop, a check can still be seeking information. It also could be a way to trap an inexperienced player into betting with a weaker hand. If a player has a pocket pair and makes it trips on the flop, he or she is likely to check to give others a chance to bet. If the checker then raises the bet, it tells its own story. This check/raise may also be a bluff. If a player suspects that the bettor was betting middle pair because in late position, he might raise his check to appear to have set a trap. Checking is only as good a bluff as the knowledge of what other players will do. If you are not sure that a player behind you will bet, then checking is a poor bluff.

This is where it is important to (1) know what others are thinking; (2) know what they think that you are thinking; and (3) anticipate what they think that you think they are thinking. Then, if you are bluffing, surprise your opponents. Here's an example of this: (1) You are in early position and you are the first to check (*inviting others to think that you don't have much*). (2) When a player bets, you just call (*they think, that you think you just have a mediocre hand and you'll be chasing*). (3) When the turn comes, you lead off by betting into the previous bettor (*anticipating that a bet will leave them thinking that you thought you'd now come out with a strong hand*). In this case, the original bettor only had a middle pair and with two over-cards on the flop, thought that he'd stepped into your trap and folded. You bluffed and stole the pot with your 10, Jack (off-suit).

Raising Bluffs

Raising, as a bluff, can be a desperation move. Good players will seldom raise as a stone-cold bluff. Their raising bluffs are more likely to be semi-bluffs. This means that they don't have the best hand; rather, they have something that could improve if called. They also have something that might cause people to fold by representing that they have more than they do. If players don't fold, they could improve what they have. Here's an example of semi-bluffing by raising the bets:

A player has middle pair on the flop. Someone in last position bets. It could be that he has top pair or that he is betting his position, since everyone checked. At this point things look like this:

Bluffer's Hole cards   Flop

The player who flopped and checked his middle pair of 10s raises the bets to two bets—representing that he has top pair (King with a strong kicker)[9] and wants the late bettor to think that he set a trap. Anyone with less than Kings is likely to fold. Some players with over-cards may call chasing to outrun the bettor. Any card under a King on the turn is likely to leave the pot when the pair of 10s bets again. However, if the pair of 10s gets raised or called, a player has some of this board as well. That's why a lot of players will check their middle pair on the turn to see if anyone improved their hand. If no bets, a bet on the river will often take the pot. That's bluffing by raising without the best hand, but hopes of improving and scaring others to fold.

Folding Bluffs

Folding can be a useful bluff; but, only if your opponents know what you folded. That's where showing your folds is likely to be a setup for a later bluff. Players, however, will show when they have garbage as well as when they have a strong pair. Suppose that a player has a pocket pair of Jacks and the flop has two over-cards to the Jacks. Two people bet, suggesting they can beat the Jacks. So, the pair of Jacks folds by muck-

9. A "kicker" is poker jargon for the value of the backup card. A King with a 4 is an example of a weak kicker.

ing his hand showing the pair of Jacks. This fold is making a statement. It's teaching people that the player can lay down a good hand when he or she thinks they are beaten. Some players are a "dog with a bone" and won't lay down a hand like this. It also may be a setup for a later bluff. Suppose that this same player later gets a pocket pair of 7s. The flop has two over-cards to the 7s and someone bets. When the pair of 7s re-raises, he's hoping that they remember his lay-down. Some may and lay down if they have a middle pair. The top pair is likely to make it three bets. If you are bluffing, a re-raise may win the pot for two reasons. First of all, you already taught the table that you will lay down a hand that is beaten. Second, your aggressive re-raise says that you have better than top pair. It suggests that you may have two pair. If you were bluffing with a small pocket pair, a fold would serve to teach a different lesson about yourself.

I knew a player who seemed to love to do this when he succeeded in getting players to fold better hands. He's most likely the best seven-card stud player that I've been up against. His reputation gave him a lot of respect. At times he would cash in on it. I'm not sure why he would occasionally show that he won the game with garbage. It didn't help his reputation and it didn't get him any more chips. He's the same player I mentioned who liked to keep "chip towers" to invite younger players to take a shot at him. He never really needed all those chips. It was just his way of inducing players to try to knock his towers down. One day he got me with these moves. I ended up head to head with him and I had a pocket pair of Queens with middle cards showing. It was Fourth Street and he had an Ace and 2 of clubs showing. Here's what it looked like:

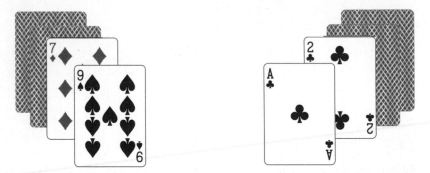

Since he was high showing, he bet $10. He was representing that he had a pair of Aces and he may have had a flush draw. Since he had brought it in with his low card (2♣), and called my raise on Third Street, his bet got my attention. I just called. On Fifth Street, I got a King and he got another club. He bet $20 and I was sure that either his Aces had me beat or he made his flush. I folded. Being the kind-hearted soul that he was he turned his hole cards over and smiled while he dragged in the pot. Here's what he was smiling about:

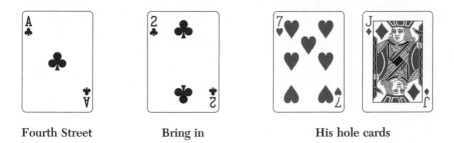

Fourth Street   Bring in   His hole cards

He was already gloating, so I didn't tell him that I laid down a pocket pair of Queens. Somehow, I think, though, he knew that.

The Foundation of a Poker Player

We have so far discussed the *Head, Shoulders,* and *Body* anatomy of a poker player. In any structure, including the structure of the poker player, the foundation is the most important element. Without a superior foundation, even the best of buildings will topple. The foundation required for success in poker is the player's ability to respond to a variety of players and table conditions. The ability to change and respond aggressively at times, passively at others, and to possess a good balance of structured play with intuitive play are ingredients that comprise the foundation of a successful poker player. This includes bluffing in response to changing conditions and players. Yes, a successful player is a responsible one.

A helpful way to define the word "responsible" is to view it as two words: response and able. This defines responsibility as having the ability to respond both positively and negatively to the cards that life deals our way. Response-Ability also determines how much a person is highly structured versus how emotionally or impulsively he or she deals with life. Players who bluff with response-Ability have three essential qualities:

1. **They like themselves AND they know how to take care of themselves during good times as well as bad times.**

   This means that a responsible player has internalized a supportive belief system. An internal supportive belief system (about self and others) is one that will sustain the player in good times and bad ones. Rather than self-defeating, they are their own best friends. This is especially true when stress happens. When they are bluffed or when a bluff doesn't work, such players will avoid whining and will not let the disappointment ruin their next play.

   Response-Able players come with an exit plan. Even when you do all the right moves, some days you "are the tree and not the dog." That means that no matter how good you are at bluffing you still might lose. Being Response-Able means adjusting to such streaks of bad luck and using a win/loss formula and sticking to it. For example, some players will leave when they win 20 to 30 times the big bet. Playing $10–$20, this means leaving when ahead by $400–$500. At the same time, good players will predetermine to leave when they have lost 60 to 80 percent of their stake. Irresponsible players will stay too long when ahead and lose what they have won and then some.

2. **They come prepared with necessary information and skills. The fact that you are reading this advanced book on bluffing means you are gaining the information you will need.**

   Responsible players make sure they have the skills and information required to do their best. This includes the wisdom to act on the knowledge and to obtain the knowledge they lack. Skills come in figuring out what hands others have and in knowing how best to play marginal hands. It also means knowing not only how to bluff but who to bluff and what kind of bluff will work on different players. Good hands play themselves. Often, the skill in living our lives is about knowing how far is far enough. Good players develop the skill to bluff in a variety of ways. Sometimes they take risks when the odds are worth it. At other times, their bluffs are passive with some and aggressive with others.

   Response-Able players learn how to figure the odds and chances of winning each hand that they play. Counting is a skill they have and by counting, dividing, and calculating, they usually are counting more money than they brought into the game. They also can alternate their bluffs by playing passively and aggressively. It's also responsible to know when thinking too much can interfere with effective play. A responsible player knows.

3. **They have permission to use their talents and to succeed.**

Many good players know how to take care of themselves. They also have obtained the information they need to get the job done. However, they may still lack the necessary *permission* to be successful and the willingness to risk. To be free to act on the knowledge and experience they have is just as important as knowing what to do. How often have you said, when you missed an opportunity to bluff and steal a pot, "I knew that! I wish I would have listened to myself."

Just as some people play until they are broke and fail to leave when they are well ahead; so, too, there are players who know better and still repeat making mistakes. They will get into staying too long, playing impossible odds, and bluffing too much or at the wrong times. This kind of player is not using his or her skills very well. The first two conditions of knowing how to care for yourself and having the information one needs seem neutralized by their lack of permission to succeed.

Beliefs That Lead to Responsible Bluffing

A responsible bluffer is a humble player. This doesn't mean being shy and self-effacing. Such humble players are truthful about themselves and life. What? Is this to say that a poker player is truthful? Perhaps authentic is a better word, since part of the skill of playing poker is to be misleading. Instead of admitting making a mistake, some players find it hard to admit and instead will blame the dealer or someone staying too long to outrun them.

Such blaming of the dealer for the bad card is the same pattern such players will use to blame life for their own ineptness. Their abilities become disabilities and their tendencies lean toward being self-defeating. It's also often an excuse to keep losing and go to the pity pot. In no other place will you find more victims than in a poker room. The victim mentality is drawn to the casino scene much like a moth is drawn into light.

I often notice players getting upset about things over which they have no control. For instance, this might occur in blackjack when another player unnecessarily takes a card and the dealer has to draw to a 6 up-card that is showing. These same players, though, will get mad when the dealer turns over and has a 5, totaling 11. I've never seen anyone get mad at the last player for holding on a stiff[10] hand, such as a 13 or 16. For example, if the dealer had a 6 showing and the next card would take a possible 10 away from the dealer, holding at a possible total of 16. However, who is to say the 10 would not have helped. If the dealer had a 5 underneath, the 10 would've given him a 21 to beat or push most of the other players. Often, when a player draws to a stiff, and when the dealer has a stiff, that player will bust and the next card up helps my hand. So, when a player does not "play by the rules," that just as often helps the table. I once saw a woman in Vegas get up and throw her drink at another player who drew to a stiff. The dealer did end up with 21 after hitting his stiff. Of course, the casino management appropriately asked the woman who threw her drink to leave the casino.

This leads to another belief that is part of responsible gaming. Namely, a responsible player is there to have fun. If I am playing at tables where the other players are rude or too serious, I will get up and find another table—not because poor players are hurting my game, such as the example given above. It's because I'm not having fun. When I'm not enjoying my play, I know that I am not playing my best. Being with people I enjoy is a big part of playing for me. I'm sure there are people who would enjoy playing at a quiet table. It may meet one's needs to play with people who are less willing to socialize and just want to play cards.

Opposite belief systems co-exist at the tables. One player told me that he never plays to have fun. He's there to make money. "Actually," he said, "if all cards had to offer is recreation, I'd never come to play." To him playing is his job, he makes so much an hour and that's what is good for his belief system. There's nothing wrong with that. However, when he's on a losing streak and not "making money," that's when we'll

---

10. A stiff in blackjack is any hand that the dealer or player has to draw to and the next card could bust them (or have them go over 21). For example, if the dealer has a 16 (a 10 and a 6) and has to draw a card, the next card could be a 9. This totals 25 and the dealer would bust.

know if he's a good "business-player." Also, we will be discussing in later chapters, what happens when people believe that they are there for one reason (like a professional earning a living) and are playing like they are there for another reason (such as losing money instead of winning).

If this player was there to make money and was successful, then he's responsible. However, if his belief system is just a way to self-deceive, then he is not responsible, even though it could be either very expensive or very profitable. One has to ask how such a player responds to losing, if his only objective is to win. This is the opposite of the belief that "It's not whether you win or lose; it's rather how you play the game." I've know many players, however, who believe, "It's not so much how you play the game, but whether you win or lose that's important." Similarly, many people will work for a living in a job they hate.

Some players make it easy to win and hard to lose. Others will come with beliefs that make it hard to win and easy to lose. For example, I knew a man who gave excellent motivational workshops. He was good at what he did. Yet, he never felt he was good enough. I asked him how he measured whether or not a seminar was successful.

He said, "Well, if everyone's pleased and I get all good evaluations at the end, then I feel great." In other words, if one person out of fifty is dissatisfied, he would feel that he had failed. That was making it hard to succeed. He changed his definition of success to make it easy to succeed.

He later told me his new decision, "If I'm being myself and have prepared a good presentation, then I've been successful." This basically put control of how successful he was in the hands of himself rather than others. In gaming, it is making it hard to win if one's goal is to always walk away with more money than one's stake. It's easy to win and hard to lose when one is playing to improve one's game, is taking advantage of the odds, and has a goal to reach over time. For example, good blackjack players are aware that the house is favored to win more than five hands out of ten. The skill is in how to win and lose at the right times. The right time to lose is when one has a small bet. Playing "smart" is in having minimum bets on the winning house hands and maximum bets on the losing house hands.

Protection in Beliefs

The first rule of gaming is to only play with what one can afford to risk and invest. Gaming is not like mutual funds. It's more like trading in stocks and bonds. Responsible gaming is very much like being an enlightened investor and putting your money where the odds are favorable. It's true that the higher the risk, the higher the payoff. However, risking money that one cannot afford to lose is being irresponsible or dreaming.

The second rule of responsible gaming is, "When it's not fun anymore, move on or quit." Responsible players play for fun because they want to be there—not because they need to be. This applies to both the professional card player and the recreational player. Players who are irresponsible are playing because they need to or have a "get-rich-quick" dream. Such dreams follow the idea of "no work but all the benefits." Now, having fun isn't necessarily always winning, although that does help. Having fun includes enjoying how one is playing, appreciating the other people one is with, and even visiting with a sociable dealer. I've often been ahead and quit because I got bored and wasn't having fun anymore. Also, I've been down in wins and having a great time. Similarly, I wasn't losing more than my limit and I had a chance to come back. However, the important thing here is that I was enjoying the process. If the process is not enjoyable, get out of the game. One can ask to play at another table and no one will think the worse for it.

Beliefs That Limit Bluffing

One rule we bring with us may be something like, "It's a sin to tell a lie." This rule about life may cause some problems in a game like poker where it's a mistake to tell the truth before the final showdown. Such a belief may serve as a tell when attempting a bluff. As mentioned earlier, a "tell" in poker is some behavior an unknowing person is doing either when they're chasing a hand, bluffing, or when they have a great hand. For instance, when a person has a great hand he may put his bet in slowly and precisely. However, when he's bluffing, he bets quickly. The speed of making bets may be the opposite for other players. Poker players are astute in noticing such tells and will seem like they're looking over one's shoulder. Some people broadcast they're bluffing as they do whenever they tell a lie. I used to be like that. My mom told me that I should always tell the truth, and if I lied she would always know it. So, whenever I shaded the truth she *did* always know. I finally figured out that my mom was a great poker player and she could always read my tells. She later told me that whenever I was hiding something I'd look her in the eyes, almost daring her to disbelieve me. Yet, when I wasn't hiding anything, I just answered her questions and kept looking at what I was doing at the time. Well, would you believe, this tell was also present when I was bluffing in poker. I used to look at my opponent when I was bluffing. Some, I'm sure, knew about it long before I was aware.

Skills and Information That Make Response-Able Bluffing

The wisdom to act on what we know and to obtain the knowledge we lack are essential qualities to build a successful foundation. It's not simply the ability to "Know when to hold 'em and know when to fold 'em." It's the skills to know the odds of staying with small pairs and to call bets against higher pairs. It's learning what you will learn for the first time in this book.

It's learning how to tell the ways that people think and how best to communicate with them. Successful bluffing follows successful people skills of communicating and speaking the language of each player (which you will learn is much different). It's not learning to speak English or French. It's learning to talk in pictures, sounds, and actions.

Here's an example of using the knowledge one already has.[11] Suppose that you have learned that a particular player only pays attention to what gets into his ears. When you are on a bluff, it would be useless to make your moves in silence. That will get some attention for such a player. To lead him where you want him to go, you will need to *talk* to this player. For example, if you said something like, "Well, I know this is foolish. You probably got a Full Boat but I'm going to bet my two pair anyhow!" I said this to an "auditory player"[12] when the third Jack showed up on the board. I had the case Jack.

He said, "You're right, it's probably a mistake."

When he bet, I raised him. He stayed in and in fact called me all the way to the river.

11. Don't worry, you'll have it by the time you finish this book.
12. We are going to go into more detail later about the different frames of reference players think in.

When I showed him the fourth Jack, he said, "It sounded like you had a full house too. I was just hoping that my pocket nines were enough."

Knowing how to bluff with words doesn't work with "visual" and "kinesthetic" players. You will learn more about this when we discuss the magic in poker in chapter 4.

Awareness can help a person develop strategies that clean up mistakes made earlier. Good players can afford to make some errors because their awareness of other possibilities and of human nature will help them to get out of trouble. For instance, in a game of seven-card stud, a 10 up on Third Street[13] bet since it was the highest card showing. A 6 up raised the 10. Well, the original bettor even said, "What? You got a pair of Aces in the hole?" So, playing and betting went on. The only pair showing at Seventh Street was a pair of 8s held by the first player. He was trying to "buy the pot," but was re-raised by a pair of Aces in the hole. The second player had no pairs showing. So, the first player—who made a mistake staying when raised—bet his pair of 8s with a full bet of twenty dollars. Well, the player with the pair of Aces folded because that was all he had and he decided that he was betting against two pairs. After the bet, the first player turned over that all he had was a pair of 8s and succeeded in getting a pair of Aces to fold. So, the mistake here was that the original bettor did not fold, since that was exactly what the raiser had—a pair of Aces in the hole. Yet, even with this mistake, an experienced player was able to semi-bluff and dig out of a hole he dug for himself.

I whispered to the veteran player, "Was that guts or skill?"

He said, "A little of both."

He later told me that he was aware that he was up against a pair of Aces in the hole. There was no pair showing except his. So, his opponent would have to have gotten his two pairs on the last card down (Seventh Street).

"So, I was risking, hoping that he didn't improve his hand and he would think I could beat Aces." This player had the wisdom to act on what he knew and to risk a full bet to represent a hand he didn't actually have.

13. In seven-card stud, each card dealt after the first two down are referred to as "Third, Fourth, Fifth, Sixth, and Seventh Streets."

Another area of skill is the ability to bluff differently to fit different kinds of players. Most good poker players who ordinarily play tightly will not change their play and play looser with a loose aggressive player. For instance, to bet/raise because one has the highest up card in a tight game will narrow the number of players, because players without over-cards may fold. This isn't true at a table where the limit is low and/or players are playing loose. So, a skillful player running a bluff won't raise loose players. However, he or she would raise a player who plays more conservatively.[14]

Permissions Needed to Succeed in Bluffing

In a later chapter, we will detail how to bluff different personalities. We will fine-tune this in how to pace and lead a player by learning to speak his or her language. Since we are discussing the foundations that good bluffing is built upon, let's first discuss the internal permissions that players bring to the table. Such permissions often make the difference between winning and losing.

In Greek mythology, Hercules was already a god. Yet, he didn't have permission to know it until he went through twelve trials. Permission has to do with a person's self-concept. People bring predispositions into adult life from the way they grew up. Their permission, or lack thereof, allow or limits people being all that they can be. Some people, for example, do not have permission to do better emotionally, financially, or socially than their parents.

To be free to act on the knowledge and experience we have, is just as important as knowing what to do. Many times I've heard people say, "I knew that! I wish I would've listened to myself." Loose players often take unnecessary and irresponsible risks. Tight players often fail to risk at all. Somewhere in the middle and acting on probabilities is the sign of a responsible player. So, tight players are actually being irresponsible. They fail to risk and to play the odds. For instance, they may have a low pair with an Ace kicker against an obvious pair of Kings, where the

14. For players who wish more information to increase gaming awareness, see Suggested Readings. Several outstanding contributions are included. For a useful summary of various casino games and reference materials see Sklansky, D. and Malmuth, M. *How to Make $100,000 a Year Gambling for a Living*. Henderson, NV: Two Plus Two Publishing, 1997.

other Kings are dead. Because the pair of 5s in the hole is smaller, a
tight player might fold, though the 5s are live and there's a chance to get
the triple card or top two pair, if dealt an Ace. That's not taking a risk
and that's being irresponsible to one's self and one's stake. Remember,
you are there to have fun and make some profit, whenever you can.

Few people understand what people like Babe Ruth and Mark Mc-
Gwire have in common. Such winners as these have three ingredients to
get where they're going: (1) they set goals, (2) they prepare themselves
for what's needed to get there, and (3) they have permission to use what
they know and desire—to be the best that they can be. Without goals
players are flopping around much like a balloon blown up and let go.
The mind is much like a guided missile. It needs a target and if used the
way it is intended, your mind will get you there. That's why Mark Mc-
Gwire is so focused. He's imaging what he's planning to do. So, too,
"The Babe" was said to point to where he hit that famous homer. What's
the image being planned for when a player sits down and says, "I've got
one hundred dollars to lose and when that's gone I'm out of here"?

So, a poker player must be able to think, figure odds, manage wins
and losses, and have the permissions to win and use his or her knowledge. We have learned that a player's belief systems about such things
as truthfulness and risk taking will influence good or bad outcomes.

Next, before we discuss how to bluff more effectively, it's important
to know what motivates players. What's important to some players is
not so with others. The Golden Rule of doing unto others as they would
do unto you will just turn out to be a "pissing contest" in poker. "You
stole a pot from me, so I'll out-run you at the river." That's the kind of
contest that you will often experience with poker players. However, if
you want to learn to bluff successfully, you must learn to change your
bluffing styles with the different types of opponents that you want to
pace and lead into folding or calling. To do this, a player needs to learn
to apply the platinum rule[15] to other poker players. That reads something like this, "Do unto others as they would have you do unto them."
In other words, learn what bluffs will work with different players and
apply them—not the way they would bluff you. Rather, use the bluff
that will meet their needs and learn about your opponents' hungers.

There's one final word I have before I move on. Namely, you can

15. See McKenna, J. *Beyond Tells,* pages 145, 147

learn a lot of things that you never knew about people and learn how best to bluff them by reading this book. However, it's imperative that you first apply this new knowledge to yourself. Until you have a handle on how people can successfully bluff you, you will never fully master the art of bluffing.

3

Different Bluffs for Different Folks

Player Hungers

I know. . . . If I asked a bunch of you what a poker player hungers for what you'd say. A lot of you would say "a table full of pigeons!" Then some would prefer the taste of "a run of good cards for a change." If you are getting bad cards and deciding to bluff with them, you are probably hungry for a lot of callers with second-best hands. But, since I can't create things like that for you, I can give you knowledge about psychological needs that can help your game of poker.

Besides food, there are three psychological needs that all of us yearn to fulfill. Even at the poker table, we will bring these needs into our game—sometimes consciously, yet always unconsciously. Knowing how to meet these needs in yourself and in your opponents will (believe it or not) improve your game and enhance the variety and quality of your bluffs. I refer to these as the "S-hungers." That stands for the hungers for *Stimulation, Structure,* and *Strokes* (recognition). If your games are not satisfying these hungers you won't settle for a blank. In other words, players will create them—sometimes in positive ways and at other times with negative moves. So, it's important to get a handle on these hungers. Again, take your time to get this knowledge before you skip ahead. I know. I know. Sometimes, getting information that will help you understand the rest of the book can be tedious. Yet, patience is, after all, the prime virtue of good poker playing.

Stimulation

All gamblers are in search of excitement. Yet, some players yearn for stimulation more than others. Many will watch your every move while others will listen to what you are saying. Others will satisfy their need for stimulation by using their feelings and intution to get in touch with others. Finally, there are players who rely on smell and will sniff out a bluff.

Some players seek excitement by creating incidents when they play. They want the greatest amount of excitement in their game in the shortest time span. Knowing this can help you determine that such a player is action oriented instead of thinking oriented. That will influence how and if you will attempt to bluff them.

At the same time, there are players who would like little stimulation. They seek solitude when they play cards. So, the absence of stimulation is their main psychological need. While charging their batteries by being alone (even in a card game), they reveal that they are non-action-oriented personalities. This too, as you will soon learn, will determine how they are best caught in your bluffs and how to trap such players.

Still, a good many players come to play for the social contact. They reveal that they are reaction oriented and will be more impulsive players. They'll moan, cheer, groan, and whine. It's all a part of their need for contact. They are the hardest players to bluff. Knowing how to meet their contact needs though can insure that they stay in longer than they should and can make you bigger pots.

Most people who play the game regularly know that it can be a pretty boring and long wait before any excitement shows up. If you are waiting for the cards to bring that excitement, you will have a much longer wait. A lot of players get excited when they get great cards and fill them into the nuts. When you win a pot every half hour, it's occasional excitement. It's exciting when you leave the table with more money than you brought into the game. For some, it's being with people and not having to be sociable or carry on a conversation that's exciting. For others, they get little excitement out of the cards. They prefer the comradery of the game.

Poker has been referred to as the "waiting game." Some are waiting for a good hand to bet. Some are waiting for someone to step into the traps that they set. And some are just waiting. If you want to increase your level of excitement by playing poker, it's time to stop waiting and become a player that creates some excitement. I know—we have a lot of aggressive players who like to raise and re-raise and play to get other players on tilt. I'm not talking about creating that kind of excitement. Most players who are not that way by nature would prefer not to be that aggressive. Then there are players who play "no fold 'em hold 'em." They are creating their own brand of excitement—usually for others who welcome them and hope they stay a long time.

Playing poker is boring for those who are just playing the cards. You can create legitimate excitement by learning to play people. That's right. When poker is played the way it is intended, it's a people game. A lot of excitement can come from creating exciting action in a game instead of waiting for that excitement to show up. All you have to do is notice the bad beat jackpots and how long they build up to realize that waiting for the right combination of cards for your excitement will be a long vigil.

You tell me. Which of these events is more exciting?

Scene one is a table where a player gets a King high straight flush. He says that was his first and he knew he had a straight; but, wow, when he realized that it was a straight flush, that was a rush. Count how many straight flushes you have experienced and ask yourself this, "How long do I have to wait to get that kind of excitement again?" That's waiting and letting things that you can't control determine how often you are excited. Remember, stimulation is a hunger that motivates us all, to various extents.

Scene two will happen over and over and doesn't *just* happen. Players who make the game exciting are doing things, engaging others, playing hunches, taking risks, playing pot odds and *playing people.* It just happens that they are doing all of this in a poker game. The cards are not that important. What they are doing with the cards is. You won't hear about it as loudly as when someone gets a straight flush; but, it will happen more often because players make it happen—not the cards.

What I am talking about is pulling off successful bluffs and never getting caught—for a whole evening . . . Wow! Now, that's exciting. So, the question is: What's more exciting, getting quads or winning a big pot with garbage? That's what I'm talking about. And, you don't have to wait for the right cards to come along to get that rush. You not only have to learn who, what, and when to bluff. You have to learn how to create bluffs that will fit different styles of players. Now, *that's exciting.*

So, playing cards without playing people is very boring. Poker and excitement, then, do go together for some. That is a rich source of stimulation that will fill you up as you go. For others, who choose starvation diets and wait for a decent hand to feed them, it's endurance.

Structure

We all need a certain amount of structure in our lives. Even the most rebellious and lackadaisical person needs to know some limits just to stay out of jail. However, those who bring a lot of structure to the way they play poker and how they bluff have an edge in the long run. In the short run, players who play with little structure and follow their whims will make some profit. They usually are reaching their goals of creating excitement. The goals for more structured players are to play the odds and not chase many pots of gold at the end of rainbows.

The need for structure is stronger in some than in others. However, limits and knowing what to expect are important to all of us. When high-structure people play poker, they bring predetermined ideas about how and when to play. Such players will use the structure of odds to determine when they play, call, raise, and fold. They are thinking or convictions-oriented and even come equipped with time structure. For example, such players will have a win/loss limit and have predetermined how much they will lose and leave when they have won over a certain percentage of their stake. When you see a very structured player, just hope that he or she is in the hand when it's down to two or three of you. Why? Because highly structured players are prime pigeons for a bluff. They pay attention to what has been played, who's betting, what you might have, and if they can't beat what they think you have they do the "right thing" and will fold. If you can "ask" them to make a call that's way out of what they will figure are good pot odds, go for it. They will predictably fold. Less structured players haven't even calculated how much a good call would be.

That said, this is a book that goes beyond bluffs. So, be sure when you decide that a player is unstructured that it's not his or her bluff. I know a player who is one of the biggest clowns that I have ever played with (except myself). That's his setup. He's actually a highly structured player and has learned to hide it well.

Strokes (Recognition)

Being recognized for the player you really are is actually sudden death to a poker player. It's a game of deception and few players want you to really recognize them. That's not what we are talking about when it comes to understanding our hunger for recognition (strokes). Even good players can become like prima donnas if they don't get the respect they deserve. It's true though, that when it comes to poker, many players don't wish to be noticed.

This deception contradicts our need for recognition. Such players want you to notice the opposite of who they are and what they have. Still, if you learn what strokes are important, you can determine how a player is prone to play. The kinds of strokes players want will let you know if they operate more out of their thoughts or their emotions.

Rather than being noticed for how they play, more and more players just want to know that you appreciate them. They yearn for the recognition of their person. Yet, some players want to be noticed for how well they know the game and how well they play. To suggest that they are doing well because they are lucky would be a negative stroke to such players. The main things to look for in stroking patterns are how players *give, take, ask for,* and *refuse*[1] strokes. This will tell you a lot about how they can be bluffed. It also will help you anticipate how they might bluff you. For example, if a player doesn't give many positive strokes and only negative ones (like whining a lot), such a player is hanging a target around his or her neck. Players love to take a shot at players who are down. Also, if you give other players a lot of positive strokes, you are probably well liked. This helps when your bluffs walk away with their former chips. It's a lot easier to lose to someone that's pleasant.

So, What!?

How is knowledge about a player's psychological needs going to help your game? By knowing what people need the most, you will also be

---

1. These factors are so important that in 1975 I invented *The Stroking Profile.* It is used all over the world by therapists and educators to arrive at diagnoses and treatment plans. For more information on this tool, which was validated by the University of Miami in a ten-year study, you can visit my website: www.JimMcKenna-PhD.com.

able to determine their personality orientation. That knowledge about your opponent will clue you into how that player is likely to play, including predicting how they are likely to bluff and be bluffed. Determining a player's personality type will warn you about what he or she is likely to call, check/raise, fold, and bluff. For example, if a player is high in needing structure that reveals that you are playing a left-brained opponent who only plays cards and hands that have good odds. You can't count on them to bet if you are into trapping with a check/raise. Why? Because they have already figured the odds and possibility that you could have the best hand. Right-brained players are less structured and more impulsive. You can count on a call, if not a re-raise. That's the reason only to bluff with the best hand (which is actually not a bluff) with loose players.

In *Beyond Tells*, for the first time, I integrated personality types with poker players. This demonstrated how players differ in the manner they play and the tells they are likely to use. I will review that information in the next chapter with an emphasis on how personality types will affect bluffing in the game of poker. Before we go there, it's important to distinguish bluffing from psychological games. Unfortunately, some players use bluffs to play psychological games where not only pocketbooks get drained but players walk away with hurt and angry feelings.

Psychological Games and Bluffing

The way a person bluffs says something about the way they deal with people in their lives outside of a poker game. Righteous bluffers are players who want to prove something like, "My skills are better than yours." It's an adult version of the childhood game of, "My dad's tougher than yours." Underneath some bluffing is an unconscious need to play a "gotcha" psychological game.

The way people set themselves up to get bluffed can also tell how people live their lives as victims. Some are playing a psychological game of "kick me." This is not saying that people who are bluffing are all playing a subconscious psychological game. All bluffs are not psychological games. However, all psychological games are unconscious and can be underneath some bluffing moves. Chances are that a bluffer or a bluffee who takes a payoff of righteousness or hurt feelings is using poker to play a psychological game. If they do the same thing with people outside of the poker game, then they are most likely using bluffing to prove they're okay and others are not okay,[2] or vice versa.

Psychological games, though, are something entirely different than playing the games of deception needed in poker. There's a difference in playing the game and "being gamy." Psychological games are unconscious behaviors that we play for feeling payoffs like being righteous, feeling ashamed, getting angry, or feeling devastated and hurt. In order to advance our life-scripts[3] (our predispositions when under stress), we will unknowing play certain favorite psychological games.

All psychological games involve a shifting from being a victim, a persecutor, or a rescuer.[4] It's amazing to see these roles played out in casinos. Remember that people only get into their scripts when they are stressed and become distressed. So, these games won't be seen when players are stress-free. However, some people are also stressed when they're doing well. So, some self-defeating plays will be seen in good times as well as bad ones.

When There's More to Bluffing Than Winning

The card table is the microcosm of players' lives. So, when we play cards we will often bring our favorite psychological game to the table. Such games serve the purpose of feeding favorite "lousy feelings," like being victimized, or proving how stupid others are.

Game Formula

The modified Game Formula[5] mentioned earlier in this chapter will go beyond bluffing. Again, it's important to stress that every time a player is bluffing, that player is not necessarily playing a psychological game. It could be a poker strategy, a psychological game to collect a feeling payoff, or both. If it is not a game (as opposed to being "gamy")

---

2. Harris, T. *I'm OK—You're OK*. See Suggested Readings.

3. Life Scripts are the unconscious predispositions, written in childhood and revealed when a person is under stress. See, Berne, E. *What Do You Say After You Say Hello* in Suggested Readings.

4. See the Karpman Drama Triangle in chapter 6. Steve Karpman, MD, has created a useful drama triangle showing these switches in game roles.

5. Ernst, F. and Berne, E. See Suggested Readings.

the payoff is winning more pots. If it is a psychological game, the payoff is bad feelings. The bluffer ends up feeling one-up or righteous. The pigeon thinks about being kicked, tricked, and victimized and feels hurt. This doesn't mean that when a player becomes a pigeon and gets bluffed that they are not disappointed. The difference is that in a psychological game the feeling stays on and is used to advance a script issue.

EQUATION 1. GAME FORMULA[6]

$$B + P = PD \longrightarrow T \longrightarrow Payoff$$

Psychological games are a variation of childhood games of "Mines bigger than yours!" or, "My daddy's tougher than yours, ha, ha!" Whether a player is "top dog" or "bottom dog," both gain a psychological advantage to feed their script.

A game-free player may use this same formula as a strategy. The difference is that the payoff is not an emotional, something-to-prove, thing. The payoff in a non-gamy bluff strategy is that it's part of the game and not a game within the game.

Games Between Players

The popular book, *Games People Play*, by Eric Berne contains many games seen at any poker table. Here's a few fine whines served by players and the psychological games they represent.

"If It Weren't for You" (IWFY)
"IWFY" is a psychological game useful for people who want to cover up their own inadequacies. The one blamed for such playing inadequacies is the dealer or another player who "got *my* cards." The lament is, "If it weren't for the lousy cards that the dealer was dealing I could be a better player." Another favorite whine when a player loses a hand on the river is, Runner, runner!"[7] This is like saying, "If it weren't for you staying in for all seven cards, I could have won!"

Each of us has to experience our share of losses. The difference is

---

6. Also referred to earlier in this chapter as the Bluffing Formula.
7. Poker jargon for someone who needs two cards in a row to make a hand.

that some lose and get ready for the next hand. Others use the loss to suffer and extract a payoff of sympathy or blaming others. IWFY players seldom, if ever, give credit to the dealer or other players for their good hands. The main advantage to this psychological game is that it's a way to hide from one's self, to ignore one's own inadequacies, and to blame the world for being a poor player. If another player stays and gets a better hand, the IWFY player will get upset not only because he or she was beat, but also because the other player stayed when (s)he "shouldn't have." It never seems to occur to such a player that the other player stayed because of skills in reading cards, people, and odds.

"Look How Hard I'm Trying"

The game of "Look How Hard I'm Trying" occurs when players lament with these whines after a spell of receiving bad cards.

"I had you before the flop!"
"I never get good cards!"
"I get the same cards every hand!"
"If I'd stayed, I would have won!"
"I'm beat more with pocket Aces than I win!"
"I can't win with good cards!"

This group, though, has many "non-whiners." Some "Trying Hard Players" will suffer in silence until they collapse to prove how strong they are. Once it becomes known that they have a bleeding ulcer, they will look up and say, "Look how hard I've been trying!" Such silent sufferers are trying hard to be strong. If they are pushed around, they'll make foolish bets, just to say, "Look how hard I tried." Often, these players are like a dog with a bone. They refuse to give up a losing hand. No one ever taught them to say, "Uncle," or to give up before things got worse.

"Blemish"

The psychological game of "Blemish" is evident with whines such as these:

"I can't believe you'd play cards like that!"
"Don't you ever check?!"
"I'll believe you next time."

"I only called [with a bad hand] because you were betting."
"I can't believe you stayed to the river with that hand."

The common denominator of a lot of these games is that someone's not okay—it's either you or it's me.

For a complete list of *Games People Play,* you may want to read the popular book with this title written by Eric Berne, MD.[8] Here are some of the more common games that show up when there is bluffing involved.

"Ain't it awful"

Misfortune is a part of living and playing any game of cards, such as poker. Some days I feel like saying, "If it weren't for disappointment, I wouldn't have any appointments today!" However, when we suffer misfortune, this presents opportunity for some to grow and others to suffer and extort sympathy. "Ain't it awful" players seek the opportunity to suffer. They are the table-whiners. When you are bluffed and lose a hand you can learn from it, treat it as part of the game, and move to the next hand. Or, you can whine about why you stayed and how sneaky your opponent was.

Responses to misfortune may be divided into these three groups of players:

1. **First-Degree Level**—These are socially acceptable games with tangent payoffs. There are players who get bluffed more often than others. Their suffering is inadvertent and they don't want it. When they get sympathy they may or may not exploit it. They generally accept the courtesy of a few "poor babies" and let it go at that.

2. **Second-Degree Level**—These payoffs are for real. There are also players who inadvertently become pigeon drops and their suffering is greatly received because it gives them a chance to exploit condolences. These players take advantage of the poor poker to get some "secondary reward" of people feeling sorry for them.

3. **Third-Degree Level**—These payoffs are for keeps. These are players who are there only to suffer or feel bad. They seek it out

8. See Suggested Readings.

and play in order to end up victims. They are the table pigeons. They stay longer than they should and play almost impossible odds. They seek suffering much like a hypochondriac will go from one doctor to another worrying about ill health. For these players, suffering is not optional. They want it, seek it, and enjoy it. In fact, they are often laughing and excited while complaining about how lousy the hands are that they have been dealt. If they get a good hand they will usually find a way to mess it up so they can suffer and play "Ain't it awful."

"Corner" (NIGYSOB: "Now I Got You, You SOB")

When playing for more than just winning a pot, some bluffing players are there to play psychological games to corner others and take a righteous payoff. However, it takes two to dance these games and some players use bluffing to play their favorite games with gullible pigeons. Probably the most frequent is the game of Corner where a player becomes the table-parent and catches other players being bad. Eric Berne called this game of corner a game of NIGYSOB, an acronym for *Now I've Got You, You Son of a Bitch.* The bluff is an efficient poker player just playing the game the proper way when a player who's the pigeon has the tendency to perhaps be impulsive and make mistakes. Any time after that the righteous player can catch the player with a bluff and collect a righteous payoff. The player who's also playing a game of "Kick Me" (below) usually gets hurt or mad and the beat goes on.

Here's a more specific example that involves a dealer and a player. Dealers have some latitude in how strictly to apply certain rules. With players that they like they may be a little more liberal than with players that they don't enjoy. When a player turns a hand face down, technically (s)he has folded. If the dealer touches the cards that "mucks" them, the hand is dead and even if it was the winner, it can't be played. I've seen some dealers allow a player to change their mind and not touch the cards too quickly, so the player might say, "Oh, let me look again, I might have had a flush." However, a dealer who's playing NIGYSOB with players might with the speed of a bullet grab the cards and say, "Sorry Sir! Your hand is dead!" You know it's a game when the player gets mad and the dealer gloats (the Payoffs). You are doubly sure it was a psychological game when the same thing happens later and the same dealer is slow to touch the cards. Players also play NIGYSOB with dealers and become the table-parent waiting for some dealers to make a mistake that they can point out.

"Kick Me"

The bluffer would not be complete without the corresponding bluffee. These are the victims who are there to get payoffs of feeling trapped, duped, and cheated. They are playing poker to get kicked, leaving broke and feeling victimized.

This group, though, has many non-whiners. Some Trying Hard Players will suffer in silence until they collapse to prove how strong they are. Once it becomes known that they have a bleeding ulcer, they will look up and say, "Look how hard I've been trying!" Such silent sufferers are trying hard to be strong. If they are pushed around, they'll make foolish bets, just to say, "Look how hard I tried." Often, these players are like a dog with a bone. They refuse to give up a losing hand. No one ever taught them to say, "Uncle," or to give up before things got worse.

Poker is ripe for the game of NIGYSOB. The whines come from the "Kick Me" players who are the NIGYSOB players' victims. Here are some whines that usually mean that the player has just been cornered:

"Oh, hiding behind the bushes again, huh?!"
"I knew I shouldn't have called that raise!"
"I didn't think you'd have those Aces again!"
"Man! You sure are lucky!"
"If I would have gotten my card, you'd have been sorry!"

The common denominator of a lot of those games is *Ain't it awful*. When we suffer misfortune, this presents opportunity for some to grow and others to suffer and extort sympathy. "Ain't it awful" players seek the opportunity to suffer. They are the table-whiners.

These are just a few of the variety of fine whines served in any poker lounge. In chapter 5, when we are unveiling the "Mysteries of Poker," we will explore the Drama that is contained in psychological games.

Telling Bluffs Apart

Sneak Bluffing

How often have you been playing in a Texas Hold 'Em game with fair cards and a player behind you who just limps in? Or, perhaps, hesitates before he calls and seems to be doing it reluctantly. Do you relax and think, "Okay, At least I've got him beat!" This is actually when you should start to worry. This quiet player who likes to just call and hide behind the proverbial bush, may already have you in his or her trap. That's why this type of bluffing I call "Sneak Bluffing."[9] It's one of the hard ones to avoid since the player is seldom aggressive yet plays a pretty tight game. One of these players is a friend of mine and I asked him once, "Do you come to the table with a short stake on purpose or do you have an angle?" He said, "I do it for the players who don't know how tight and conservative a player I am. I'm hoping that such players will make the mistake of going after me when I play good cards and get caught up in my act that I haven't been doing too well." Wow! I knew my friend was much better than he appeared. However, I thought that his short stacks meant that he wasn't doing very well. That's exactly what he wanted me to think. Now that's pretty sneaky and pretty clever. Another type of player likes to be sneaky when he or she bluffs. This highly structured player plans his every move. He only plays good cards and maximizes plays when in position. This system player even has a system for when and how he or she bluffs. The problem this player has is that he or she is so structured that when they bet, most people with marginal hands will fold like trained pigs. So, I asked another friend who is like this how he handles his tight reputation. I wasn't surprised to hear him say, "I take advantage of it. Sometimes when I've got lousy cards and I am in a good position, I'll bet or check/raise with a stone-cold bluff!" I wondered if he was setting my up to call him next time that he has a great hand.

Dare Bluffing

There's another kind of bluffing style that I refer to as dare bluffing. These players are daring you to call them because they know they have

9. McKenna, J. *Beyond Tells*, pages 199–215.

you beat. They are bluffing with the best hand and they seem to know it. These players are also highly planned in their actions and they are aggressive when they play. That's because they only play with winning hands and will make you pay if you are chasing with a mediocre hand. Their dares, however, are not always obvious. They could be checking and re-raise a bet when someone bets. Their bets are always at least semi-bluffs. In other words, what they have is already good and there's a chance of improving if you call them.

Both of these bluffers who are highly structured, have a plan, and differ in how aggressive they bluff. The Sneak Bluffer is slow to bluff and plays a more passive game. The Dare Bluffer is equipped with a plan to at least semi-bluff and does so in a more aggressive fashion.

Attack Bluffing

A whole set of players out there are not so well planned in their bluffs. These much looser players bluff and keep the action going. Some I refer to as employing "attack bluffing." Others are less aggressive and seem to be playing hands they don't have but wish they did. I refer to these as using "dream bluffing." Structured players are bluffing with their eyes wide open.

Next there are many players who like to close their eyes with little regard to planning when they bluff. Unlike players who either dare you or sneak up on you, a whole set of players are not so well planned in their bluffs. These much looser players bluff and keep the action going. Some of these unplanned bluffers are employing attack bluffing.[10] Other unstructured bluffers are less aggressive and seem to be playing hands they don't have but wish they did. These players are using dream bluffing. While structured players are bluffing with their eyes wide open, there players like to close their eyes with little regard to planning when they bluff.

Attack bluffs are aggressive and unplanned bluffs. When one of these "no fold 'em hold 'em" players splashed the pot with a raise, I had already pegged him for an action-oriented guy—a High Roller. So, it wasn't a surprise to me that he chose an attack approach to bluffing. Often, when you see such bluffing occur aggressively, with flare, the

10. McKenna, J. *Beyond Tells,* pages 199–215.

bettor hasn't even looked to see what he or she is betting into. Such players take risks more liberally, will bet into over-cards, and can be a threat to the most seasoned of players—particularly if the loose player is catching their hands. They will give you action and stay in longer than they should. However, this high roller deserves a word of caution. Since they are closer to the center on a scale of Responsiveness/Aggressiveness, they can modify impulsive bluffs and become more structured when needed.

Dream Bluffs

Dream bluffs occur from players whose bluffs are passive and unplanned. These bluffers play more with their hunches. They will do little to influence play and pretty much let the cards play themselves. They are bluffing as if they are strong because they actually believe that they are going to win the hand. They are dreaming of the hand they are going to get. It can't even be called semi-bluffing, because they are bluffing on their dreams and don't even have a pair or a gut-shot straight. Recently, I was playing with a very friendly player who seemed to play a lot of hands. Some people would have called him a calling station. People were filling up on his frequent calls. I began to wonder about how he was playing. So, I asked him when he showed his hand (Ace high, no pairs), "That wasn't even a 'semi-bluff.' What were you thinking?"

He replied, "Well, I would have had him beat if I got another Ace!"

These "dreamers" will bet more on the come and play as if they already have the hand. They are playing more from emotions while being passive.

Both these styles of bluffing come from loose players. The difference is that the Attack Bluffer is aggressive; while the Dream Bluffer is much more passive. There's an expression in poker to "play 'em like you've got 'em!" Well, this is more of a way of life for all bluffing styles. However, the Dream Bluffer is more of a stone-cold bluff. They tend to play every hand as if they already have what they are representing. The Attack Bluffer, while misrepresenting his or her hand, is motivated more from seeking excitement.

So, how does one tell whether a person is dreaming, daring you, sneaking up on you, or attacking you? The answer is simply, "Know your players!" By determining the personality types of players, you will know how to determine whether they are structured or loose. The highly structured players will favor planned bluffs ("dare" and "sneak"). The looser players will lean toward impulsive bluffs ("attack" and "dream").

Chasing Smart

How often have you had a pocket pair before the flop and wondered whether they were worth playing. Let's look at three pocket pairs and you are in middle position with each of these:

No one has raised the bet before you. However, there are a number of players behind you (*including the blinds*) that could raise the bet. Or, you might get these before the flop in your middle position:

The same middle position conditions exist and your pocket pair is:

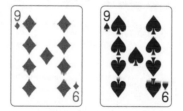

Do you *call, raise,* or *fold*? Finally, for this discussion, suppose that you are dealt this pocket pair before the flop and you are in middle position:

What's your play? All three pocket pair are being played, pre-flop, from middle position, and no one has raised the bet before you act. From the start, everyone is chasing to make the best hand at the flop or the river. Some chase "impossible dreams" while a few are chasing smart.

Let's see what kind of chaser you are. We know only one thing for sure. The odds of your getting a third matching card (on the flop) are about 8 percent or 11 to 1. After that, it drops to about 4 percent or 22 to 1. So, how stubbornly do you usually play these pocket pairs? Do you just play the odds? Do you take into consideration what position you are betting from? Who and what type of players will act after you? Of course, a seasoned player will take all of these into account.

Most players in low-limit games will play any pocket pair as long as there are no raises. Some more disciplined players will fold the 2s if there are any raises before or after they call. Some players will slow-play the 9s and the Queens to see what the rest of the table is doing. With medium pairs, there's really is no right or wrong answer to whether to simply call or to raise the bet. Raising has its advantages to narrow the field of Aces and Kings with small kickers. However, in low-limit games, these small-kickers players will act like a dog with a bone and call to the river. Let's suppose that the flop comes to:

Flop

And, two players bet before you. With three over cards, do you get stubborn and call with your pocket pair? What are the odds of chasing this hand? Well, with the 2s, you are three times beaten—maybe more if someone also has a pocket pair. Now the pocket nines and the pocket jacks have some possibility of improving and may be worth a chase. What do you think? If you have the pocket nines, the flop gave you a "runner-runner"[11] flush draw and a "runner-runner" gut-shot-straight draw.

---

11. "Runner-runner" is poker jargon for chasing two miracle cards to make a hand.

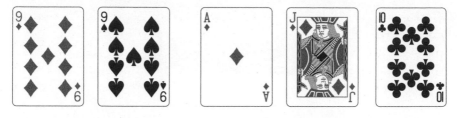

Your Hole Cards   The Flop

What are the odds of chasing this hand with three over-cards, even though you have a distant gut shot and a flush draw? To get trips on the turn, it's still an 11-to-1 shot. Then if the 9 came, it could give someone holding a Queen, King a higher straight. To get either the straight or the flush you'd have to get two needed cards in a row (runner-runner). Your odds of getting another diamond on the turn is about 35 percent or 2 to 1. However, to get the fifth diamond, it's only a 5-to-1 chance. Do you hold your breath and "runner-runner" a flush? So, go figure! Would you lay down this pair? I hope so. However, in low-limit games the cost of going to the river is often so little that many players would chase this hand. It could be that the odds of making "trips" are 11-to-1 with two outs. In a low-limit game (like $3–$6), it's worth the chase if there is at least $66 in the pot. Of course, even if you make it, you'll probably get beaten by a straight or flush. So is this chase smart or dumb?

We had so much fun with that, let's take the same flop if you held the pocket Queens:

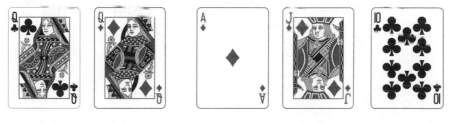

Your Hole Cards   The Flop

Now, you only have one over-card to worry about. Yet, you have a runner-runner Royal Flush draw, a flush draw, a gut-shot-straight draw, with a runner-runner full house possibility. So, what do you think? Yeah! Go ahead play it, that's gambling and that's chasing smart.

4

Bluffs with Personality

If ever the personalities of players are on display, it's when players are bluffing as well as when they are responding to being bluffed. Players will attempt to hide their personalities with acts like being tired, being new to the game, being influenced by alcohol, playing stupid, or even acting like they know a lot more than they actually do. Still, if you listen to how they talk and notice how they behave, you will discover their true personality types. This will guide you into how they can be bluffed, what their hungers are, and how to pace them and lead them with your bluffs. It will also help to anticipate how different personalities can go on-tilt. Let's review what predispositions different personality types bring to the tables.

Responses Based on Personality Predispositions

The common denominator that accounts for the variety of responses to bluffing is personality differences.[1] Our personalities can be understood from a variety of theories. However, the basis of one's personality is a mixture of four elements: our *thoughts, feelings, beliefs,* and *behaviors.* The last component of personalities (behaviors) can be further divided into *actions, reactions,* and *non-actions,* which include introversive and

---

1. For the readers who have already read *Beyond Tells,* this will be a review of things I introduced in 2005. However, I will be integrating personality information with a new focus on bluffing.

extroversive behaviors.[2] Personalities, then, comprise the unique combination of these six orientations:

1. Thoughts
2. Beliefs (opinions)
3. Feelings
4. Actions
5. Reactions
6. Non-actions

Players make sense of the world around them primarily in one of these ways. They organize their thoughts and their cards by their favorite one of these six perceptions.[3] The also will choose the style of bluffing based on their favorite orientation. Later, this combined with the differences in how various players think will become invaluable tools to improve your own bluffs.

Thinking-Oriented Bluffers

These are primarily left-brain players and very organized. Thinkers know the odds and can quote the latest statistics. They usually do quite well. Many handle bad times by beating up on themselves. "How could I have been so stupid?" They're continually analyzing their mistakes and licking their wounds when they're down. They will blame themselves when a loose player successfully bluffs them into calling. "I should have known . . ."

Their pleasure in playing is doing a good job. Their psychological need is for people to recognize them for how well they play poker. In other aspects of their lives, they display a lot of plaques and trophies to show how proficient they are. If they make a mistake, they hide it like it was a hideous sin. To make an error is the epitome of failure for

2. Kahler was the first to add three behavioral components to C.G. Jung's two basic components. See Kahler, T., *The Mystery of Management* and Jung, C. G., *Personality Types: The Collected Works of C. G. Jung*, in Suggested Readings for more details.

3. The Personality Pattern Inventory (PPI), developed by Taibi Kahler, Ph.D., will determine people's base personality as well as the phase they are currently using. For more information on obtaining the PPI contact Kahler Communications, Inc., 1301 Scott Street, Little Rock, Arkansas 72202.

thinking-oriented players. One such player would comment on how people were playing, much like a coach would. When he got caught trying to steal a pot with a hand he should've thrown away much earlier, he was embarrassed. In fact, he got so flustered he began saying he misread his hand. This distracted him so much that he stopped "coaching" and became very quiet and withdrawn. He eventually lost his stake and left—all because he wasn't perfect and others saw it. These thinking-oriented players are also the keepers of the "towers of chips." They'll display their winnings as proud posters attesting to how accomplished they are.

Conversely, these bluffers are much easier to bluff because they pay such strict attention and anticipate what you are representing. Thinking-oriented bluffers have a lot in common with the next personality type—beliefs (opinions)-oriented bluffers—the difference is that "thinkers" are harder on themselves than others.

Belief (Opinion)-Oriented Bluffers

These are also very methodical players who tend to be hard on other players. The major difference from thinking-oriented players is that these players are also very opinionated. Thinking-oriented types are hard on themselves. Opinion-oriented players are hard on everyone else. These are the "parents" of the poker tables. They know a lot and they let others know what they think. They expect others to play poker the way it was meant to be played—whatever that is. They will critically comment on how others play and can be off to the side mumbling with other conviction-oriented players. They like to gossip about whether what they are witnessing is a bluff or a real hand. To catch them making a mistake is certain to put them on tilt and make them more vulnerable to being bluffed. Their fear of making mistakes and being criticized will also make them prime targets to lay down good hands when bluffed.

In the game of Texas Hold 'Em, a great many comments are overheard about how other players play their cards. For example, suppose a player comes in with a King and a 4 (unsuited) and gets beat by a player with a King and Queen in the hole. The opinion-oriented players at the table will be quick to criticize the player who got beat for even playing with such a low "kicker" as a 4. Hold 'Em may even attract a higher percentage of such opinion-oriented players. Since they seldom will play little kickers, they seldom will create any excitement by bluffing such a hand. Generally, if they are betting, they are not bluffing. This could work to their advantage.

Feeling-Oriented Bluffers

Players who use intuition and hunches to play cards will do well at times. Most of the time, particularly in the midst of some stiff competition, they'll make many mistakes. A lot of feeling-oriented players don't seem to learn from those mistakes. In fact, they just seem to keep asking to be kicked. What they want is to be accepted. They're there more to socialize than to win. They'll get kicked if that's the only way one can be noticed. A friend of mine has a major psychological need to be recognized as a person. It's important to her that people like her. She knows how to play stud poker and is proficient at it—most of the time. I noticed that when she'd play at a hostile or unfriendly table, she would begin to make errors. She played best when she was playing at a friendly table where people appreciated her as a person. This resulted in the absence of errors to get attention. My friend is typical of feeling-oriented players, whose need for acceptance is greater than how well they can play the game.

When bluffing, though, this type of feeling-oriented player is very hard to read. That's because when they are betting "on the come," they actually believe that they already have the hand. If they think that you like them, they will stay with you all the way when you are bluffing them. If they think that you don't really like them, they may lay down their chase just to avoid playing with you.

Action-Oriented Bluffers

These players are in the game for the excitement, the risks, and the stimulation. When things go wrong they get tough. They usually are expecting others to be tough and will get pretty pushy. "If you can't stand the heat, get out!" is their motto. Creating negative excitement is better than no excitement at all. So, these players know how to get others upset. They seldom, if ever, admit to creating problems when things are bad. It's always someone else's "dumb actions" that caused the problem.

Action-oriented players are often the targets of the opinion-oriented players. Such belief-oriented players will comment their convictions and challenge the action-oriented "upstarts." It's more exciting for the action-oriented player to take chances and break the rules of safe and good card playing. Often, an action player will just infuriate the more conservative player.

I noticed this at a Texas Hold 'Em table where an action-oriented player was creating negative excitement. He had loose play and a loose mouth. He'd make comments like, "Come on you guys! Let's get some action. This is boring." Once he criticized an opinion-oriented player who was careful and prone to study the cards before betting. So, after that comment, when the action got to this slow-paced player's turn to bet, he took even longer—just staring at the cards and peeking at the other player who wanted things to speed up. After about sixty or ninety seconds (so it seemed), the player bet and then said, "Is that fast enough for you?" This didn't upset the other players who were also annoyed by the loud-mouthed player. It didn't even upset the action player. He'd succeeded in getting some action going. He got another player to get angry.

Sometimes, making other players angry is a strategy used to get upset players to bet looser. One retired sales executive whom I met tells an amusing story of his using this technique with another action-oriented player. It was working and the upset player was betting looser. Finally, the other player stood up and said to my friend, "One more word out of you and I'll meet you outside."

The older retired sales exec stood up and said, "Can you back up what you are saying?!"

"You're damn right I can!"

So, my friend sat down saying, "Well then, okay, I'll shut up and behave." Everyone had a big laugh and two action-oriented players got the excitement they like without anyone getting hurt.

Reaction-Oriented Bluffers

"Have you heard any good jokes lately?" This is how a reaction-oriented player sounds. These bluffers come for a good time. They enjoy contact with the game and with people. They'll get high on good hands as well as second-best ones. They like to see action and are easily bored. For this reason, reaction-oriented players aren't too patient. They will even make mistakes to get some action going. Playing "stupid" and acting confused is a favorite way to handle bad times for these players. After all, if a reaction-oriented player is confused, he or she is making people contact—even though it's negative contact. Other players will either try to rescue or explain, or some may even get annoyed at the delay.

If there's a player that other players will miss, it's the reaction-oriented player. These players are fun and they like to tease. Some tables like this type of player more than others do. One such player would tease when he had a good hand. If someone would check, he'd say, "Oh! Showing weakness, hey!" Then he'd go through the motions of betting before he'd also say, "Check!"

Reaction-oriented players are at their best when they're having fun. This may be true of everyone. It's especially so for reaction-oriented players. When they're down, they'll play dumb and invite criticism rather than laughter. Sometimes, one will see a direct relationship between how many chips a reaction-oriented player has and how cheerful they are. In bad times, they become the scapegoat and stop teasing. They require connecting with others, whether doing well or poorly. Instead, one will see them looking around the room at other tables when bored to see if there's more fun someplace else.

Non-Action-Oriented Bluffers

Playing cards is probably the most social thing that non-action-oriented players do. They are withdrawn and don't participate in much of anything that happens except the hands they play. They handle stress by getting quieter and stronger. These introversive types are usually good players. They make good employees because they follow directions and listen well. They don't take many risks and they aren't self-starters. They will play very tightly and won't win or lose much.

They would really rather be alone.[4] In their private lives, they'll spend most of their time in solitude. This doesn't mean that everyone who is quiet and withdrawn at the poker table is a non-actions oriented player.

Occasionally, I'd meet this type of player who would take pride in his or her "poker face." My attempts to engage them in small talk would

4. Kahler, T. *Mystery of Management.*

usually prove futile. They are there to play cards—not to socialize. In fact, one such player told me, "Playing cards is the one thing that I enjoy doing most with people—because we can play all night and not have to talk."

Player Perceptions

How players perceive things will influence how they can be bluffed. The ways that they think and make sense of the world around them, including their cards and their opponents, will influence what types of bluffs will work with some and not with others. We will spend a whole chapter later on how players make different sense out of the same information. Suffice it to say here that if you are giving a talk and are only using words, without any slides, stories, examples, and exercises for people to participate in, you are going to miss two-thirds of your audience. To limit your bluffs to just making certain moves will also miss two-thirds of your opponents. You must learn how to bluff with actions, words, and pictures. Some players will respond to what you say, others to what you do, and still others to how you look. I will tell you more about that later.

While some players say that gaming may be 90 percent luck and 10 percent skill, it's the skill to know how to handle both good and bad luck *and* how to bluff differently (for different players) that makes the winning difference in the long run of success. More than either luck or skill is the bluffing attitude that players bring to the gaming table. In this sense gaming is 25 percent luck, 5 percent skill, and 70 percent attitude.

Player Perceptions and Bluffing

Most of us are predictable. When things are going well, as players, we seldom present a negative attitude. However, when under stress, *playing styles* can change into *survival styles*. Such survival styles will reveal winning, losing, or breaking even attitudes. When players discover they have been bluffed and laid down their best hands, stress may turn into distress. Some of their ways to survive will involve blaming, finding fault, or becoming victims of the house. Others under stress will assume an attitude of being challenged and literally turn bad lay-downs (lemons) into opportunities to use their practice wisdom (lemonade).

Some of the best players also know how to use their position and opportunities to bluff with "lemon hands."

Understanding players and their different playing attitudes will help identify ways to avoid being bluffed and then turning stress into distress. Staying in a positive frame of mind is as much a playing skill as playing that is based on odds versus gut feelings. When players are getting their needs met, their attitude is more effective or at least in bad times, they are less likely to become distressed. When players are meeting their psychological needs, they are staying longer, are putting more money into action, and are more likely to be winning, or at least are better managing their win/loss goals.

Some players will do things to change attitudes in others. They will make moves to get other players to play "on tilt." In fact, that's the only way that some less skillful players can get an edge over more skillful players. Even though a player will assume a negative attitude and even lose more than usual, in the long run players will handle stress better when their psychological needs are being met. Knowing how to manage such distress is part of the skills that good players and casino professionals provide.

Assertive Versus Responsive Attitudes

There are two main differences in how people approach the game of life and casino play. First, players approach games and their bluffs at different levels of assertiveness. This can range from very passive players (introverts, who slow-play) to very aggressive players (extroverts, who use raising to intimidate). Second, players will respond to life and others with varied attitudes, ranging from *reserved* and logical to *responsive* or emotional players. The former are very structured and have their bluffing plans and procedures predetermined. Others bring little or no structure to the game and play only from their guts, their hunches, or their intuition.

Carl Jung noticed such differences in attitude in the early twentieth century. He noted:

> For us, attitude is a readiness of the psyche to act or react in a certain way. The concept is of particular importance for the psychology of complex psychic processes because it expresses the peculiar fact that certain stimuli have too strong an effect on some occasions, and little

or no effect on others. To have an attitude means to be ready for something definite, even though this something is unconscious; for having an attitude is synonymous with an a prior orientation to a definite thing, no matter whether this be represented in consciousness or not.[5]

If we compare a player's aggressiveness and attitude, we can determine different player styles[6] and predict their ways of bluffing. This comparison will produce a useful assessing grid such as in Chart 1.:

Bluffing Attitudes and Personalities

Playing styles come from noticing the players' personalities and their attitudes. How assertive and structured their approach to gaming will reveal playing styles that later will be valuable in revealing their favorite ways of bluffing. When we notice how differently each personality type approaches the risks of gambling there are at least six basic styles of play revealed.[7] Each style comes complete with its own pre-existing attitudes about people, money, risking, problems, frustration, losing, and winning. This combination of personality types and player styles are referred to as:

High Roller
Party Hardy
Hunch Player
Loner
System Player
The Boss

As we will show, each of these styles of playing present good and bad aspects. The ideal player combines elements of each style. This composite style may rightly produce a seventh player style, which I referred to

5. Jung, *Personality Types*, page 414. The noted Swiss psychiatrist Carl Gustav Jung was the first to create the words extrovert and introvert. He compared his personality types by looking at such levels of assertiveness and combined these with what he called attitude or what we are calling degree of structure.
    6. To explore styles used in communication work, see Suggested Readings for Carlson and Brehm, who have done extensive research applying a similar model.
    7. Again, this will be a review for those who have read *Beyond Tells*. I will, however, integrate bluffing with styles.

Chart 1. Bluffing Attitude Assessing Grid

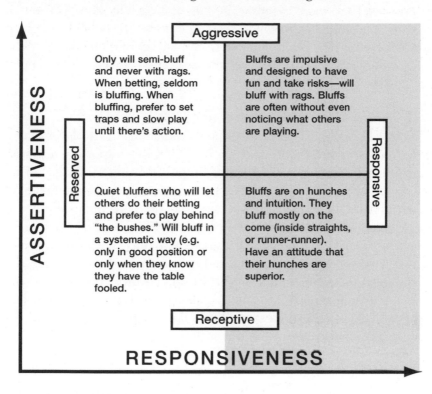

as the Winner in *Beyond Tells.* To understand the above playing styles, it's important to understand a range of ***attitudes*** that combine both a player's *Assertiveness* and *Responsiveness.*

Comparing Responsive and Assertive Attitudes

Players respond to the game with varied structure and logic versus their hunches and intuition. Players also will vary how passively or assertively they bluff. Styles will evolve from measuring the way players respond (structure vs. emotion) to opportunities to bluff with how assertively they apply their skills (receptively vs. aggressively).

In this way, one will notice players who respond to tasks more with logic and odds (they're left-brain). Left-brained players are very logical, structured, and unemotional. They use averages and percentages as their basis for decisions and plays. Others respond more with their impulses or intuition (their right brain). Right-brained players are more unstructured and more impulsive in their approach to playing. They use intuition and hunches to guide their decisions. It's possible to gauge how structured (left-brain dominant) or unstructured/emotional (right-brain dominant) a player is. You can also rank yourself on how much you approach gaming with structure or emotion.

Gauging a Player's Responsive Attitude

Notice how players respond to poker situations? If a player is very logical and structured, rate that player "0" on the responsiveness scale shown below. Some players behave by predetermined designs. They call, raise, and fold their hands based on logic, odds, position, and close observations. Others respond with their hearts more than their heads. These latter players don't have a plan for raising, calling, or folding. Their only plan is to follow their instincts. So, the other extreme would be if a player were very emotional and impulsive. In this case, rank "10" in responsiveness for such a player. In other words, how emotionally does a player respond? (0 = Not at all; 10 = Most Always) Or, how structured does a player respond? (0 = Most Often; 10 = Not at All) How might others rate you on this scale?

Figure 2. Gauging Responsiveness

Structured Play 0—1—2—3—4—5—6—7—8—9—10 **Unstructured Play**

(Reserved)   *(Responsive)*

R E S P O N S I V E N E S S

Gauging a Player's Assertiveness

However, understanding how a player responds to tasks is not enough to reveal the player's style of bluffing. Next one must notice how assertively each player bets or applies their skills.

Some players approach the game very passively, let the cards play themselves, and may routinely slow-play good cards. Such players do little or nothing to influence other players. They essentially play a "show down" game and let the chips or cards fall where they may. Their ways of bluffing are also passive, preferring to let others do their betting and waiting to spring traps. Others will be very active and play aggressively to influence play with betting, raising, and check/raising. Their bluffs are more like attack and challenges.

You can rank yourself on how assertively you play with passive play being "0" and very aggressive play ranking "10."

Figure 3. Gauging Assertiveness

Passive Play 0—1—2—3—4—5—6—7—8—9—10 Assertive Play

(Receptive)   *(Aggressive)*

A S S E R T I V E N E S S

Determining Bluffing Styles

First, determine how structured a player handles play. Is the player reserved, demonstrating left-brain dominance (has a lot of structure)? Or, is the player more responsive, indicating right-brain dominance (plays more out of hunches and impulses)?

Next, decide how assertive a player handles playing and betting. Is the player more of an introvert, quiet, and does little to influence the game? Some passive players only play or bet if they have good cards. Such players are more in a receptive frame of mind, just there to see what's going to happen next. These are passive players who can bring a lot of structure to the game (left-brain passive players). Other passive players will bet on impossible odds and chase[8] possible pairs, straights, and flushes a lot. Such passive players call too many bets and play more by their hunches and intuition (right-brain passive players). Or, is the player more of an extrovert? Such an aggressive player bets when showing strong cards, tries to influence other players a lot through talking and betting. These aggressive players will bet rather than check, will

---

8. "Chasing" is poker slang for running after possible hands (like having a pair and chasing three of a kind). Chasing can refer to staying in when other players have higher cards than a player has, trying to outrun the higher pair (like a pair of Jacks bets and is chased by a pair of 10s).

check and then raise any subsequent bets, or will bluff more often than most players. I've heard it said by such a player, "I'd rather lose my money betting than calling!" Some aggressive players will be very opinionated and even openly critique other players' mistakes. Such left-brained aggressive players are experts in determining the odds and use statistical estimates to guide their play. Other aggressive players will bet more on their hunches and intuition. These right-brained aggressive players will take too many risks and are playing more for the excitement than anything else. Some do well. Most create more excitement than profit. Chart 2 will summarize these bluffing styles.

Chart 2. Bluffing Styles

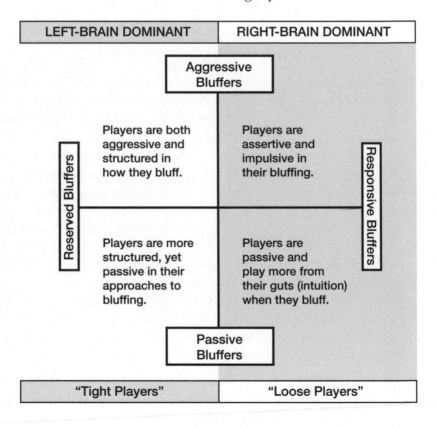

Bluffing Style Traits

The attitude players have toward other players will also tell their bluff-ing styles. Each player is communicating with other players either pas-sively, assertively, with reserve, or with enthusiasm. When a player's assertiveness and responsiveness to others are compared, four basic playing styles[9] emerge:

1. Players who are **Receptive and Reserved** are passive and struc-tured toward others. These players are the System Players who are there more to *analyze* the cards and other players. Theirs is a conservative attitude—polite, yet distant from other players. The Loners are also in this quadrant. Theirs is an attitude of solitude and withdrawal from any conversation—"just the cards, please." Both the System Player and the Loner are serious about what they are doing and are focused more on the cards and the actions of other players than on socializing. Their bluffs sneak up on their opponents. Since they prefer passive bluffing, they generally are letting others do their betting.

2. Players who are both **Receptive and Responsive** are passive and impulsive in their approach to others. Such players are the "Hunch Players" whose communication with other players is more to *facilitate* and socialize with others. These are the "table opti-mists," whose favorite style of play is to chase hands based more on intuition than on odds. Hunch Player is there more to enjoy others, be noticed as a person, and to socialize than to play out-standing poker. They play the hands that are in their heads and are usually bluffing "on the come."

3. Players whose play is both **Aggressive and Reserved** are assertively logical toward others. These players are "the Bosses" whose communication with other players is designed more to *con-trol* and to be critical. They often present an attitude of arrogance with their confidence. The Boss has many opinions about what's right and what's wrong. If others players should want to improve their game, the Boss will stand ready to give free coaching. The Boss loves to be asked for an opinion. They have so much confi-

9. Carlson and Brehm, op. cit.

dence in their bluffs that when they are bluffing, they always have a hand that can improve when called (semi-bluffs). Their bluffs are more like dares (silently saying), "Call that, if you don't like money!" Finally,

4. Players who are both **Aggressive and Responsive** will be assertive and unstructured toward others. They are the "High Rollers" and the "Party Hardies" who communicate with others much like salespeople to *advocate* or be *promotive*. Their attitude can range anywhere from being flippant with others to reckless abandon where risking takes precedence over noticing what the chances are of making nearly impossible hands they are chasing. High Rollers demonstrate more thinking in their risk taking. Party Hardies are there more for contact and to generate excitement. Both will be on a steal when they get serious. When they are bluffing, their actions seem more like they are attacking you or the pot. They will splash the pot, throw in their raises, at times be boisterous, and generally be creating excitement with their bluffs.

Each of these styles will behave in predictable ways while bluffing. However, you are dealing with poker players. In other words, beware of Bosses dressed up like High Rollers. Particularly after reading a book such as this, it wouldn't be long before players will identify their own bluffing tells and start masquerading. In the next chapter, you will learn how to know how players think and be better able to spot the actors. Knowing what is normal for such styles will help to understand how bluffing styles, for instance, will differ from each other. Simply stated, when any ordinarily responsive/receptive player (Hunch Player) becomes less reserved and more aggressive, you can be sure you are being conned. More detail about this will follow.

Chart 3 offers a diagram of communication styles showing how players treat other players:

Notice that the closer a person is to the center of this grid, the more positive player attitude is. The farther a player is judged to be on the outer edges of this grid, the more negative their attitude is toward others. For example, while the Boss is controlling, that control can be more benevolent (center) or autocratic (outer edge). Similarly, while System Player is forever analyzing, how such a player thinks can be strictly (outer edge) or with compassion (center). While some Hunch

Chart 3. Player Attitudes and Bluffs

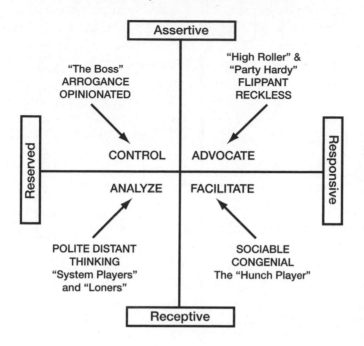

Players are effervescent (outer edge), others are more serious and balance their hunches with discerned observations (center). Finally, there are serious and informed salespeople and there are flightly ones. So too, High Rollers and Party Hardies can be reckless (outer edge) or take more calculated risks (toward center).

Determining Your Bluffing Style

Using the earlier scales used to rate assertiveness and responsiveness, rate yourself in the above grid. For instance, if you thought that you were "6" in how you respond and "7" in being assertive, then you would be in the upper right quadrant. This would suggest that you are high in responsiveness (lean toward unstructured) and high in assertiveness (tend to be more aggressive). Such a rating would suggest an action-oriented or reaction-oriented player (High Roller or Party Hardy).

Attitude is not set in stone. A player's attitude may change with surrounding conditions.

Chart 4. Sample Rating Grid

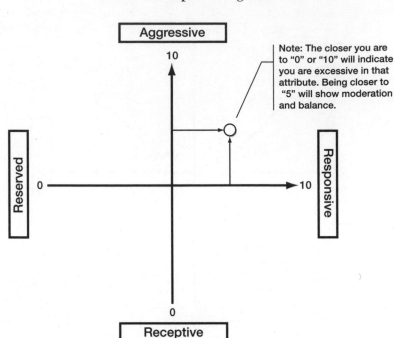

This means that sometimes players will change the quadrant out of which they are operating. However, based on personality orientations each player has a favorite (or home quadrant) attitudinal set.

Jung also observed:

> Attitude is an individual phenomenon that eludes scientific investigation. In actual experience, however, certain typical attitudes can be distinguished in so far as certain psychic functions can be distinguished. . . . There is thus a typical thinking, feeling, sensation, and intuitive attitude. Besides these purely psychological attitudes, whose number might very well be increased, there are also social attitudes, namely, those on which a collective ideal has set its stamp.[10]

To take Jung's idea of attitude a step further, the four quadrants of the above grid will produce at least six types of bluffing attitudes that

10. Jung, *Personality Types*, page 417.

correspond to six personality orientations of *emotions, actions, reactions, non-actions, thoughts,* and *opinions.* Some of these personality orientations are more structured. Others lean toward being more impulsive. Some are more prone to being passive, while others are more aggressive. Namely, *thoughts, beliefs,* and *non-actions* orientations are more structured (left brain). The more unstructured orientations (right brain) will be *emotions, reactions,* and *action*-oriented personalities.

Favorite Playing Atmospheres

In *Beyond Tells* I introduced a chart that summarizes the characteristics of how these different personality types will reveal themselves during a game.[11] Please refer to appendix D, for that chart. There is a column that tells you what to use and what to avoid with the various personalities of players. In order to succeed in bluffing other players, it's important to be aware of the atmospheres that each prefers.

Not all personalities are attracted to the same playing atmosphere. In fact, in the absence of the right conditions, most players will create the atmosphere that best fits their needs. Atmosphere also refers to the attitudes that other players and dealers bring to the game. Attitude and atmosphere go together and must match the individual differences of players to insure good and effective bluffs. Here's how some people prefer different surroundings:

1. Some people like a playful atmosphere with lots of noise and distractions stimulating their senses. These players don't want a bunch of rules and do best if other people seem more "laid-back." They will bluff more in autocratic atmosphere. **(Laissez-faire)**

2. Other players prefer an atmosphere that is quiet, subdued, predictable, and considerate. These players like things to be fair and conditions to be equal for all players. They will fold in an autocratic approach and prefer to be asked questions, rather than be demanded. They will call requests and fold demands. **(Democratic)**

3. Then, there is a whole bunch of people who just want comfort and a place to be noticed and appreciated. They will respond to

11. McKenna, J. *Beyond Tells,* page 174.

kind and gentle bluffs and fold to autocratic approaches. (**Benevolent**)

4. Finally, there are many players who want to be dealt with directly with no frills or manipulations. These players might say, "Just let me know what you want and let me loose!" These players will get out of your way when you are direct. If you want them to stay just tell them with a check. (**Autocratic**)

These four playing atmospheres (laissez-faire, democratic, benevolent, autocratic) are preferred differently by each of the six playing styles. The chart in appendix D will outline these atmospheres and how each player attitude (style) corresponds.

Now that you have blended the various playing styles with bluffs, you are ready for the next level of reading players. That will reveal for you the secrets that successful players know and the magic ways they use the art of pacing, leading, and misdirecting to reach their goals. Those goals are usually aimed at getting others to fold their better hands or to call when their opponents hands are second-best.

5

Magical Secrets Revealed

The secret in magic is often "misdirection," pacing where the audience is and then leading them to where they think, see, or feel what the magician wants them to. The illusions present in magic are only effective if they believe that what they are experiencing is real. Poker is often such an illusion. More specifically, bluffing is the magic of misdirecting, pacing other players, and then leading them to act in ways that will trap them into calling or folding. Poker demands advanced people skills in communication. It requires knowing how to best communicate with players who have a variety of ways of thinking.

In 1975, Richard Bandler and John Grinder were students of language. They launched a way to understand how people think and make sense of their worlds.[1] They established a system referred to as Neuro-Linguistic Programming (NLP). It became a valuable tool for industry and the mental health profession. It also is a valuable tool for surviving and thriving in poker.

To develop NLP, the originators studied three different very successful professionals. They looked closely at how Virginia Satir,[2] an extraordinary family therapist, got such successful results. They studied Milton Erickson, MD,[3] a highly effective hypnotherapist, to learn what

1. Bandler, R, and Grinder, J. *The Structure of Magic, I: A Book About Language and Therapy.* Palo Alto, CA: Science and Behavior Books, 1975.

2. Satir, V. *Peoplemaking.* Palo Alto: Science and Behavior Books, 1972.

3. Bandler, R., and Grinder, J. *Patterns of the Hypnotic Techniques of Milton H. Erickson, M.D.—Volume 1.* Cupertino, CA: Meta Publications, 1975.

accounted for his high rate of success. Finally, they studied Fritz Perl,[4] the father of Gestalt Therapy, to learn what his effectiveness could tell them. Although none of these mental health professionals worked in any way alike, they all had one thing in common. That one thing was their ability to know instinctively how their patients were thinking. Unlike so many psychotherapists at that time, they were able to match how their patients made sense of the world. They connected almost instantaneously with their patients. They were masters at communication.

This study of the magic of poker will follow Bandler and Grinder's approach. I have studied what effective poker players have in common. It's not my purpose to negate the magical powers of good poker players. Rather, I want to show how the magic of playing good poker is a complex activity and has structure. As so aptly stated in *The Structure of Magic*, when Bandler and Grinder were talking about observing "therapeutic wizards," they said, ". . . like other human activities, has structure and, given the resources, is, therefore, learnable.[5]"

Poker players who are the wizards of the game are complex and deserve to be observed. Poker players are also learnable. A good player knows how to read not only the cards and people. They know how to distinguish how their opponents are thinking. This gives them an invaluable poker skill—the ability to communicate and lead players where they want and the ability to annoy players into acting the opposite of the way they appear to want. It gives good players the edge to know how to get players to call when they want a call and how to get other players to fold when they are bluffing.

Referential Indexes and Frames of Reference

Players differ in several ways in how they approach poker. As mentioned, some are aggressive while others are passive in how they play their hands. Still some players play their hands in very structured and predictable ways. Yet, we have all experienced players who play impulsively, based on hunches and/or the need for action. Quadra sizing these players has been useful[6]:

4. Perls, F. *The Gestalt Approach: Eyewitness of Therapy*. Palo Alto, CA: Science and Behavior Books, 1973.
5. Bandler, R. and Grinder, J. *The Structure of Magic*, page 179.
6. McKenna, J. *Beyond Tells*.

Chart 5. Playing Styles

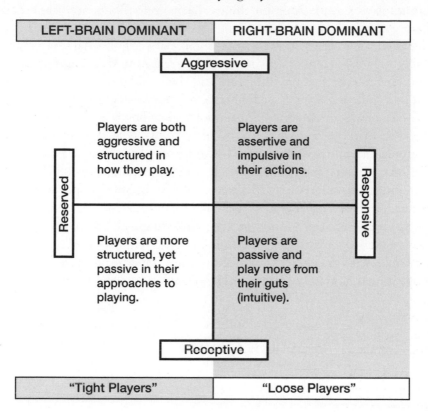

LEFT-BRAIN DOMINANT	RIGHT-BRAIN DOMINANT
Aggressive	
Players are both aggressive and structured in how they play.	Players are assertive and impulsive in their actions.
Players are more structured, yet passive in their approaches to playing.	Players are passive and play more from their guts (intuitive).
Receptive	
"Tight Players"	"Loose Players"

(Reserved — left side; Responsive — right side)

However, within all these styles of playing, close observations may tell how players approach bluffing. They don't, in and of themselves, tell us how players think and make sense of the cards. We will need to draw from other ways to observe to learn that. For the first time, applied to poker, we will be describing MAPS that will guide us in understanding how differently players think.

NLP refers to these ways as "representation systems."[7] Whether being aggressive, structured, passive, or responsive, players think sometimes in pictures (Visual Thinkers), at times in sounds (Auditory

7. Bandler, R., and Grindler, J. *The Structure of Magic II.* Palo Alto, CA: Science and Behavioral Books, 1976. Pages 6–12.

Thinkers) and often in feelings or motions (Kinesthetic Thinkers).[8] Some players are looking for things that you do. Some are listening to how you talk. And some are paying attention to your actions. These are the three main ways of thinking and making sense of what's happening at the table. They also tell you how players are making sense of things and how to pace them and then to lead them where you magically want them to follow. Pacing is matching how a person is representing things (whether in pictures, sounds, or motions). Leading is a technique developed in hypnotherapy that makes suggestions to lead a person where you wish them to go. Pacing and leading are also valuable poker tools and can enhance the quality of your game, including your bluffs.

Conversations are a rich source of not only how people represent things but how they reason as well. They can represent things in one of "4–tuples": Visual (V), Auditory (A), Kinesthetic (K), or Olfactory (O) terms. How people reason is revealed by their patterns of thinking. For example, while I was recently waiting for a hand to be played, I heard this conversation between two other players not in the hand.

Player 1.	"You know, I was in a tournament last week that looked at first to be easy to beat." (I noticed the choice of the word "looked" (V) followed by "beat" (K). That let me know that Player #1 thinks in pictures and then gets a hunch V → K, from pictures to actions.)
Player 2.	"Yeah? Tell me more. I'd like to hear that." (The choice of the word "tell," suggests that Player #2 thinks in auditory (A) terms.)
Player 1.	"Well, I saw a couple of moves that looked like a lot of players were going to get wiped out early and then I could clean up." (Again V → K)
Player 2.	"So what happened? Did you see players knock each other out for you?" (I noticed how player 2 switched from his auditory (A) way of thinking to pace player #2's visual and kinesthetic frames of reference.)

---

8. NLP refers to these as "4-tuples." There are also people who organize their thoughts around smells (olfactory frame of reference). However, most clues are around these three: Visual, Auditory, and Kinesthetic.

Player 1.   "Yeah! It was lookin' pretty good until I discovered those
            moves ended up trapping me later on." (Still thinking and
            reasoning V → K)

Player 2:   "What do you mean, you were trapped?" (Leading with players
            last reference (K) and still pacing)

Player 1:   "Well, it looked like one of those players was a lot tighter than
            he appeared. I went all-in with a pair of Kings. He called with
            a pair of Aces. The rest was history." (Still thinking from
            pictures to actions)

Different Frames of Reference

The first survival technique at the poker table is to know you. The
second is to know your opponents. Thinking styles will give you a head
start in classifying how both you and your opponents think. Listening to
the predicates, adjectives, and verbs people use is like having a personal
dictionary to learn how players make sense of things and organize their
thoughts. Ask yourself *How much do you think in pictures, sounds, or
feelings?* Figure 4 will be your guide to how people can lead you and
how to pace other players.

Figure 4 Reference Words

Visual	Auditory	Kinesthetic
focus	sounds good	feel
see	shouts	pull together
picture	tell	grip
look	say	handle
bright	yell	hold
color	harmony	cold
perspective	whisper	close
view	quiet	depressed
eye to eye	tune in	step
a big	dialogue	fall upon
a little	rings a bell	trip
"*See* What I Mean?"	"How's that *sound*?"	"How'd that *grab* you?"

Two important things to remember:

1. We all make sense of the world in different ways.
2. One way is not better than the other—*just different.*

You may be asking yourself, "Why is how a person thinks that important to a game of poker?" If you want to be able to predict how a person will act, you have to start with what comes before actions. How and what we think leads to feelings. When we have a thought we either feel good or bad; but, we will feel something. What we feel is determined by how we interpret what is happening. In other words, what we are thinking includes how we are interpreting things.

Here's a picture for those of you who think more in pictures:

Figure 5. Thoughts First

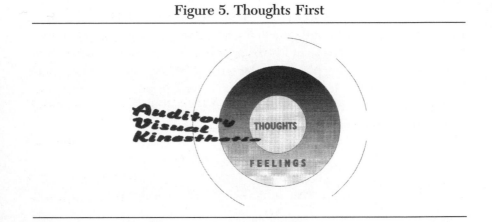

Notice that the last thing, the thing that we see, is the action a player takes. If you knew the thinking behind those actions and the feelings that that thinking generates, you would have more than behavior to guide your responses. Knowing the thoughts behind your opponents' actions can protect you from their bluffs. If you can master how an opponent thinks, you can also know how best to bluff them. Remember, thoughts lead to actions. So, if you want a player to fold, what do you want him or her to think? If your goal is to keep them calling your monster hand, what do you want them to think? Simply put, when an opponent thinks you are weak, he or she will behave very differently from when thinking that you are strong. Unfortunately, no one can tell *what* a person is thinking. You can determine whether they are picturing or remembering things. You can also determine whether they are constructing pictures. For example, if a player looks at a flop that has a possible straight and bets while looking up to his right, you know that he is constructing a hand. It could be that he has two pair and is constructing a full house. He may, when you raise their bet, and look up to the left and then to the right, seeing his two pair and constructing that you must have made a straight. So, you can affect how a person is thinking. You can't, however, make them think. You can certainly lead them into thinking certain ways and that's what bluffing is all about.

Finally, if you want a person to think certain things about your hand, be sure that you are communicating on their channel. Speak their language—not yours.

As mentioned earlier, if you listen closely to how each player organizes things with words, you will know how that person thinks.

Main Frames (How Players Think)

- ♠ Some organize their thoughts around pictures. They are primarily Visual Thinkers.

- ♠ Some prefer to listen and must hear first. They are Auditory Thinkers.

- ♠ Still, we have those who get hunches and are very intuitive. They prefer to organize things around their feelings. These are Kinesthetic Thinkers.

- ♠ Some (although not as many in our Western culture) like to put their nose to the grindstone and sniff things out. These are Olfactory Thinkers.

Using References to Keep Players In

Let's return to the earlier example of a conversation between two players (pages 96–97). I decided that by listening to the patterns of table talk that I gained some information that I could use to bluff either player #1 or player #2 later in the game. That opportunity came sooner than I thought. I was head to head with player #1. The flop looked like what's shown at the top of the next page:

Flop

I had previously raised the bet (pre-flop) with a suited big slick—

—and said, "Let's see who's got enough to call me." This was carefully aimed at player #1, who was behind me and in a better position. I was talking his language (V [*see*] → K [*call me*]). Everyone except player #1 folded. Now that I had him, I wanted to make sure he was following and not leading. So, when I flopped top pair with a great kicker (and a runner-runner flush draw), I checked while saying, "It looks like it's you and me. I'm not doing any more betting for you!" I was leading with the aggressive talk and still representing things from pictures ("*Looks like . . .*") and ending up with action words (". . . betting for you"). If he followed and bet (as I wanted him to do), my check may have led him to think I didn't have top pair. What I said was the bluff because he was a good enough player to know that when someone is speaking strongly he is usually weak. I was speaking semi-strong—hoping he would think that I had a middle pair. By saying that, I was acting strong and hoping he would interpret that a weakness. If I would have said, "If you bet, I'm in trouble," he would have known I was at least semi-bluffing. He looked at his Ace—

—and bet his pair of 10s into me. He said, "I can't see giving you a free card." He was still seeing things the way I was leading him to think. I simply called and the Turn came:

Flop   Turn

Although this looked like it couldn't have improved either of us, it gave me the nut flush draw. I bet into him this time and said, "Looks like it's time for me to come out of hiding." He just called. I was hoping he wasn't bluffing me with two pair. Along came a spider and sat down beside the river.

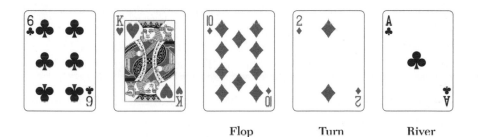

Flop   Turn   River

I relaxed and bet my two top pair. Player #1 raised me, thinking that his Ace, 10 had out run me. I re-raised to three bets and player #1 just called. What won this hand was not just the best hand. I succeeded in keeping the second best hand in and got better value out of my hand. It was possible because I was able to pace (V $\rightarrow$ K) and keep him communicating (playing) with me. This is an example of how learning a communication model (NLP) can enhance your people skills. It's also an example of a way to make sure players stay in when you want that.

Using Referents to Get Players to Fold

By knowing how a player thinks, it's possible to lead him or her into folding. The above example showed how a player could be encouraged to stay. Good therapists have this communication skill and will encourage patients to follow and return for counseling. The same is true of poor therapists who mismatch their patients' referential ways of thinking. Patients leave therapy too soon. So, if you want to get a player to leave, try to mismatch how he or she thinks. Let's use that same example of player #1 who thinks first in pictures and then in feelings. Suppose that we both have the same hands above: Suite Ace, King against unsuited 10 and Ace. I've got the same odds of improving and the advantage with the flop that gives me a pair of Kings and player #1 a pair of 10s. This time, though, I bet instead of checking. I also mismatch by saying something like, "I've got a bad feeling about that King. Sure hope you don't like it more!" I've mismatched him by using kinesthetic (K) words, which should annoy him a little. If he looks up to his right, he's probably constructing what I have, like King, 10. My showing weakness might also suggest strength to him. If he calls with his pair of 10s, I still have him beat because my pretending weakness is actually a semi-bluff. Since I mismatched the way he thinks, he may fold. If he stays, I still will have the edge when the Ace comes on the river. He's not likely to fold and at this point I would want him to stay. So, I might go back to matching him with, "Oh, oh! That looks like trouble. I should have gone with my feelings." Now I have made sure he will call because I am painting pictures followed by feelings. In other words, I am talking his language.

So, how is mismatching a way to get players to fold or leave the hand? It will definitely annoy the other player. When we mismatch, we represent things in a different way, and if the other person wants to communicate with us, he or she has to *translate* your words into his or her way of thinking. That can be annoying. For example, suppose you sit down and start telling me something that happened to you. You say, "I can't believe my eyes. I thought that I'd play the slots while waiting to play poker. I saw this machine that just got free and I sat down and noticed one win after another. Then I got a Royal Flush." Then, I'd say, "Sounds like a fish story to me. Are you trying to tell me that all you have to do is follow the advice, 'No dime before its time,' and I'll win jackpots?" You'd have to translate all my auditory language into your visual way of thinking. Otherwise, you'd just scratch you head and think something like, "He looks like he's having a bad day." That would be annoying and you are not likely to want to share any more stories with me. I got you to fold your excitement by mismatching and speaking in a language you'd have to translate from auditory to visual referents.

Let's play a hand. Suppose you have a fairly good starting hand, K♥ and Q♦:

You get excited and bet while looking up to your left and then down to your right. We'll talk more later about what your eye movements mean. Then you say, "We must both be looking for good cards. I don't think you'd have called with garbage." I say, "Sounds like you've got me figured out. I might just call for help right now." It annoys you a little because you're not sure I heard what you said and maybe I am just pretending to have weaker cards than you, which I do, 10♠ and 7♥:

The only thing I've got better than you is better position and a way to mismatch you into folding your better hand. The flop comes (8♦, 9♦, and 5♥) and gives me an open ended straight draw. You check and I bet while saying, "Sounds like a garbage haul to me." The flop looks like what you'll see on the next page:

You fold instead of raising because you are still trying to make a picture out of "sounds like a garbage haul." Of course, this is all speculation but we all know that players don't play their best when they are annoyed. Mismatching is a way to annoy others and get them to leave you.

Silent Clues

So far, we have been learning how players think by listening to their words. By watching closely, players will reveal with their eye movements how they are thinking. Unfortunately, we have not discovered a way to know exactly what they are thinking. That's up to your imagination. We will know, though, if they are thinking in one or more of the 4-tuples (V, A, K, O). At this point, we are not listening to their words. We are watching their eyes. They can be talking or they can be silent. Sometimes, you may be playing a table where there are not a lot of verbal clues. Watching eye movements will tell us how they are thinking at any given point in time. It's a little harder when they are wearing sunglasses; but, it's possible to know which way they are looking.

First here's what eye movements will tell us, or *reveal* if you prefer a more visual word:

Eye-Leading Systems

The eyes are a window to how a person is thinking. The position of a person's eyes reveals whether he or she is thinking in pictures, is talking to one's self, or is searching for the right word. It also reveals if that person is drawing from previous visual memories or is constructing new pictures. This mostly applies to right-handed people and may be different for some left-handed folks. If you are looking at a person, when their eyes move to a certain direction, this figure will let you know how they are thinking (not what they are thinking):

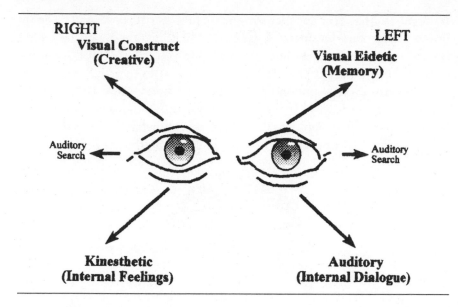

RIGHT
Visual Construct
(Creative)

LEFT
Visual Eidetic
(Memory)

Auditory
Search

Auditory
Search

Kinesthetic
(Internal Feelings)

Auditory
(Internal Dialogue)

Thinking in Pictures

When we are thinking in pictures, whether our eyes are open or shut, our eyes will move up and to the left or to the right. That's because when our brains are accessing pictures it's like a computer mouse either right-clicking or left-clicking. When you left-click your brain your eyes will move up and to your left hemisphere. That's where memories are stored. When you right-click your brain, your eyes will move up and to your right hemisphere. That's where your creativity is lodged. Instead of remembering pictures, you are constructing pictures that you haven't seen yet.

Remembering and Dreaming

When a person's eyes are looking upward, they are either remembering images they have already seen or they are constructing images they are hoping to see. When our eyes are looking down, we are either talking to ourselves or having some feelings about what we are thinking about.

Remembering the Past (Visual Eidetic)

Some people will remember what they heard. When your eyes are looking up and to your left, you are remembering things you have seen.

It might be that you are picturing your hole cards, or you are seeing how a player played a similar flop and was bluffing. You might be seeing how you got caught "speeding" the last time you tried to bluff with this hand. When you see a player's eyes look up and to their left, you know that they are seeing something. You need to know more to figure out what they are thinking. If the player says something when he or she looks up and to their left, you'll have a clue as to what they are thinking. All you know for sure is that they are seeing something in the past.

Photo 2. Photo Memory

Imagining the Future (Visual Construct)

At other times, players will be constructing pictures. Their eyes are looking up and to their right. That tells you that the player is imagining and creating things not actually seen. It might be how they were able to get you to fold the last time they raised. It might be the hole cards that they wished they had. Or, sometimes loose players will imagine the hands that they are chasing. Once, when a player stayed in with a middle pair, I asked what kept her in. She said that she just knew that trips were coming. I wished I had paid attention to her eyes. They were surely up and to her right constructive side.

Just because you notice that a player is constructing images that haven't yet happened, doesn't mean that you know what they are constructing. Recently, in a no-limit game, I noticed a young player had a short stack. So, I was expecting him to go all-in when the opportunity was ripe. Sure enough, it came when he was the big blind. Several players limped in and one player in late position made a $30 bet. Just before the big blind acted, he looked up and away to his right. In fact, he even turned his head to the right and looked away from the table. I knew he was constructing something. Then, he went all-in. I knew that he was seeing himself doing something—only he was visualizing himself going all-in with pocket Kings. The flop came with a top card being another King. When he won the pot, I couldn't resist saying, "You saw yourself going all-in as soon as someone raised the bet, didn't you?" He nodded with a slight smile and I said, "Good hand!" I wasn't in the hand; but, I can assure you that when he was constructing going all-in, and seeing his short stack, I would have folded in a heart beat. That is unless, of course, I had a premium pair. His all-in only amounted to $75.

Photo 3. Constructing a Picture

The important thing to remember is that knowing that a person is constructing visual images that they have not yet seen doesn't tell you what they are imaging. The context of such eye movements will give you a clue. For instance, the player in photo 3 was responding to a player who asked her, "Do your have one or two pair?" Players will often ask questions like this to get a read on how a player reacts. In this case, the player said, "You'll soon find out!" Her looking up and to her right suggested that she wasn't being truthful. She was constructing two pair rather that remembering two pair. If she had looked up and to her left, I would have believed her.

Thinking in Sounds

Some players pay more attention to things that are said, sighs, laughs, and anything that comes into their ears. They are auditory thinkers and you will know that they are searching for a word or talking to themselves when you watch their eyes. If they are looking down to their left, they are saying something to themselves (internal dialogue). When their eyes are level and moving back and forth, such players are searching for the right word, much like a computer scans to find a word.

Auditory Search

If a player is looking directly in front of them and then moves his or her eyes to the left and the right, they are searching for a sound. It may be the word to describe their hand. It may be the right word to call you. Eye movement (not looking up or down) that moves back and forth is called visual search. When a player bets and starts moving his eyes back and forth across the table it could mean that they are seeing how many people are going to be calling.

Photo 4. Auditory Search

It could be that they are searching to hear what the words are to describe the unbeatable hand they are playing. Beware of players who are rolling their eyes up, back and forth, and down and around. Why? Chances are they are accessing all 4-tuples and are playing in a way to have more awareness that anyone else at the table. After this book, though, I wonder how much eye rolling I'm likely to see.

Photo 5. Auditory Search

Self-Talk

When a player is looking down and to their left they have an internal dialogue going. Again, it would be nice to know what they are saying to themselves. All that we know for sure is that there is an internal dialogue going. When you see this and you want to connect with someone to improve you communication at the table, you could ask, "What are you thinking?" If you noticed a player looking down to his left after he called a bet, you might ask, "Well, are you saying good or bad things to yourself?" He or she might just think you are kidding. However, on some level you have established a rapport with that player because you caught him thinking or saying something to him- or herself. If you catch yourself looking down and to your left, listen to what you are saying to yourself at that point. Therapists use this tool frequently to establish rapport and learn how to help their clients. A patient may not answer a question and instead may just look down and to their left (sometimes moving from left to right and back again). That's when an astute therapist might say, "What are you saying to yourself about that?" It's clear that they also were feeling something about their internal dialogue.

Suppose you notice a player has just bet and looked down and to his left. You just know that he's saying something to himself. Like the therapist, you could inquire, "Now you're saying to yourself, 'I hope my pair holds up.' " You've caught him talking to himself and you've thrown out a verbal net. Now, listen for what you might catch. He might say, "No. I was hoping someone like you might raise." (*This strength suggests weakness.*) He might looked surprised that you caught him in an internal dialogue and say, "Uh, what!? Oh, just call and see." If you have the top pair and a great kicker you should raise and watch him fold with his weak kicker.

Photo 6. Internal Dialogue

Internal Feelings

The same is true of when we look down and to our right. We are experiencing an internal feeling. Again, if you want to establish rapport, you can connect with a player who's looking down and to his or her right side. If you have a relationship that will stand some comradery, you might say something like, "How are you feeling, Punk. Are you feeling lucky? Did I bet with top pair, or did that King give me trips? How're you feeling, huh?" What you have established is that you have caught the player in feeling something. Again, knowing that eyes down and to the right occur when people are into feelings, when you catch yourself doing this ask yourself, "What am I have a feeling about right now?"

A word of caution when noticing a person is looking down (either to the left or to the right). Make sure that it is a stare into space and that they are not looking down at their chips. That's usually a "tell" that they are going to bet.

A word about feelings is important. If your feelings are interfering with your poker playing, you will notice that your eyes are looking down a lot. If you want to get out of such a slump, *don't look down* unless you have to. Keep your eyes level or looking up. That will help you get away

Photo 7. Internal Feeling

from whatever you are feeling. I occasionally use this technique with patients who are depressed and doing a lot of negative self talk. It helps to relieve depression[9] for many without medication.

Hidden Poker Eyes

Having reviewed representation systems,[10] let's talk about players who wear sunglasses to hide the movement of their eyes. They think that players can't read their eyes. To a certain extent, this is true. However, it's possible to know which direction they are looking during play. It might not be possible to know when they are studying another player with their head turned away and looking out to the side. Yet, during play they will be looking in the direction of the flop as in photo 8.

Even though his eyes are shaded, it's possible to know that his eyes are looking up and to the right, since his head is tilted down.

Lines of vision are important not only to the player, but to other players at the table. In Texas Hold 'Em, players are looking at the flop before deciding what their next action will be. In what direction (right or left) does each player have to look to see the flop?

9. For my therapist readers, relax. I am not suggesting this as a treatment of clinical depression. It's a way to give a patient a tool to use for temporary relief while other therapies are applied.

10. Grinder, J., Delozier, J., and Bandler, R. *Patterns of the Hypnotic Techniques of Milton H. Erickson, M.D., 1 & 2,* Cupertino, CA: Meta Publications 1975.

Photo 8. Hidden in Plain View

NLP has documented that *the movement* of eyes[11] reveals how a person is thinking or making sense of the world. So, players in seats 1, 2, 6, and 7 are going to be regularly accessing their right brain. If they are also loose players, they are probably in the right seat. While players in seats 4, 5, 9, and 10 will be regularly accessing their left brain. Such players who are also tight are probably in their correct seat. The players who are centered will tend to be seats 3 and 8. Of course, seats 5 and 6 could also be centered. Look for moving the eyes back and forth.

Finally, if you are playing too loose, try moving to one of the left-brain seats 4, 5, 9, or 10. This will force your brain to use the left side more. Also, if you are playing too tight, try moving to a loose seat (1, 2, 6, or 7). This will allow you to access your emotional side more. An interesting observation might be to notice what seat is your favorite. What seat do you do best in? Which do you do worst in? Now you know why. Just remember this, **no matter what seat you're in, there you are**. Or, as some players have said, "Bad cards will change, but bad players seldom do."

Since we are talking about eye movement, wearing sunglasses can have another meaning. We will explore this more in the next chapter on

---

11. The directions of eye movements are related to different parts of the brain as in the diagram in the paragraph under section "Eye-Leading Systems."

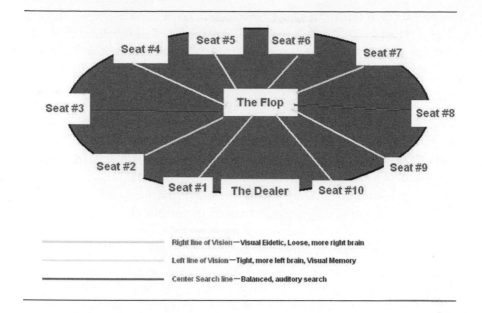

the mysteries of poker. The role of hiding and concealing are special types of bluffing. Players who like to hide will wear sunglasses; however, there are other ways to play the hiding game. Also, at times sunglasses are used to conceal the player's scare (that they are afraid you will see in their eyes). I have noticed when a player takes his sunglasses off and on that it means just that. When he's scared of his hand he will put his sunglasses on. Conversely, when he likes his hand he will take his sunglasses off. Go figure!

Meta Awareness

I once had the quickest brief therapy of my practice. A woman whom I used to counsel many years ago called me and told me how much in love she was with a man who was everything right. Her problem was that her biological clock was ticking and she wanted to get married. Every time she mentioned marriage to him, he would at first agree that she was the only one for the rest of his life, but he just was so afraid that marriage would spoil what they had. His previous marriage of nine years had ended in a bitter divorce. He'd been single for about ten years. So, he made an appointment with me and I saw him. I already knew that he had a problem with the word "marriage." So, I avoided using it until after we had built a little rapport. Then I said, "I understand that you and Jane have been discussing marriage." Then, I watched his eye movement. At first he looked up and to his left, and then he moved his eye up and to his right.

Almost immediately his eyes looked down and to his left when he blurted out, "Oh, no . . . no chance. I've been that route and it was a disaster!"

When I asked what he was feeling, he said that he was frightened and wanted to keep things as they were. His eye movement told me how he was thinking. When I said the word that was anchored in bad feelings, he immediately accessed visual memories (his first disastrous marriage), then he went into visual construct, imaging himself married to Jane. From there, he dropped into his internal feelings (eyes down and left). So, knowing this I had to get him to let go of the past and collapse his negative anchor with the word "marriage." First of all, I reframed the word "marriage." I started repeating his metaphor about his first marriage. Then I said in no uncertain terms, "That nine years was not marriage. You have never really been married. That was two immature people who didn't know how to be close. That relationship was infested with games, not love or intimacy. You have never been married." I then asked him to think of how close he has been to Jane. I said very distinctly, "That's more what true love is like."

He said, "Maybe you're right."

Then I said, "Let's do an experiment. I don't want you to look to the left (in the past), so put you hand over your left eye." He was anxious to get over this, so he cooperated. "Now I want you to look up and to your right." He did. "While continuing to look up and to your right, imagine what you have with Jane and imagine yourself married *for the first time* to her." He did and his eyes dropped to his left side. Only this time he felt hopeful and more positive.

He said, "You know, Doc, being married to the right person can't be all bad. In fact, it'd be like I finally got married for the first time." He left and I didn't have to see them again. Three months later they were married and since I haven't heard otherwise, I assume that they are married successfully—a first marriage for both of them.

Of course, this kind of therapy is possible when a therapist goes beyond simple awareness and uses NLP tools to access how patients are thinking and making sense of their worlds. So, how could I use this awareness to go beyond simply calling, raising, checking, or folding in a poker game? In fact, how could I use this awareness of others to enhance my bluffs? Would I be taking unfair advantage? I'll address this later. Right now, let's look at how the metaphors that patients bring to therapy can be translated to the metaphors players bring to the poker game. Any story (such as the story I told about player #1 and player #2) could be used as a metaphor to communicate an implied message to an opponent.

Use of Metaphors

Therapeutic metaphors[12] have been used for years by therapists to effect needed changes. Poker is a game that would lend itself to the use of metaphors. Usually, particularly in the lower limit games, a lot of socializing goes on. People tell each other stories about bad beats, getting "sucked out on," and other pastimes. Sometimes the talk is more gossip than pastiming. On other occasions, players might talk about the action while they are playing a hand. Some will never tell a story or get into the table talk. However, they will listen and silently react to what's being said. So, let's suppose a player loses with pocket Aces. He gets beaten by two small pair. He leans forward, looks at the player who beat him, and says, "What kept you in? You didn't get that second pair until the river!" His rival says, "Well, I only called because you were betting. I didn't believe you had anything." With that, the player with the beaten "Aces and spaces" looks across to another player and rolls his eyes. How he rolls his eyes will be as useful as when the patient rolled his eyes around the word "marriage." He first looks up and to his left, and then he just sighs and looks down and to his right. That told me he was remembering and then felt bad. Then he looks up and says, "I can never win with pocket Aces! Either a King will flop that will make a third King for someone or a player will suck-out on me with garbage!" Yeah, I know. You feel like saying, "Poooor baby!" But the way this player thinks $(V_m \rightarrow K_i \rightarrow A_i)$[13] give you clues to the kind of metaphor that will reach him and how to bluff him. Suppose he's a friend of mine and I want to give him a gift of being freed from his "never" script of not being able

12. Gordon, D. *Therapeutic Metaphors*. Cupertino, CA: Meta Publications, 1978.
13. The subscript letters mean m = memory and i = internal.

to win with pocket Aces. I might tell him this story in between hands.

I once knew a gal who had the same problem. I can see that same look she had on her face. She got over her problem, though. I asked her one time what she did to start winning with pocket Aces. She rolled her eyes, leaned back, and said, "I got smart. I learned how to fold when I thought I was beat." I said, "Well, how do you know when someone can beat your Aces?" She said, "It's simple, I discovered that I wasn't paying attention. Now, when someone in the big blind stays with me and there's garbage on the flop, I can lay down pocket Aces in a heartbeat." (Of course, I now know how to play her when I'm the big blind and there's a garbage flop.)

Well, guess what? He suddenly began the proper care and management of pocket Aces. I didn't tell him directly but the woman in my story was really him. I had noticed how he'd get beat because he could not lay down a good hand even if he knew he was probably second best. I know, if the pot odds were better, he was right to chase. They never were when I played with him. Now that was a "nice guy" story. What would happen if a player used metaphors to set up a steal? First let me tell you a story:

I heard about a fight that almost broke out down the street. These two guys were playing Omaha Hi-Lo and really got upset with each other. I don't know what they were fighting about. Finally, the older guy said to the young player, "Do you want to take this outside where I can whip your ass!?" The youngster said, "I sure as hell do!" With this the senior citizen started to get up and then sat right down and said, "Not me. I'd get my ass beat and then I'd go home and get more abuse from my wife." With that they both had a laugh and the fight was over. In fact, they seemed to get along the rest of the night. That's what I heard anyway. But, I thought it was pretty funny. Also, it proves that you can catch more flies with sugar than with vinegar—but then, who wants flies?

Now, suppose that you are listening to this story in a poker game. After hearing that story, what kind of mood are you in? Are you amused and wondering whether that actually happened? Are you annoyed and wanting to get serious and play some poker? Or, do you just not care and wonder what this has to do with a book on bluffing?

Remember, we are discussing the use of metaphor. This story actually happened and I was there to see and hear it. When a player at the table was being negative and trash talking other players a lot, I watched his eye movements and told the story so he would connect to it. It was clear that the other players, including me, wanted him to leave or get a more positive attitude. Then again, it could have been his way of getting players on-tilt. Another player I know is such a bad card player that he can only win if he can get other players on-tilt. Anyhow, I began to notice that he paid more attention through his ears. He looked around very little and when he was talking he wasn't painting any pictures. He'd listen to what others were saying and drop his eyes to his left and just shake his head. He was telling me that he was an auditory thinker and that he was critical and used poker to fight with people and feel disgusted. So, I told that story and I got his attention. First of all it was aimed at his ears (A). I used auditory reference and kinesthetic reference (e.g., "heard a story" and "got upset"). Second, it was about a fight at a poker table. He was all ears. I could have told the same story differently if he turned out to be a visual thinker. So, what happened? It seemed like magic. Even the other players would say to the side, "What happened? I'm glad he decided to cool down." What happened was that the metaphor hit home. He started to be nice. At first I thought it was a "tell"—that he had a strong hand and didn't want to lose callers. But, the rest of the evening went better. He even did better. I guess he discovered that he could catch a lot more players with sugar than with the vinegar he was serving.

Anti-Bluffs

I've noticed that a lot of players will mix up bluffs with tells. While all bluffs may have their own tell, all tells are not a bluff. It's easier to bluff a tight player. Yet, there are ways to ensure that players will not attempt to bluff you other than being too loose to bluff. Early commitment is one of these ways.

Position, as most players know, is another weapon to consider when distinguishing a bluff from a "tell." However, until recently, I never thought of using the position of the "Big Blind" as a place to ward off bluffs. For example, a friend of mine routinely plays his big blind in the dark. He even announces it to let people know he hasn't looked at his hole cards. If a player in late position raises the bet, he still will call without looking. He generally wants to see the flop before he will look at his hole cards and let players know that they are not going to successfully attack the blinds. I asked him how he did with this strategy and why he did it. He said that he did fairly well and, "It usually keeps players from needlessly attacking my blind. They know that I will call. So, it cuts down on bluffs."

Well, does it really? I asked, "What if there is a re-raise?"

He said, "Then I'd look before I'd call."

It's an interesting move. So, I experimented with it to see how it felt. I wouldn't recommend this in high-limit games. However, in low-limit games, it might have some merit. When I was the big blind, I played it in the dark. There was a raise and that cost me $6 to see the flop in a $3–$6 game. I thought that this is not like me and it was scary being that loose.

Then the flop came:

Everyone checked, so I did, too—still not knowing what my hole cards were. Then, on the turn came a Queen of spades and a comfortable "rainbow" board. Then someone bet the Queen; I then looked at my hole cards. The board looked like this and everyone folded to me:

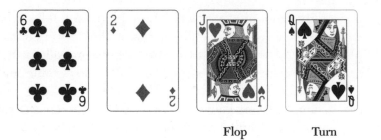

Flop   Turn

I could hardly believe my eyes. I had pocket Kings and I was head-to-head with at least a pair of Queens. Needless to say, I held my breath, thinking my opponent might have two pair. And, I was relieved that I could stay. Anything else and I would have folded in a heartbeat.

When a "hold 'em card" (a card that didn't help anyone) came, I won the hand. Now I know what loose players feel when they outrun good hands. I felt no shame. However, as I told my friend, I probably would have played my blind differently if I had looked at my hole cards. Since everyone checked, if I bet my pocket Kings, everyone would have probably folded and I would have ended up with the blinds. So, not knowing what my hand was turned out better for me. The big advantage that I found in playing my big blind in the dark was that it notified people that I would defend my blinds without even looking.

Players generally bluff the opposite of what they want you to think. For instance, if a player has a strong hand, he or she may bluff by "showing weakness." A check is often that sign of weakness. Or, if a player is on a stone-cold bluff, he or she may bet strong on garbage. I don't mean always calling a barking dog off the porch. However, if there are ways to avoid being bluffed, commitment will put players on notice that you are there to stay. Commitment can come in several ways:

Commitment
First, of course, if the pot odds make the risk of a chase worthwhile, a player will be committed to stay. Next, the belief that you have the best hand will confirm your commitment. Being committed to stay will come from knowledge of your opponents. Some players are easy to get out of the way. Others, whom you know like to steal, are the kind that you tend to commit early in a hand.

Appearing Loose
In order for you to bluff other players, those players need to be paying attention to your moves. Some players have the ability to pay strict attention while they are appearing to be distracted. So, a way to avoid being bluffed is to convince your opponent that you're "out to lunch." Some, even professional players, have other players convinced that they are good, but that they are "mad." Pretending to be distracted is a way to avoid being bluffed. That is, of course, that you are playing against someone who *is* paying attention. Don't try this with another player who is truly not paying attention and only knows bluffing for thrills.

Calling Stations

Most players like a player that is a "calling station" and will call a barking dog off of a porch. Howerver, that's when they have a hand and there's no need to bluff. When bluffing, however, a calling station will not be deterred by your bluff. If you can give the impression that you are a player who makes bad calls, you can avoid being bluffed by most good players. If you have succeeded in misleading the table in this way, however, beware of those whose bluff is to bet the best hand.

Appearing Distracted

You will notice, though, players reading while playing or talking to other players. Make sure that this is not an act. You can notice how well they are actually paying attention or how good they are at acting. If a player is a good bluffer, he or she wants to know that you are thinking about what they are doing. If you succeed in pretending to be distracted, you can avoid a bluff. That's because good players know that a player must be paying attention to be bluffed. Also, as I will cover later, once you are appearing distracted and come out knowing what's happening, that bluff won't work twice with the same players. You may need to search for a different ploy.

Player Images

We've all heard the expression "dress for success." Dress is important as it shows us a person's self-image. Johnny Moss is one of the most famous and successful poker players. He once said, "A poker player dresses like a millionaire, even if he's busted." What he was saying is that how we image ourselves is how we'll behave. Your image can abort or invite bluffs. It's important to know which one.

I've been asking people about players' images. First, what comes to mind when you think of a player's image? What image do they want to have at the table? And then how much can you believe the images that players show?

I've received a variety of answers. Most good players say that they want to have the image of being unpredictable or inconsistent. When it comes to what image means, it can be anything from the image of a good player, a loose one, a stone-hard killer, or whatever you want to think up. When a player is whining or complaining about bad cards, what image is he or she projecting? This is how a loser will talk, and other players will jump right on their "misery wagon" to take advantage of their poor image. This could be a way to invite bluffs if you have a strong hand and want whining to sound like an unlucky streak.

Psychologists know a lot about image and how it is reflected by actions. Behind every action there must be an image. Simply stated, images (about self and others) precede our actions. If we believe a certain way, that belief or image will be reflected in how we behave. This is not the case in poker where the image often reflects the opposite of behaviors.

A lot of players will dress like bums to pretend that they're lousy players or poor drifters who don't know what they're doing. This may work for them and can be a good bluffing maneuver. At the same time, however, some will be inconsistent and buy in with stacks of chips to look successful. Image is everything in playing cards, as well as in living life. It's essential, however, that the images being projected match. In other words, just playing like you've got good cards needs to match the way you handle good fortune.

It's amazing, for instance, how many people take their money and expect to lose. They keep talking about how much they're going to lose, and even though they may be ahead now, they expect to be broke before they leave. Many players leave the table only when they are busted. These same players may have been far ahead at one time. They weren't there to win; they were there to lose.

The mind is like a guided missile. It must have a target and it'll most often arrive exactly where it is aimed. No goals or the lack of any images of success will act like unguided missiles. Like a balloon that flops all over the room if blown up and released, a person without goals will flop from game to game and occasionally hit a win. Such wins, however, are more by accident—much like the unguided balloon may accidentally hit a lamp in the room.

A lot of leveraging in card games is based on "play 'em like you've got 'em!" Well, along the lines of what we're discussing, what image does a player project who bets and plays like he or she already has the best hand? If one has the scare cards to back up such moves, such a player might be semi-bluffing to gain control. Sometimes, a good player does this and isn't called. When everyone folds, he or she sometimes will show high cards—without even a small pair. True, this is often (as I will detail later) a setup for the next time he or she is not bluffing.

Does the image you project at the tables match how you actually are playing? Just taking the time to ask yourself this question can change your actions.

Reputation

Earlier I said that "behind every action there must be an image." Normally, when we look at actions and the images behind them we expect to find some congruence. In other words, if a person thinks of himself as serious, he will generally act studiously and look serious. If people think of themselves as being friendly or humorous they will smile and joke around. These are the images that are consistent with their actions. That's in real life. However, the poker table is far from real life.

Players are not there to be who they are; rather, most of us are there to pretend to be someone we are not. That's part of playing poker. Some will be aggressive, pretending to be strong. Some will be passive, pretending to be weak. And some will come in and clown around, pretending to not be paying much attention to the game. How do you tell when a person is being herself or is projecting an image to fool you as an opponent? Just know that you are in a poker game, and most of what is happening is designed to either get you to call or to fold.

Players spend time building a reputation as being solid or loose players. It's safe to say that all players want their reputations to make money for them. How? They do this by getting people to fold or call their actions, that's how! In the final analysis, a person's reputation is only as good in a poker game as the amount of folds and calls it gathers. The bottom line about your poker reputation is how often you walk away with more than you brought. If players are not "showing respect" for you, it generally means that you have a reputation as a thief. If, on the other hand, players are paying a lot of respect, it means that you have convinced them that what you do is truthful. "I never bluff!" is probably the most blatant bluff (lie) that I've heard at a poker table. Even the tightest and most predictable players will use their reputation to buy a pot now and then. In the 2004 WSOP tournament, Dan Harrington used his tight reputation to bluff Greg Raymer who folded to Harrington's garbage hand.

In the end, if you are not winning more than you are losing, then your reputation sucks and needs to be revisited. If you are a serious player who wears sunglasses and hats to hide your eyes, you may think that you are being intimidating. If you are walking away as a loser, you succeeded in only fooling yourself. Most good players are not threatened by hats and sunglasses. Many think that players who are afraid of being found out will do such hiding. If it works, fine—as in the case of the 2004 World Series of Poker winner, Greg "Fossilman" Raymer. Otherwise, find another image that will work, or maybe some acting lessons would be better.

I mentioned before that players who use their images as ways to bluff are found out by being inconsistent. For example, a clown who's joking and carrying on a side conversation will look like he's not paying attention. Or, a guy who's dressed like a bum will pretend to be a melon off the last truck. When such players end up making solid plays, it will make you stop and think, *Some melon!* Such players may actually be the most structured player with the strongest hands.

When you make such switches, it's time to build a different reputation. By your inconsistent actions, you just blew the old reputation. You acted impulsive and turned out to be paying attention. In my book, *Beyond Tells*,[14] I discuss six personality types[15] and their playing styles. Try to build six types of reputations—you never know when you might need to change and you can keep your opponents guessing. It's a good idea that if you are using your reputation to bluff, learn to play like the six types outlined in chapter 3. Learning how to switch roles and bluff as a conservative player, an impulsive one, as well as being able to match the play of passive and aggressive players are needed skills.

14. McKenna, J. *Beyond Tells*, pages 150–171.

15. Kahler, T. *Mystery of Management*. Kahler discusses in detail the characteristics of these personality types. See Suggested Readings.

6

The Mysteries of Poker

The dictionary will refer to a mystery as an enigma or something that is "puzzling, ambiguous, or inexplicable."[1] As such, an effective bluff in poker is also puzzling, must be ambiguous to be effective, and can be difficult to explain. In other words, bluffing becomes one of the mysteries of the poker world.

Unraveling the Mysteries

Understanding a player's personality predisposition is the first clue to unraveling the mystery of bluffing. Players characteristically will handle life[2] the way they bluff:

Photo 9.
The Boss

♦ *The* (self-appointed) *Boss*[3] at the tables will have an opinion about most everything and everybody in their lives. They expect others to be perfect and want people to notice how good they are both at work and at the tables. Such people need their opinions recognized. They will bluff "by the book," because, for instance, their position dictates that a bluff would be

1. Please refer to an online dictionary: www.dictionary.com
2. In Kahler's *The Mystery of Management* as well as Caper and Kahler's "Mini-Script," there are valuable clues about how people handle stress differently. Kahler's distress sequence is especially helpful—see Suggested Readings.
3. For a summary of the playing styles, see appendix D.

proper. Bluffs may or may not include sandbagging[4] depending on their current opinion about sandbaggers.

♦ *Party Hardy* is looking for contact with the world around her. Getting people involved is more important than the task at hand—whether playing cards or working in an office. If they have a problem, they will blame everyone else. Look for impulsive bluffs with chips thrown toward the active player(s).

Photo 10.
Party Hardy

♦ *High Roller* is looking for excitement in the cards and in his personal life. These players want to create fun or conflict—anything to get things going. Winning or losing is not as valued as taking risks. Such players love to manipulate. Whether they win the money or not, if they can create incidents they are happy. Their bluffs are more like challenges or attacks.

Photo 11.
High Roller

Look for dramatic chip handling, such as splashing the pot or bets down slamming.

♦ *Hunch Player* is there to feel rather than to think. In their personal lives these players are sensitive and tend to help others more than themselves. They play cards the same way. "Oh, I'm sorry" is often said by Hunch Player when winning the pot. Hunch Player is more interested in being accepted for who she is than for how well she plays. If they lose or make mistakes, "poor babies" and knowing

Photo 12.
Hunch Player

that people still like them are more important than how much others like their work. They bluff accidentally, playing hands on the come, or because they have a hunch. When a bluff works, they will often act surprised—an act to keep the "bluffee's" good graces.

♦ *Loner* is in the game and life to be strong and suffer silently. These types will be the most observant about what's happening around them, and if they could find a solitaire game of poker they'd be there. Look for more of these players at the video poker machine

4. Checking and then raising any bets that limp in.

(the closest to poker solitaire away from home). In their personal lives, they prefer solitude. Loner will do a good job if given clear directions and left alone. Poker has the structure and solitude that Loner will thrive on. When bluffing, it's usually because everyone else has checked and they are pretty sure that there will be no calls. Loner pretty much does what is expected. However, when bluff-

Photo 13.
Loner

ing, they quietly refuse to do the expected. They will check or just call the nuts to the end. Then to everyone's surprise, Loner steps from behind the bushes and silently announces, "Ah, ha, I have the nuts!" He or she would never be so bold as to outright say this. They speak more in passive-aggressive actions.

♦ *System Player* is all logic with no feelings. "Just play the cards, sir." They are workaholics in their personal lives and love to play cards because of the structure it brings to their lives. Like *The Boss*, these players relish being recognized for how well they play or how well informed they are on odds and other game statistics. The rest of their lives are usually overstructured and require punctuality and

Photo 14.
System Player

schedules. Their bluffs are likewise planned and on schedule. For example, look for mostly semi-bluffs when they have the highest exposed cards (in seven-card stud). That's their system.

Bluffs Reveal Playing Styles

How a player bluffs will shed light on the type of player he or she is. As we will discuss in more detail later, knowing how a player thinks and makes sense of the world will also shed light on how best to bluff that opponent. An effective bluff can be *bright, varied,* and *well hidden.* An ineffective one is more apt to be *dumb, obvious,* and *impulsive.*

The brighter bluffs are those that are planned and vary with the type of person being bluffed and the positional advantage of the bluffer. On a continuum of planned and unplanned bluffs,[5] the more effective ones are those that fit the conditions at the table. The more conservative

5. McKenna, J. *Beyond Tells*, page 200.

players (The Boss, System Player, or Loner) are more apt to plan their bluffs. On the other hand, players such as the Party Hardy, High Roller, and Hunch Player are bluffing by the seat of their chips. They seldom plan a bluff and let their moods determine their bluffs. The playing style of a player will also influence their choice of bluffing methods. Some prefer to be aggressive when bluffing; others are more prone to be passive in their bluffs.

Responsive Versus Assertive Bluffing

We previously learned there are two main differences in how people approach both the game of life and casino play.[6] Players will likewise bluff at different levels of assertiveness as well as in planned and impulsive ways. Bluffs can range from very passive to very aggressive bluffs. Also, in addition to assertiveness, there is the factor of whether a player responds to things more with their emotions or more with logic. Some players are very structured and so their bluffs are predetermined. As mentioned earlier, their bluffs can also be paradoxes. Others bring little or no structure to the table and will bluff only from their guts, their hunches, or their intuition. If we compare a player's aggressiveness and responsiveness,[7] we can also predict how they are likely to handle good and bad times. We can determine different bluffing styles that fit players' styles of play. This comparison will also produce another useful grid for assessing bluffs.

Just as players have different styles, so the same bluff can have different meanings when the factor of personality differences is added. Some players naturally bluff softly. For others, it's natural to aggressively bluff. Both are bluffing according to how responsive they are. It's important, then, not to assume that all soft bets are good hands and that all aggressive bets are bluffs. Some soft bets may not be bluffs—particularly if coming from a passive playing style.

6. McKenna, J., *Beyond Tells*.

7. For more information on this comparison of aggression and structure, see Jung, C. G. *The Collected Works of C. G. Jung*. Vol. 6. Princeton, NJ: Princeton University Press, 1971. Also see communications styles discussed by Carlson, R. K. and Brehm, R. T. *Understanding Communication Style*, and Thayer, L. *Communication and Communication Systems*, listed in Suggested Readings.

Responsiveness in Bluffs

Players respond to the game with varied structure and logic versus hunches and intuition. Players normally vary how passively or aggressively they bet. Players will respond to cards and to life in different degrees of responsiveness to their surroundings. Many people respond in planned ways. If a player is logical and structured, planning is their way of life. Such a player would score as "0" on the responsiveness scale. The other extreme would be people who are very emotional and impulsive. They usually fail to plan. Such players will usually bluff impulsively and be scored as "10" on a bluffing-responsiveness scale.

Figure 6. Gauging Planned and Unplanned Actions

0—1—2—3—4—5—6—7—8—9—10

Planned Actions   **Unplanned Actions**

Ask yourself, "When I am representing a hand I don't have, do I act in a planned way or am I more impulsive when I bluff?" Then, rate yourself from 0 to 10 on the above scale to rank how you respond when bluffing.

Assertiveness in Bluffs

Some players approach the game passively and let the cards play themselves. Others will be very active and play aggressively to influence play with betting. You will notice people who just play the cards and others who play the people. The professional will play both. You can also score yourself on how assertively you play with passive play being "0" and very active or aggressive play ranking "10."

Figure 7. Gauging Passive and Aggressive Play

0—1—2—3—4—5—6—7—8—9—10

Passive Play   **Aggressive Play**

How would you score yourself in the manner in which you tend to bluff? When representing a hand other than you actually have, do you bet softly or do you get aggressive. Ask yourself, "When I am bluffing, do I hide or do I attack?" Bluffing styles evolve from measuring the way players respond (planned vs. unplanned) with how assertively they apply their bluffing skills (passive vs. aggressive). You can graph yourself or other players on this grid. Use the scales above to score your responsiveness (0 = Reserved 10 = Responsive), then mark your score on the horizontal arrow. Next enter your scores on the assertiveness scale (0 = Receptive 10 = Aggressive), then mark your score on the perpendicular arrow.

Since others might see you differently, ask some players who know how you play to rate you on the scales of responsiveness and assertiveness.

Here's a sample of how to graph you on the above bluffing grid:

Now that you have yourself in one of the above quadrants, let's see what your bluffing preference says about you.

Chart 6. Sample Rating Grid

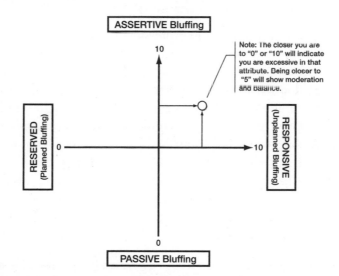

Bluffing Preferences

When both attributes are compared, the four basic styles described in later chapters and with more detail will produce these bluffing preferences: (1) "Sneak Bluffing" (passive and planned), (2) "Dare Bluffing" (aggressive and planned), (3) "Attack Bluffing" (aggressive and unplanned), and (4) "Dream Bluffing" (passive and unplanned).

If a player is bluffing the way his personality dictates, then such bluffs are congruent. It's when the bluffs change characters that the next level of awareness is required to survive the deceptions of Meta-Bluffs. Conservative players can be expected to be "straight bluffers." This means that they will mostly semi-bluff[8] and will demonstrate the usual unconscious bluffs. When on a steal, however, such conservative bluffers may do the opposite as part of their strategy. On the other hand, loose players will do the unexpected and become "paradoxical bluffers." Their bluffs are impulsive and/or flamboyant. If a loose player is not overly impulsive, many bluffs are semi-bluffs. However, most of a loose player's bluffs are high-risk bluffs, involving low-odds chases and "on the come" bets. An Assessing Grid for Bluffing then becomes apparent.

Composite Bluffing

The ability to change styles of bluffing is the skill of a composite player. Such players will player around what I referred to as the "winner's circle." Composite (as well as the professional) players will hover around the middle of the assessing grid. At times, such winners will be very aggressive and then will back off to let someone else bet. Also, they will at times abandon the logic and statistics and will allow themselves to also play their hunches. I heard a player say, "I thought you had the nuts." To this, the winner said, "Thinking can sometimes ruin your game." Such changes for the composite player are more out of flexibility and playing based on changing conditions. These changes are not unconscious. They may be habits. These are part of the tools the good player brings to the game of life. Those in the winner's circle (center grid) know that tells don't fit all and that all tells fit the player.

8. A semi-bluff occurs when a player has a good start, like one pair or four cards to a flush, with potential to improve.

Chart 7. Assessing Grid for Bluffing Preferences

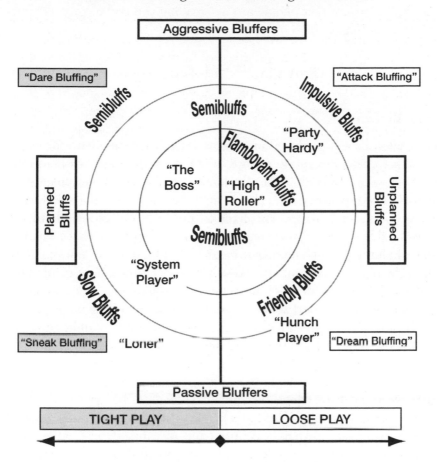

If you are not doing well while playing, adjust your sights by moving toward the center of the scales for responsiveness and assertiveness. Imagine the dynamic of aiming at a target with the cross-hair lines representing the center of the playing grid. The more you have yourself in the cross-hair of the grid, the more of your bluffs will be on target.

Likewise, when you are doing well, it's also a good idea to move around the grid to ensure that people are not reading you and to protect yourself from getting into an inflexible routine.

Tight Players' Bluffing Style

Slow Bluffing

How often have you played in a Texas Hold 'Em game with fair cards and a player behind you just limps in? Or, perhaps, hesitates before he calls and seems to be doing it reluctantly. Do you relax and think, *Okay, at least I've got him beat!* This is actually when you should start to worry. This quiet player who likes to just call and hide behind the proverbial bush may already have you in his or her trap. That's why this type of bluffing I call "sneak bluffing."[9] It's one of the hard ones to avoid since the player is seldom aggressive yet plays a pretty tight game. One of these players is a friend of mine and I asked him once, "Do you come to the table with a short stake on purpose or do you have an angle?"

He said, "I do it for the players who don't know how tight and conservative a player I am. I'm hoping that such players will make the mistake of going after me when I play good cards and get caught up in my act that I haven't been doing too well."

Wow! I knew my friend was much better than he appeared. However, I thought that his short stacks meant that he wasn't doing very well. That's exactly what he wanted me to think. Now that's pretty sneaky and pretty clever. There's another type of player who likes to be sneaky when he or she bluffs. It's the highly structured player who plans his every move. He only plays good cards and maximizes plays when in position. This is a system player who even has a system for when and how he or she bluffs. The problem these players have is that they are so structured that when they bet, most people with marginal hands fold like trained pigs. So, I asked another friend who is like this how he handles his tight reputation. I wasn't surprised to hear him say, "I take advantage of it. Sometimes when I've got lousy cards and I am in a good

---

9. McKenna, J. *Beyond Tells,* pages 199–215.

position, I'll bet or check/raise with a stone-cold bluff!" I wondered if he was setting me up to call him next time that he has a great hand.

Semi-Bluffing

There's another kind of bluffing style that I refer to as "dare bluffing." These players are daring you to call them because they know they have you beat. They are bluffing with the best hand and they seem to know it. These players are also highly planned in their actions and they are aggressive when they play. They only play with winning hands and will make you pay if you are chasing with a mediocre hand. Their dares, however, are not always obvious. They could check and re-raise a bet when someone bets. Their bets are always at least semi-bluffs. In other words, what they have is already good and there's a chance of improving if you call them.

Both of these bluffers who are highly structured, have a plan, and differ in how aggressive they bluff. The sneak bluffer is slow to bluff and plays a more passive game. The dare bluffer is equipped with a plan to at least semi-bluff and does so in a more aggressive fashion.

Loose Players' Bluffing Style

Splash Bluffing

There are much looser players who bluff and keep the action going. Some of these unplanned bluffers I refer to as employing "attack bluffing."[10] A whole set of players who are not so well planned in their bluffs. Others are less aggressive and seem to be playing hands they don't have but wish they did. I refer to these as using "dream bluffing." Structured players are bluffing with their eyes wide open. These loose players like to close their eyes with little regard to planning when they bluff.

Attack bluffs are aggressive and unplanned bluffs. When one of these "no fold 'em hold 'em" players splashed the pot with a raise, I had already pegged him for an action-oriented guy whom I refer to as "High Roller." So, it wasn't a surprise to me that he chose an attack approach to bluffing. Often, when you see such bluffing occur aggressively, with

10. McKenna, J. *Beyond Tells*, pages 199–215.

flare, the bettor hasn't even looked to see what he or she is betting into. Such players take risks more liberally, will bet into over-cards, and can be a threat to the most seasoned of players—particularly if the loose player is catching their hands. They will give you action and stay in longer than they should. However, this high roller deserves a word of caution. Since they are closer to the center on a scale of responsiveness/aggressiveness, they can modify impulsive bluffs and become more structured when needed.

Come Bluffing

Come bluffing occurs when players' bluffs are passive and unplanned. These bluffers play more with their hunches. They will do little to influence play and pretty much let the cards play themselves. They are bluffing as if they are strong because they actually believe that they are going to win the hand. They are dreaming of the hand they are going to get. It can't even be called semi-bluffing, because they are bluffing on their dreams and don't even have a pair or a gut-shot straight. If you notice their eye movements, they are continually looking up and to their right (visual construct). Recently, I was playing with a very friendly player who seemed to play a lot of hands. Some people would have called him a "calling station."[11] People were filling up on his frequent calls. I began to wonder about how he was playing. So, I asked him when he showed his hand (Ace high, little unsuited kicker), "That's wasn't even a 'semi-bluff.' What were you thinking?"

"Well, I would have had him beat if I got another Ace!"

These "dreamers" will bet more on the come and play as if they already have the hand. They are playing more from emotions while being passive.

Both these styles of bluffing come from loose players. The difference is that Attack Bluffer is aggressive, while Dream Bluffer is much more passive. There's an expression in poker to "play 'em like you've got 'em!" Well, this is more of a way of life for all bluffing styles. However, Dream Bluffer is more of a stone-cold bluff. She tends to play every hand as if

11. Schoonmaker, A. *The Psychology of Poker*. Las Vegas: Two Plus Two Publishing, 2000.

she already has what she is representing. Attack Bluffer, while misrepresenting his hand, is motivated more from seeking excitement.

So, how does one tell whether a person is dreaming, daring you, sneaking up on you, or attacking you? While I go into more detail in my book on tells (*Beyond Tells*), the answer is simply, "Know your players!" By determining the personality types of players, you will know how to determine whether they are structured or loose. The highly structured players will favor planned bluffs ("dare" and "sneak"). The looser players will lean toward impulsive bluffs ("attack" and "dream").

Drama of Bluffs

Bluffs in poker can be full of joy, full of pain, at times miraculous, and glorious when they work. Just because a player is fun and humorous doesn't mean he or she is safe from bluffing you. In fact, some well-known players are the friendliest players you can meet. They genuinely enjoy people and may even act a little crazy. This act doesn't mean that they are not paying attention or that they are stupid. In fact, he or she could be the most intelligent player at the table. Playing the "fool" is their bluff.

Another ploy that works well in bluffing is the act of appearing to not be paying attention. I once heard it said, "You can't bluff someone who's not paying attention."[12] Recently, a player to my left was the big blind. He was talking to the waitress while others were betting and tending to the game. He turned away, didn't even seem to have looked at his hole cards. While he was "looking out the window," talking to the waitress, he appeared not to even know what was going on. When it was his turn to check his big blind, he said, "Is it my turn?" Then, he raised the bet. It turned out that he had a suited Big Slick (Ace, King) and he was hard to beat. By acting like he wasn't paying attention, he was actually inviting bets and bluffs. There are a few good players who do this with newspapers, magazines, and earphones, pretending to be in another zone when they could probably get on a witness stand and not miss a beat of what's going on.

12. This is a line in the film *House of Games*. It was spoken by a character named Mike. The film was written and directed by David Mamet (and released in 1987).

You'll hear moans and groans when things happen. You hear things like, "Oh, oh!" when the flop or turn comes. As Mike Caro pointed out in his Law 24 of poker tells, "Beware of sighs and sounds of sorrow." These acts are designed to mislead you and bluff you into thinking the opponent's hand is weak, or to think what just happened hurt him. It probably helped his hand.

So, you will find a lot of players masquerading as victims. This drama can be on a conscious level or on an unconscious one. When masquerading as a Victim, Persecutor, or Rescuer, it's a strategy. When the masquerade also involves an unconscious agenda, it's a psychological game. You may want to review the Drama Triangle discussed above.

The Drama of Psychological Games

Bluffing can come complete with the drama of **Victims, Persecutors,** and **Rescuers.** When used as games between players, the bluffer, the pigeon, and the table can form a triangle. For instance, a player was on a bluff and got beat on the river. She immediately moved from Victim to Persecutor, complaining about why the pigeon stayed in so long. Although the bluffer is now on the attack, persecuting the former pigeon, she won't stay in either Victim, Persecutor, or Rescuer roles. As soon as the player who "sucked out" and won on the river is a Victim, someone at the table will Rescue, with something like, "Well, it is 7-Card Hold 'Em." Then the original bluffer who became the pigeon's Victim may switch to becoming the Persecutor to the table Rescuer and snaps back with, "Yeah, opinions are like navels, everyone has one."

A psychiatrist friend[13] of mine in San Francisco developed what he calls the Drama Triangle.[14] It's very useful to understand the drama of bluffing in poker. I once had the chance to play my friend in poker when I really didn't have much experience with the game. I wonder now if Steve was putting me in his drama triangle. As a matter of fact, it can be very useful to understand the drama in bluffs. The drama comes from shifting roles between the Victim, Rescuer, and the Persecutor. Here's what that triangle looks like:

13. Steve Karpman, M.D., won the Eric Berne Memorial Award for creating the Drama Triangle.

14. Karpman, Steven B., M.D. "Fairy Tales and Script Drama Analysis." *TAJ* (Transactional Analysis Journal) 7:26, 1968.

Figure 8. The Karpman Drama Triangle

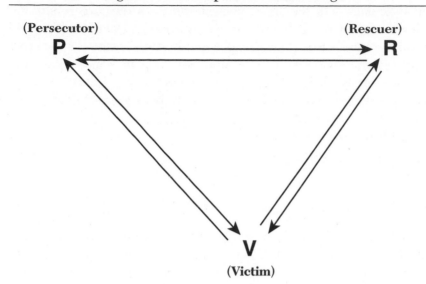

(Persecutor)   (Rescuer)

P ──────────────▶ **R**

V

(Victim)

Lure of Bluffs

Greek mythology tells the story about Sirens who lured sailors into the sea and their ships onto rocks.[15] The myth describes these Sirens as birds with women's bodies that lived at sea. They would trick sailors to jump in the sea with their intoxicating singing. Odysseus managed to save himself and his men from the Sirens. He put melted wax in his crew's ears and then had them tie him to the mast, making the crew swear they would not release him no matter how desperately he begged. So, he heard the song but made it past the sirens. The lure was mysterious and succeeded in getting experienced sailors to wreck their ships. Odysseus found a way to overcome the lures.

Bluffing in poker involves this same mysterious luring of players to do things that will wreck their stacks of chips. So far, in unraveling these mysteries, the importance of taking into consideration the six personality types and the kinds of bluffs they are likely to use have been revealed. This does not account for the varied skills (luring songs) that a successful bluffer brings to the table. These skills include being effec-

15. *Odyssey*, Book 12, pp. 208–224. Princeton, New Jersey: Princeton University Press, 2000.

tive liars who can lead people to the shores to wreck their ships. It also combines skills with the art of painting bluffs in the foreground, the background, and in plain view. Successful poker bluffers are influenced by bluffing modes that they can spot in others and know how to avoid using the same mode with each opponent. Let's look more closely at the poker sirens' skills in these areas. As Odysseus did, let's put some wax in your ears so you won't be as susceptible to these bluffing lures.

Using Bluffs to Lure Wrecks

The arsenal of bluffing weapons for the successful poker player include the ability to mislead, misdirect, to pretend, to be deceitful, and to outright lie without being caught. What's a lie that is obvious? It's a lie that told on itself. Much like the way my mom, and moms all over the world, know when their kids are lying. Any unsucccessful bluff is often one that the bluffer gave away to the perceptive player who is good at reading "tells." However, many people come to the table with the belief that lying is a sin. They think, *It's wrong and that's what makes poker the devil's playpen.* The fact, though, is that it's a sin not to ever lie in a poker game. It's not only wrong; it will result in your being a "nonwinner" or a "loser." So, if you want to learn to lie and wear it as a virtue, here are some lessons in deception.

Bluffs by Omission

Just as a person can lie by not telling you the whole truth, a poker player can bluff by omitting information that would get you to call or fold—depending on what the bluffer wishes. If the purpose is to get calls, a bluffer in poker may omit betting or raising bets. Slow-playing is by its very nature a way to lie through omission. Since a good hand would normally bet or raise a bet, the omission of such actions is the bluff. Suppose that a player in early position checks when the flop is:

With this "rainbow"[16] flop, there's not much a player can be chasing. There's an absence of a flush and straight draw, unless it would be a runner-runner. If anyone bets, it's likely to be the top pair of Jacks. If several people fold when someone bets and the early player just calls, this could mean that the caller can match the Jacks or may have two pair. Who knows? This is where knowing your player is important. Would such a player even come in with little cards in an early position? Or, the caller could be slow-playing a pair that is better than Jacks and doesn't want to raise and lose the pair of Jacks' money. By omitting to raise with a pocket pair of Kings, the early player was indeed bluffing. That's lying by not letting an opponent know he's beat. That's luring a player into shallow water to wreck his or her chips.

Slow-playing good hands is a way to get calls when you want people to stay in. Suppose, though, that you want the other players to go away—particularly if they are likely to have better cards than you? By omitting your usual way to play, you could bluff. This takes a careful application of your reputation. For example, you are a tight player who plays with a lot of structure, like the system player in this photo:

Photo 15. System Player considering a bluff

This player ordinarily would fold if she couldn't beat the high card showing. However, this time, she decides to omit her usual play and, with her pair of 5s, re-raises a bet where the high card on the flop is a King. The pair of Kings folds his hand. Why? Not because he had the

16. Poker jargon for a mixture of suits that limit the flush draws.

worst hand, but because he figured that he was beat with a pair of Aces. That's what a tight reputation can buy you and that's bluffing by omitting your usual way to play. If this didn't work, what do you think System Player would have done? If the Kings re-raised, the 5s might have re-raised. In this case the Kings were asking, "Can you beat my Kings?" System Player was answering, *"Yep!"* by re-raising. Another omission that System Player would more than likely do is to omit ever showing her hand, whether the other player folded or she folded. A showdown, though, would ruin this poor System Player's reputation.

Bluffs by Misdirecting

Misdirecting is a move that is used in many sports, like basketball, boxing, and even in baseball. This deceit can cause an opponent to move the way you want them to and then switch and move in the opposite direction. Whether faking passes, punches, or bunts, the power of misdirecting is proven. Just as a fighter can get an opponent to swerve with a fake left jab into a right upper-cut, so, too, a poker player can get other players to make the wrong move. This is leading (or really misleading) players where you want them to go. When we discussed how a player organizes thoughts in visual, auditory, or kinesthetic ways, we showed how a person can be led. It's using their language (V, A, K) to lead them. This is where auditory bluffs are more noticeable. Players are saying things that are misleading. The sounds of these bluffs are usually mourns, sighs, or expletives, like, *"Oh, no!"* When you are misleading to bluff an opponent, it's important to know how that person makes sense of the world so that you can pace them and then mislead them where you want them to go. Pacing is matching the way your opponent thinks. For example, if you have determined that your opponent thinks in pictures, then it's best to speak with visual references. Suppose you want a visual player to call because you are sure that he or she has the second-best hand. You might say something like, "I can *see* that you want to bet, so I'll just hope you can *show* some mercy." You are speaking his visual language. You are pacing him ("see") and then leading him ("show") to call your bet by suggesting that you are afraid he might raise another bet. You might even get him to raise that bet. In which case, let's hope you read him correctly as having the second-best hand. Don't try sounding weak to a veteran player—it won't work.

Bluffs by Misleading

Misleading may at first sound like misdirecting. However, it's really not. When you are misdirecting, you are matching the referential index language of your opponent, as in the above example. Misleading is to purposefully not speak the opponent's language to create tension. Instead of misleading, it's really mis-communicating. When done on purpose, it's mis-communicating to mislead someone to confuse things. For example, suppose you are talking to the same visual thinking opponent above and say something like, "I'm going to bet so much this time that it won't be poker to call." Not one visual reference in that sentence. You are failing to communicate with your visual opponent. You are using kinesthetic language. He might even say, "Huh? What's that mean?" If you wanted him to call, you've succeeded in getting him upset, confused, and probably wanting to fold. Now, if that was your intention, you used misdirecting (actually, mis-communication) to bluff an opponent into laying down a hand.

Recently, in a no-limit game a young player attempted to get me to fold. The only reason that I called him was that he seemed to be mis-communicating with me (misdirecting) and I only had the middle pair. He had already checked the top pair, and on the turn I bet my middle pair. He went all-in with a short stack (a little over $100). That raise represented a third of my stake, since I had just come into the game. I called his all-in and he mucked his hand, saying, "That was a bad call!" He got up and left on-tilt. Another player said to me, "I guess he hadn't read your book on tells." Actually, I wasn't reading his tell as much as I was sensing that he was wanting to scare a senior citizen who had just sat down to play.

Bluffs by Pretending

A great many bluffs are pretending to have the worst, the best, or a mediocre hand. All bluffs involve pretending. The pretenses can come in the forms of actions, sounds, and gestures. The statement of, "Play 'em like you've got 'em," encourages pretending. So, that's all some players know how to do. How often have you heard it said, "Play 'em like you *don't* have 'em?" Probably, about as often as I have—zip. Yet, a good many players will play garbage like they have the nut while playing the nuts like they have garbage. How does playing like you don't have much look like, what's it sound like, and how does it feel when it happens? We've already talked about slow-playing. However, there are other ways to pretend that your hand is no threat to an opponent. Besides slow-playing, it's important to be aware of sounds and actions that signal pretending. A player who flops three of a kind may sigh, mourn at the sight of a pair on the flop (the rest of his trips), or say something like, "I'll check!" He or she may even bet and say something like, "Well, two pair may get this pot." The important thing is to figure out if it is a pretend bluff. As we mentioned earlier, the eyes are the window to the truth and to lies. By watching the movement of the speaker's eyes, you might learn if this is a pretend-bluff statement. If the bettor is looking up and to his or her left, the player is accessing visual memory. You'd better take this statement as more truth than not. On the other side, if the bettor is looking up and to his or her right, it's probably a construction of what he just said.

Bluffs by Trash Talk

Position usually refers to when a player acts (early or late). Acting after everyone else has its advantages. However, some players use their mouth to gain a positional advantage. Position also refers, in the study of psychology, to the psychological position a player takes with others in the game. In this case, position is not so much when a player bets or calls, it's how players win or lose that will reveal their true *life positions*. Some players will be accessing your ears with trash talk, compliments, mourns, and groans to gain an advantage or to disarm you. At times, a compliment is designed to get you to play less aggressively. In that sense, it's a bluff because it's treating you like you are a pigeon. Sincere compliments are never bluffs. Negative remarks are always designed to put you on-tilt or gain a psychological advantage. It's good to have your own arsenal of trash talk to counterattack when someone aims at you. For example, I out ran a pair of Aces with a straight. The defeated "trasher" said, "Why did you call with only a 1-to-7 chance." I replied, "Oh? I only called because you were betting!" He quieted down and my $20 bet rewarded me a pot of well over $140.

Players in good times will have good attitudes and take a position with others that says, "You're okay and so am I." However, the true attitude about others will be showing more when a player is experiencing bad times. When a player loses, is outdrawn on the river, or comes in second-best, attitudes will be stretched. Some will then start throwing jabs, such as, "Why would you stay for such a gut shot?" Or, "That was stupid!" Both reactions are saying, "Well I'm better than you are!" When players engage in such "trash talk" it's usually because another player chased a low-odds draw and beat the player who had the better hand (until the end when the runner-runner made the hand). Other players will trash-talk from the time they sit down and call it comradery.

Some players operate out of the psychological position of *I'm a better player and you are just lucky.* Others will position themselves like, *Well, you know more than I do. So, I guess you're right.* Either way, trash talk is not fun or comradely behavior. It's just a sore loser trying to save face and get even.

Most professional players seldom get caught up in such trash talk. When they lose a hand, it's more about wondering if they would do the same again and hoping that the player who is playing long shots doesn't leave the table too soon. When they are beaten by a runner-runner who made a gut straight on the river, the attitude of patience is more prevalent than trash talk. Over time the loose player who bets poor odds and chases slim chances will leave more than they will take.

Trash talkers are usually tight rigid players who believe that everyone should play a certain way (like them) or that there is something wrong with other players who don't. Other players are often more creative and are not stuck in the same old patterns. They will take risks and make even low probability hands. Unfortunately, players who make such "miracle hands" often have a false psychological position about themselves. Such a player may actually think, *I'm the best player at the table and the rest of these tightwads don't know how to play this game.*

Pretending that you are better than others is not the bad thing. Believing that you are better than you are is the problem. Either way, it's when a player is rude enough to tell another player that he or she is making mistakes. That is the bigger mistake. Why? Well, for one thing, it hurts the game. The player who did make the error in judgment and won might not stay very long if the bashing is so negative. Then the table lost a call station, or some easy money.

This is not to say that playful comradely talk is the same as trash talk. There is sometimes a fine line as to where comradely talk stops and trash talk starts? Is the talker kidding or are serious things being said in jest? Two friends who know each other can say things that strangers would seldom utter. Generally, if you are upset about being beaten by a runner, it's best to say a prayer instead of trash-talk. Pray that the runner-runner stays long enough to get even. Winning back your loss will get you farther than trying to shame or humiliate a loose player.

As the saying goes, "Never try to teach a pig to sing. It annoys the pig and frustrates the hell out of you." That's what I'm talking about!

Bluffing by Hiding and Concealing

Remember this: We are talking about ways to lure others into doing things that will wreck their piles of chips—much like the sirens of Greek myth. Hide-and-seek is a game that even children become good at doing. Some players will hide to get you to come looking for them. Whenever they have good hands, they know how to hide them. When they have poor hands they also know how to hide by betting, raising, or mucking their hands. Concealing is one of the tools of successful bluffing. To succeed in poker your opponent must not be given free information. For this reason, you will not see a veteran poker player ever show his hole cards if he is not called down. When players are showing their hole cards, either to be proud or to be spiteful, they are usually being stupid. That's because they are teaching opponents how they play: what kind of cards they will limp in with, how much they will chase, whether they are bluffing, and so on. Concealing how you play is probably going to be a useful tool when you want to bluff. I know players who will show their hole cards to set you up for a later bluff. But, if you do this, be sure that it is for that reason only and that you are not being spiteful or proud. Just remember what comes before the fall.

I mentioned earlier players who wear sunglasses to hide their eyes. Some of these players are actually hiding from people. They may be afraid that you can tell what they are thinking and want to distance themselves to avoid getting too exposed—especially when they don't have much. As mentioned earlier, when they are afraid of their hand they will put their sunglasses on. When they like their hand, off come the glasses. I think this has some validity but will have to be put in context with each player who wears sunglasses—particularly if they take them on and off.

The Art of Bluffing

Playing poker is more art than science. True, mastering the science of math and knowing the proven theories of personality theories will give a player needed edges. Yet, in the final application of skills comes the art of playing and of bluffing. When Michelangelo painted the Sistine Chapel in Rome, he used knowledge, skill, and his own artistic signature. If another artist did the same drawings, they would look quite different. The same is true of the art of playing poker. Each player who applies his or her own strokes (bluffs) will make such moves in unique ways. Yet, they will still apply the science of such moves as pacing and leading. This is where being creative in the ways to bluff opponents is crucial. The same bluff won't work for everyone and often not even with the same player. So, in studying and going beyond bluffs, good players integrate their creative right brain with their scientific left brain.

Bluffing Modes

How to bluff other players will require knowing not only how different players think but knowing what predispositions they bring to the table. Chapter 3 reviewed personality orientations and bluffing. Go back and review and you will realize how different personalities bluff and be able to tell the difference between aggressive and passive bluffs.

Bluffing with the Best Hand

Before moving on to how players give away whether they are bluffing or not, a lot of players will have the best hand yet they will play it aggressively and will appear to be buying a pot. First of all, bluffing is not even necessary when you think that you have the best hand. Just like some players take their sunglasses on and off, because they are afraid and don't like their hand, some players get afraid that their good hand will get outrun. So, they may bet a good hand aggressively, saying, "I'd rather win a small pot than get outrun by weaker hands." This happens often when some players have pocket Aces and their greatest fear is to end up with "Aces and Spaces"[17] and get beaten by two small pair. This is not to say that a good hand should always be played in the slow lane.

17. Poker jargon for a pair of Aces only.

Again, the conditions at the table and the possible ways players can beat you has to be considered. That said, there are times and conditions when having the best hand deserves a bluff. It's true that a good hand like trips will be hard to beat. Some people will check and give the impression that their hand isn't that strong. Still others will bet strongly pretending that they don't have much. After all, someone wrote a famous book[18] of tells and said essentially that "weak means strong and strong means weak."

How to manage the best hand, whether to check, raise, or just call, comes with years of experience to gain an understanding of when it's safe to slow-play, when to bluff, and when to just drive to get everyone out and win a smaller pot. Most veteran players want to get the full value out of their hands. Sometimes, however, with some players, and with some flops, the value may be less than usual. Here's an example. Suppose you have pocket rockets (Aces) and the big blind raises your bet after the flop. That's when it might be wise to consider that the value of your hand has suddenly diminished.

18. Caro, M. *The Body Language of Poker*. Hollywood, CA: Gambling Times, 1984.

7

Bluffs That Tell on Themselves

Players will give away what they are going to do in a variety of ways. If a player is just going to call when it's his turn, you will see him pick up the bet from his stack. Players who avoid this kind of "telegraphing" will not make such premature moves. In fact, a lot of players won't telegraph whether they are going to call, fold, or raise. You will see them do the same ritual of, for instance, putting a protecting chip on their hole cards whether they are going to stay or not. Sometimes they will then remove the chip and fold. At other times, they will go ahead and bet or raise. The important thing is that you will not know what they are going to do until it's their time to act.

Another frequent telegraph is peeking at hole cards a second or third time. If there are two or three cards of the same suit on the flop and a player takes another peek, it usually is sending a telegraphed message, *Is one of my cards in that suit?* If they already have both cards in that suit, you will not likely see this peek—unless the player is sophisticated enough to be bluffing that he hasn't made his flush.

All tells are actually ways to telegraph messages to other players. For example, Caro reminds us that peeking and then betting usually means that the player is not bluffing.[1] Of course, it could be some players' way to bluff—realizing that others have read Caro's book. Similarly, players will telegraph when they are bluffing, if you know what to look and

---

1. Caro's Law #10, *"If a player looks and then bets instantly, it's unlikely that he's bluffing."*

listen for. As mentioned previously, it's possible to predict how different players are likely to bluff.

Predicting Bluffs

People will characteristically handle life[2] the way they bluff. For example:

♥ *The* (self-appointed) *Boss* at the tables will have an opinion about most everything and everybody in their lives. They expect others to be perfect and want people to notice how good they are both at work and at the tables. Such people need their opinions recognized. They will bluff "by the book," because, for instance, their position dictates that a bluff would be proper. Bluffs may or may not include sandbagging,[3] depending on their current opinion about sandbaggers.

♥ *Party Hardy* is looking for contact with the world around her. Getting people involved is more important than the task at hand—whether playing cards or working in an office. If they have a problem, they will blame everyone else. Look for impulsive bluffs with chips thrown toward the active player(s). However, remember that throwing chips is normal behavior for impulsive players. Where others will splash the pot to bluff, that's what Party Hardies do. These bluffers seldom plan a bluff—they just get the urge and "Ready, fire, aim!"

♥ *High Roller* is looking for excitement in the cards and in his personal life. These players want to create fun or conflict—anything to get things going. Winning or losing is not as valued as taking risks. Such players love to manipulate. Whether they win the money or not, if they can create incidents, they are happy. Their bluffs are more like challenges or attacks.

♥ *Hunch Player* is there to feel rather than think. In their personal lives these players are sensitive and tend to help others more than

---

2. In Kahler's *The Mystery of Management* as well as Caper and Kahler's "Mini-Script," there are valuable clues about how people handle stress differently. Kahler's distress sequence is especially helpful—see Suggested Readings.

3. Checking and then raising any bets that limp in.

themselves. They play cards the same way. "Oh, I'm sorry" is often said by Hunch Player when winning the pot. Hunch Player is more interested in being accepted for who she is, than for how well she plays. If they lose or make mistakes, "poor babies" and knowing that people still like them are more important than how much others like their work. They bluff accidentally, playing hands on the come, or because they have a hunch. Their bluffs are hard to read because they really believe that they are going to win. Their bets are usually "on the come,"[4] as they are hunching that their *inside straight* or *three of a kind* are already theirs.

♥ *Loner* is in the game and life to be strong and suffer silently. These types will be the most observant about what's happening around them, and if they could find a solitaire game of poker they'd be there. Look for more of these players at the video poker machine (the closest to poker solitaire away from home). In their personal lives, they prefer solitude. Loner will do a good job if given clear directions and left alone. Gaming has the structure and solitude on which Loner will thrive. When bluffing, it's usually because everyone else has checked and they are pretty sure that there will be no calls. Loner pretty much does what is expected. However, when bluffing, they quietly refuse to do the expected. They will check or just call the nuts to the end. Then everyone's surprised, when Loner steps from behind the bushes and silently announces, "Ah, ha, I have the nuts!"

♥ *System Player* is all logic with no feelings. "Just play the cards, sir." They are workaholics in their personal lives and love to play cards because of the structure it brings to their lives. Like *The Boss*, these players relish being recognized for how well they play or how well informed they are on odds and other game statistics. The rest of their lives are usually overstructured and require punctuality and schedules. Their bluffs are likewise planned and on schedule. For example, look for mostly semi-bluffs when they have the highest exposed cards or good cards with good position. That's their system.

---

4. This is betting like you have the hand but only have part of what you are betting on.

Beyond Bluffs (Meta-Bluffs)

In *Beyond Tells,* I introduced the idea of Meta-Tells.[5] That's when a "tell" is telling on itself. That's also the next level of reading bluffs. Most experienced players never view a tell at face value. Tells don't happen in a vacuum; the content of any given bluff must be viewed in the context of the process going on at the table. Most discussions of bluffs focus on the content or behavior of the player and generalize the behavior for most players.[6] To fully understand bluffing is to be aware of the *process* of each bluff. For example, a move, such as check/raising, is really meaningless if not taken in the context of the process going on at the time of that move. The content of a bluff looks at *what* is happening. Process takes into account "how" and "by whom" a bluff is performed. The same action (checking and then raising a bet) can mean different things at different times, when done by different players.

By being cognizant of the process of bluffs, we can fine-tune playing skills and powers as a player. The process looks beyond the content of bluffs. The process looks at the *hidden* tell within any given bluff. "Hidden tells" may seem like a contradiction or an oxymoron.[7] That's because many tells are contradictions to what is expected. Contradictions occur when the conscious actions do not correspond to the unconscious tells. In Caro's terms, when the act of an impostor is not congruent with his or her unconscious tell. As an oxymoron is a contradiction of words so bluffs can be contradictions and mean different things for different playing styles. So we'll refer to a "bluff" that tells on itself as a meta-bluff—that's going beyond bluffs. Meta-bluffs come in two levels: aware and unaware actions. That's why every bluff will tell on the player *and* on itself when one has weighed enough factors. The body language of each bluffing move contains both a social level (the content) and the psychological level (the process).

A bluff not only reflects valuable information about the user's playing

---

5. McKenna, J. *Beyond Tells*, pages 175–176.

6. There are some excellent books that outline the contents of bluffs. See authors Lessinger, M. *The Book of Bluffs*, and Alvarez, A. *Poker: Bets, Bluffs, and Bad Beats* in Suggested Readings.

7. For example, "The roar of the grease paint" is an oxymoron. It attributes sound "roar" to smell ("grease paint"). This contradicts the statement, "The roar of the crowd and the smell of the grease paint."

style, but also it can reveal the player's personality orientation. Likewise, if we already know the person's style for handling life, we can also predict the kind of bluffing that person is likely to employ.

Freudian Chips

Sigmund Freud's theories on the subconscious and how actions will reveal what's going on inside of us predates the study of poker bluffs and tells. Tells are also outside of the player's awareness. In other words, it's a bluff designed to mislead. Often aggressive play reveals that a player is weak. Yet, mild plays say that the player is strong. Of course, veteran players who know this will throw you a curve and pretend to have a bad hand by being aggressive, attempting to trap an informed, unsuspecting player.

Freudian slips are actions full of contradictions. For instance, a person says he's feeling great and has a frown on his face. When I see this conflict, I usually think something like, *Notify your face!* Such contradictions occur when we say one thing and are thinking something else. Like the story about the guy who is distracted by a ticket agent with a see-through blouse. He says, "Could I have my change in nipple and dimes, please?"

Poker players are often contradicting themselves. When an ordinarily aggressive player places a bet softly, he or she is usually on a bluff. Similarly, a quiet player who gets "mouthy" usually signifies a red flag. The important thing is to know what is normal for each player.

A lot of bluffing tells have to do with how a player handles his chips. I call these "Freudian chips." They are unconscious nervous habits or signals that tell different stories. Recently, a player wanted to call but threw in too many chips. The dealer said, "Is that a raise?" The player said, "Oh, uh no. Uh, I mean yeah. Let it be a raise." Of course, you guessed it. He wanted to slow-play some good cards and ended up winning that hand. Not before I got out of his way, though.

Freudian chips come with variety. Some juggle, others shuffle chips. Many don't touch their chips until it's time to bet or raise the bet. Players will put some chips on top of their hold cards only when they plan on playing the hand. Others will do this routinely whether they are going to play or not. Incidentally, notice when players shuffle their chips. Some players will shuffle their chips only when they are nervous about something. A player who raised in late position started shuffling his chips. He was on a steal. When this same player has a hand he will freeze, hold his breath, and look around hoping for calls. It could be just the opposite for other players. When scared of a call they may freeze. When confident in their hand, others may shuffle their chips. You just have to put the actions in the process again—not the content.

Here's another example. I noticed a player who routinely puts about five chips on his hole cards. If he likes the flop, he stacks five or ten more on top of them (as if getting ready to bet from the chips on his hole cards). If he is just calling or staying, he will take the bet from the five he has on his cards. Then he will replace the chips from his stake. Needless to say, after the flop, I'd watch how he stacked his chips with a Freudian eye.

Chip nests reveal player attitudes brought to the game. Some players are loose; others are very structured. They usually will nest their chips in the same manner. For some, chips are stacked in high towers symbolizing fortresses or virility. A few will pile all their chips together with no order whatsoever. Others will arrange their chips in stacks of five or ten to facilitate betting and raising bets. Often, players will divide what they brought to the table by what they are ahead to help them manage win/loss goals. Recently, I played with a guy who came complete with a white shirt and tie. He piled his chips up in a random pile. Seemed like an act that didn't go with his appearance—so, I kept an eye on him. That ploy wasn't really working. He refused to play many hands and that didn't match his "bone yard" pile of chips. Finally, he arranged his chips in piles of five and systematically placed them in a circle, building a sphere. That matched his personality and he stopped bluffing.

All these chip rituals tell a different story about their chip masters. The important thing is to determine if people are handling their chips in a conscious or unconscious manner. A very systematic player, who likes to parade as a disorganized loser, will randomly pile his chips up. This is deliberate on his part like his strategy to appear loose. The way he bets may reveal that he plays tighter than a bark on a tree.

Finally, it's useful to notice how and when players shuffle their chips. Some only shuffle when they are chasing. Others stop shuffling when they have made their hand. Pay attention and you could slip into some extra chips for your nest.

Fitting Bluffs

It's important to fit the bluff to the player and not attempt to fit a player to a bluff. In other words, different personality types of players will attempt to bluff more in line with their styles. When a player departs from his or her usual style, look for a bluff. For example, where betting in a flamboyant way may mean bluffing for some, for others it means that they are excited about what's happening and are impulsively throwing in their bets. This factor changes the context and is seldom a bluff for an impulsive player. It's more the impulsive player's nature to be flamboyant. Staring at the cards may show weakness for most players. And, staring away from the action can mean that he or she has a good hand.[8] However, Party Hardy will bet impulsively and often not even look at the other hands at the table. Such players are looking away from the action, yet they are betting into straights and flushes and don't seem to care. So, it's important to weigh such factors and to fit bluffs to the player rather than try to fit all players into any given bluff.

Photo 16. This would be a bluff for a player who
usually is less dramatic.

8. For more detailed descriptions of tells, see *The Body Language of Poker: Mike Caro's Book of Tells*, in Suggested Readings.

While Caro's body language of poker will usually stand up, one must also pay attention to differences of who the player is. A very good player will use known bluffs to bluff. For example, he or she may sometimes carefully place bets and at other times will string the chips in—just to throw tell readers off. Such tells could also mean one thing for High Roller and the opposite for System Player. High Roller, who carefully places a bet with scare cards[9] showing, may very well have the best hand. Usually, such a player is aggressive and will bet aggressively. *The change in routine is the process and it's what's significant.* At the same time, semi-bluffing Systems Player may place a bet in softly with scare cards showing and even look away to suggest that she has the hand. After all, most serious players would have read Caro's *Book of Tells* and will do the opposite of what ordinary tells mean. That's their system. If weak means strong and a system player is holding a weak hand (e.g., three suited cards showing, no pairs, and garbage in the hole), then he or she may create a paradox—bet weak to appear strong. Similarly, a veteran player might bet the nuts[10] by showing strength—figuring that appearing strong may suggest that they don't have the hand. This might be called using a bluff to bluff. Similarly, just throwing a bet in may mean a loose bet for some, a bluff for others, or it may be the normal betting style for others. Using bluffs to bluff are for sophisticated players. Weak players are usually bluffing on impulse.

In order to go to the next level of reading bluffs, players will need to join each move to the personality of the bettor. For example, just throwing a bet in may mean a loose play or a bluff for some. For others, it may be normal betting style to throw bets in.

In photo 17 we see that High Roller has the "nuts" on the turn, Kings full of 5s. Yet he is throwing in his bet. That's his normal way to play. If he changed and was placing his bet in softly, put him on a steal.

9. In seven-card stud, a pair of Aces or three suited cards up are scare cards because they look like the rest of a strong hand.

10. The "nuts" is poker colloquial for the best possible hand. Why? Probably because poker was a male-dominated game for years *or* when people bet like they have the "nuts," most aware players will "bolt." Who knows for certain? Story is that in the old West, when a player would bet his nut off of his wagon, he was betting his wagon on that hand.

Photo 17. High Roller betting

Here's the same player placing the bet slowly and carefully.

Photo 18. Typical bluff of High Roller

It's important to avoid the mistake of reading all bluffing moves in the same way. That's making all bluffs a simple statement of behavior without the context of who, what, and how the action was happening. Whose bluffing takes into account the players' usual style of playing. How he or she is bluffing considers their patterns of thinking. Remember earlier we discussed three skills in successful bluffing:

1. Knowing how your opponent thinks
2. Knowing what your opponents think you are thinking
3. Knowing what your opponents think you think they are thinking

To excel in reading bluffs, it's important to realize

1. Every bluffer thinks and makes sense of the world in different ways. Bluffers come with a mixture of thinking in pictures, words, and actions. The same action by different personality types will mean different things.
2. Your opponents can only know what you are thinking if you let them know. It would behoove you to keep your mouth shut and be aware of how your eyes are moving. Good players are observing your every move, including listening to how you talk. You wouldn't show your hole cards to give players a read on how you play. Why, then, would you give them other clues, like talking and moving your eyes around? (Unless, of course, you are misleading them.)
3. If others know what you think that they think that you are thinking, they have probably already bluffed you. If you are leading them into a bluff, why not talk as if you know what they are thinking—only be wrong. That way they think that you think that they have good cards when you actually don't think their cards are as good as yours. It's complicated; but, so is bluffing.

Lots of players are good at acting to control how you read them. Some will play the clown when they know a lot more than it appears; others will hide who they really are and how successful they can be. This was driven home to me recently when I met several players outside of the poker rooms. In chatting with them on separate occasions, I learned that one was the president of a multi-million-dollar corporation. He sure didn't act like he was that smart in the poker room. He did very well in both arenas. The other guy let it be known that he just sold a very large golf course and was enjoying the relaxation of poker times. He also was well hidden from people with whom he played.

Neutralizing Bluffs

Have you ever noticed when some players pause and stare at the flop and seem to be focused on whether to call, raise, or fold? Sometimes these pauses seem like forever before the player bets, raises, or folds. Often such focusing is meant to be a hoax and get other players to think twice before they call a raise. Such moves are designed to get noticed. I call this "hocus-focus" in poker. Although, the "focus" word is used a lot, I wonder how many players know what it really means. Or, is focusing just another way to bluff? Learning how to cancel out a bluff with getting the bluffer to notice you is a way to neutralize bluffs. We mentioned earlier that a player needs to be focused on what you are doing and what you might have in order to bluff that player. There are ways to redirect a player's attention to get him or her to lay down their bluff. Before going there, here's a brief story about how to get people to notice what you want them to pay attention to.

I often think of Dr. Milton Erickson, a famous hypnotherapist, who knew the real value of being focused. He demonstrated that people will do what they are noticing themselves doing. For example, another psychiatrist brought him a ten-year-old boy that was in constant trouble at home and at school. After sitting is silence for about five minutes, Dr. Erikson asked the boy, "Young man, would you be surprised if in the next two weeks you noticed yourself doing everything right and others noticed how well you were doing?"

"I sure would!"

To this Dr. Erickson dismissed the boy with, "*Very good. I'll see you in two weeks.*" Well, you guessed it. On the next visit, the consulting therapist reported that the boy had turned around. He started noticing himself doing well. That's the power of focusing. We will usually reinforce what we notice.

Players notice how much they are losing. That's why you will hear a lot of whining in a poker game. People will talk about the bad hands, or the big fish that got away. Seldom will you hear about how good a hand worked out. When was the last time you heard a player commenting on how lucky he or she has been or how well they have been doing? Of course, etiquette would limit such bragging. Yet, how often do players tell themselves how good things are in their lives? We tend to notice the bad hands, the cut finger, the headache, or the tired back. Players have "short-term focus" as opposed to "long-term focus." A good player will count on how often certain hands will win and how much playing a hand is worth the risk. In the long run, their focus is on what works over time.

Directing focus is an important bluffing skill. When a player raises a bet three or four times the bet, that player is directing your attention to his hand. The player is saying, "Notice me. I think I've got you beat." Now you can fold and, if that raise was a bluff, it worked. If you had the absolute nuts, you wouldn't fold. What would you do? You certainly would not fold and it would be a mistake to just call. It's fold or go all-in. Remember the story about how Dr. Erickson got the misbehaving boy to notice himself being good? This is where you want the bluffer (or raiser) to notice that you have the better hand. Unless the bluffer has a great deal of extra stake, this is a good time to go all-in. Chances are that if he was bluffing he will fold. However, if he has a good hand and was semi-bluffing, you have to have made it insane for him to call you. That's one way to neutralize a bluff and to get a player to notice that you have a better hand. There are other ways, but most of them only work well in pot-limit and no-limit games. The important skill here is coming over a bluffer's raise. It must be timed and it requires conditions that won't encourage a "pissing contest" and minimizes loose play.

Bluffing Styles

Different playing styles come with different or preferred body language. Bluffs can be subtle as well as flamboyant—just as some players are passive and others are aggressive. Also, people tend to be either very structured or emotional in their approach to bluffing. So too, bluffs will range from well-planned actions to impulsive ones. As Mike Caro[11] points out, some tells are unconscious and others are acts by an impostor.

Knowing how people make sense of things can help to predict the type of bluffing-tell such people use when stressed. Remember that each person has a unique survival style when under pressure. Whether a person has good fortune or bad fortune, predictable coping styles will

11. Caro, M. *The Body Language of Poker.*

be noticeable. For example, we know that Hunch Player is pretty laid back, lets the cards play themselves, and at the same time tends to follow their intuition and hunches. Now, what kind of bluffing-tell would you expect? On the unaware level of tells, Hunch Player might bet confidently—either placing bets gently or splashing the pot with his chips—even though he may be chasing and doesn't have a hand yet. But, in Caro's body language, we learned that when a person is bluffing they are more apt to forcefully throw their chips in and when they have a good hand will tend to place their bets softly. Remember, though, Hunch Player believes his hunches are more than the cards. If Hunch Player has a pair of Queens and gets the hunch that he is going to get a third Queen, then he will play like he already has three Queens. Players like this are hard to read because they will play like they have the hand and bet "on the come."[12] A professional's ploy often will overcome this doubt. For example, by reaching for his or her chips while Hunch Player is betting, a veteran player can see if they can force a second peek. When bluffing, even Hunch Player will look again, if nothing else than to imagine what the third Queen would look like.

The important skill is figuring out when a player's unaware actions are congruent with their personality playing styles.

Photo 19. The Boss betting normally.

Photo 20. The smiling Boss is out of character (on a steal).

12. When a bettor is betting on the come he or she doesn't have the hand they are representing. This can be a semi-bluff or it can be pure recklessness.

It's important to learn the style of each player. When a player changes style, there's a bluff in progress. In photos 19 and 20, The Boss, who is normally serious and judgmental (#19) suddenly starts betting in a friendly manner (#20). This sudden socializing can be disarming. It's also an impostor because it's not The Boss' style.

Loose players are in character when they appear loose. When they are not, look for bluffs.

Photo 21. Sloppy Party Hardy

Photo 22. Carefree Loner
dressed for comfort

Loner (photo 22) is actually feeling great. He likely loves solitude and just may need to notify his face that he's having fun.

Body Language and Personalities

It doesn't take long, though, to figure out the body language that fits each personality difference. By using body language and personality differences, the science of tells gets that much more interesting. Add eye movement and the science of bluffs gets revealing. Here are some examples:

♣ *The Boss* will frown a lot in judgment of others' actions. Look for them to normally tilt their heads up and look down their nose at people and the cards. Any other gestures, like peering up, head cocked to one side, and smiling will mean the Boss is speeding.[13] The eyes of the Boss will also reveal when they are bluffing. Generally, they are more apt to be looking down and to the right or looking back and forth searching. That's because of the constant internal dialogue that structured/aggressive players are used to doing. Calculating odds, predicting their next move, etc.

♣ *Party Hardy* will be noticeably sloppy in appearance and in how they manage their chips. Their faces are also often wrinkle-free as they take this carefree approach to life. When they are serious or studious they are on a bluff. Their eyes are often looking up and to their right since they are frequently constructing pictures and skimming their next moves.

♣ *High Roller* is more on the flamboyant look and talk. They will dress sharply and act like showy salespersons, who know how to "work" a sale. When on a bluff they will suddenly get quiet and less aggressive. Their eyes also like to look to their right, either up or down. That's because they are constructing moves or playing on hunches.

♣ *Hunch Player* is there to look good and can be expected to smile a lot. Being sociable is more important than being withdrawn into the game. Notice how much they raise their eyebrows in half moons while smiling at you. Their eyes are often looking up and constructing hands that they are sure they are going to have.

13. "Caught speeding," is poker jargon for being caught bluffing.

♣ *Loner* is dressed for comfort (vs. style). Look for brown shoes with blue pants. Or, wrinkled clothes that don't seem to go well together. Loner will seldom, if ever, make eye contact with other players. Eyes are usually down, either engaged in self-talk or listening to their feelings.

♣ *System Player* is neat and will keep his or her chips in orderly fashion. They may even line up the stripes on the chips and like to make towers of success with their chips. Some systems players will buy more chips when losing—just to keep a show of chip towers. System Player's chips are like trophies  or plaques on a workaholic's walls. Their eyes favor the left as they are remembering images or engaging in self-talk.

Simply put, loose players are in character when they appear loose and conservative players are doing what's expected when their play is tight.

In photo examples 23 to 25 there are three different body languages that are all congruent with the individual playing styles:

Photo 23. Flamboyant High Roller

Photo 24. Businesslike
Systems Player

Photo 25. Smiling Hunch Player
(eyebrows raised)

So, it becomes clearer that all types of players at the table speak not one body language. Some players speak in "loose-ese" body talk. Others are speaking "tight-ese." Yet both languages have their own dialect that is peculiar to each personality type.

Conflicts in Body Language

So, how can you believe body language? If the same body language means something different for different players, how reliable are tells? Extremely! If read in the context of who is "speaking." It's just that *no tell fits all, yet all tells fit the player.* This is where being congruent, described in chapter 6, helps to tell players' tells apart. Remember the example of a person saying something positive, like, "I really like you," while shaking his head "No?" His actions didn't agree with his words. So, it's always best to believe the actions and ignore the words.[14] For example, if a person, say a Hunch Player, places a bet carefully (thinking her hand's coming), and then stares at the cards or the pot, then we can say that player is caught speeding.

Why? Because Hunch Player is betting as if she already has a good hand.[15] At the same time, the player is staring at the action. At any rate, it would be best to believe the unaware tell that says the player's bluffing and ignore the soft betting. According to Caro, players who look at you or the action are most likely bluffing. (I wonder if my mom read Caro's book of tells.) When an impulsive player slows down and stares, or when such a player places bets carefully, it means that speeding is in progress. This is the case for this Hunch Player in photo 26.

Photo 26. Placing bet carefully, yet staring at cards

It helps to remember the normal betting for this player.

Often, when a player is being friendly, this means that they have a great hand and don't want to scare anyone away. However, when friendliness is a way of living, then there is no conflict. That's why Hunch

14. That could be the origin of the expression, "The way to tell that a poker player is lying is to watch his lips. If they're moving don't believe him."

15. Caro's theme of "weak means strong and strong means weak" would say that placing the bet softly is to suggest weakness and not wanting to scare anyone out. Ordinarily, by itself this tell would reveal a strong hand. In this case, because we have a Hunch Player placing a bet softly (suggesting strength) while staring at the flop (suggesting weakness), this conflict makes the tell an act.

Photo 27. Hunch Player placing bet carefully and smiling

Player being serious is more a threat (photo 26) than when she's being friendly (photo 27).

The Boss in photo 28 is placing his bet in softly, representing that he has a good hand. However, he usually has his head tilted up. With his head tilted to one side and looking slightly up reveals that the Boss is on a bluff.

Photo 28. The Boss with head down and peering up is on a bluff.

With his head up and level, as in photo 29, the Boss likely has a real hand.

Photo 29. Boss with head up has a strong hand.

Here's another example of normal style versus a bluff when this Party Hardy is pretending not to notice:

Photo 30. Party Hardy betting and talking to another player

It helps to remember Party Hardy's normal actions.

Photo 31. Party Hardy throwing chips.

There's no conflict in body language when a person is true to form. For example, High Roller, in photo 32, just got caught stealing and is not taking the defeat quietly. This mild "table tantrum" is negative excitement for a player there for thrills.

Photo 32. High Roller caught stealing

Often, when a player is being friendly, this means that they have a great hand and don't want to scare you away. However, when friendliness is a way of life, there's no conflict. For example, in photos 33 and 34, Hunch Player is being at times cheerful and sometimes she is being serious. While smiling is normal for Hunch Player, being serious usually means she's on a bluff.

Photo 33. Hunch Player being
serious (bluffing)

Photo 34. Hunch Player being
nice (normal)

In photo 35, System Player is betting with a pair of Aces in the hole. That's his system to avoid being outrun and to narrow down the field of players.

Faking Frames of Reference

If you listen and watch players carefully, you will often notice inconsistencies—particularly when such players are on a bluff. You will hear

Photo 35. System Player betting versus checking high cards

such players representing things with visual terms (e.g., see, look, sharp) and behaving more like they are playing with their emotions, like a hunch player (kinesthetic frame of reference). Whenever you see this conflict, it usually means that the player is acting. Believe his talk (visual) and not his actions (kinesthetic). The way he talks reveals unconsciously how he really thinks, in pictures. This is particularly true if you have previously assessed the player as a conservative player who relies on a system rather than his feelings and intuition, such as Hunch Player would. This is a visual player masquerading as an action-oriented competitor. It's not that an ordinarily conservative player can't suddenly be acting like Party Hardy. In fact, if the player is a good enough bluffer, he could pull this off as an act to throw opponents off.

It's a tournament and the blinds are $40,000–$80,000. It's down to four players (two aggressive players, a much more conservative one on the button and probably the best hand (A♠Q♣) in the Big Blind). The aggressive players are the chip leaders and the player who is on the button shared a short stack with the player in the big blind. You know them. It happened in the 2004 WSOP tournament. You may even have seen them on the event televised by ESPN. The chip leader was Greg Raymer who had almost $8 million. The second chip leader was Josh Arieh with a stake of just under $4 million. The button was Dan Harrington and he had a measly (comparatively speaking) $2.3 million. Usually, you can expect one of the short stacks to make a move. Was this going to be it? And, if one makes a move, how can you know for sure it isn't just that—a desperate attempt to double up. Well, as many of you saw, Arieh raised the blinds to $255,000. He did this with a Kh9s, not a bad hand but definitely a shot at stealing. What was convincing about this semi-bluff was that Arieh who is aggressive just gently placed his raise. Raymer must have sensed this because he just called the raise with As2s. One thing about Raymer is that his weird glasses make it impossible to see which way his eyes are looking for sure. However, he turned his head slightly to the right (suggesting he was visual constructing). He too was on a semi-bluff. With that, Dan Harrington looked slightly up and away from the bettors. He said, "I'm going to raise it," and he didn't go all-in. Rather he pushed $1.2 million to the pot. Now, since Harrington had such a tight reputation, this made his shift into an action mode more convincing. He did this with a lot of skill, nerve, and determination that all outweighed his hand, 6♥2♦. I don't know if this would have worked without a reputation like his. If you noticed his eyes, however, he was constructively visualizing and his words were action-oriented. Again, whenever you notice this kind of contradiction in frames of reference, suspect a bluff. I'm sure both Arieh and Raymer suspected that it was a bluff. While waiting for his opponents to decide whether or not to call him, Harrington gave a visual clue that he was on a steal. The other players missed it. Harrington's eyes kept looking up and to his right. He briefly would look left, but his eyes seemed drawn to his right side. He kept visually constructing something. Maybe it was the hand that he was pretending he had (like pocket Aces). Maybe he was constructing a picture of his opponents folding. Whatever, we know that he was not looking at the hand he was betting on. If he had the Aces, he would have been moving his eyes to the left (visual eidetic) to remember his hand. Yet, Raymer and Arieh's respect for Harrington and the fact that he was asking them to increase their bet by over five times their bets made the pot odds less attractive. If you recall, the big blind (David William) had the best two holes cards. He folded in a heart beat. Harrington won the pot when both Arieh and Raymer folded.[18]

Skill of Hiding

The process of bluffing involves one of five activities: semi-bluffs, impulsive bluffs, flamboyant bluffs, friendly bluffs, and slow bluffs. Any one of these, except semi-bluffing, can also be stone-cold bluffs. Each of the various styles prefers one of these. The Boss, who is both aggressive and applies planned bluffs, will prefer to use semi-bluffs. However, such ordinarily tight players will occasionally use a cold-stone bluff to trade in on their reputation. Their bluffs are more like dares. On the other hand, System Player, who is also tight but passive in actions, will lean toward slow bluffs. He has a hand, maybe even the "nuts," and prefers to stay hidden and bet or raise after other players commit themselves. Impulsive bluffs will come from the other styles: Party Hardy, High Roller, and Hunch Player. The most impulsive is Party Hardy, whose bluffs look more like attacking the pot. This is also true of High Roller with the exception that High Roller's bluffs are flamboyant. Since High Roller is closer to the center between *planned and unplanned bluffs*, High Roller can switch to being more gentile and less attacking.

Once you are aware of the different personality types, look for sudden changes in their normal styles. First, determine what a person's normal style is. Then notice any sudden change in either responsiveness or assertiveness. That's a sure sign that bluffing is going on. As an example, if Loner is suddenly playing like High Roller, cover your chips. Also, notice when Hunch Player becomes very aggressive. It's likely that this ordinarily passive player in on a steal. The ordinarily aggressive Boss who suddenly becomes friendly and supportive is likely to be picking your pocket. This kind of switching is noticeable in even professional players. Usually, it's very hard to find a consistent tell in a professional player. However, sudden changes in unconscious actions will be there for them as well. A professional poker player, with whom I have enjoyed playing seven-card stud, is joking and being friendly whenever he is

---

18. To review this on DVD you can order a set of three discs on the Internet at www.championshipdvd.com. Also, look up Bluff #20 in Lessinger's *The Book of Bluffs*, page 97. See Suggested Readings.

chasing or has little but potential. When he suddenly gets quiet, however, I will bolt and lay down my hand faster than a fox chasing a squirrel. Whenever he changes his mood and plays quietly, he's working on
a monster hand. From being friendly and aggressive he will often get
quiet and serious. When this happens, one can expect the best hand
will be his. If he reads this, though, I can expect when we play again
that he'll stop being cheerful when he's playing garbage. That's how
"tells" work. Once a player knows you're on to him, expect his tell to be
used as a bluff in the near future. Again, bluffs must be taken in context
of the player. Another player that I know only is talking (joking, etc.)
when she has a good hand. When she's chasing a hand, she is quiet and
studious.

Reads

If you know how to read, you won't have many surprises. This is true
in life as well as at the poker table. I was recently working with a
fifteen-year-old young man and his family. He was getting into trouble
daily at home, but not at school. It was obvious that he was setting himself up to be "kicked." He was genuinely surprised when they got upset
with him. The social skills he lacked at home were his not knowing how
to read his parents and how to "grease the wheels." When he would say
"no," he'd be sarcastic or do it in front of his parents' friends. He was
confused because his parent always told him to be honest with them,
and when he said a truthful, "no," they would predictably go "on-tilt."
What he was not computing was their previous behaviors when they
were embarrassed or he was being disrespectful.

While learning the odds of making various hands in poker is an
important skill, *it is surpassed by the ability to read people*. That was
important enough to emphasize. A lot of professionals will tell you that
playing the odds is more important. A few will admit that playing the
person, in the end, is a more important skill. Mike Caro recently admitted this in print when he said, "At poker, math is meaningless and psychology is paramount."[19] What's available are past actions (particularly if
they are unconscious) that give you much more valuable reads. What
the young man mentioned previously forgot was how intolerable his

---

19. Caro, M. "Lies Told About Psychology in Poker." Atlanta: *Bluff Magazine*,
November, 2005, pages 96–97.

parents were to being embarrassed. They could stand the refusal. They couldn't tolerate his disrespect. Once he began to read their need for respect, he learned to grease the wheels, and call them off to the side before saying a respectful "no."

It is one thing to know about the various tells in a game of poker. It's quite another, though, to read what those same behaviors mean to different people. Most poker books and articles don't take into account the various personality types and how the same behavior can often mean something totally different from one person to the next. For example, to place a bet in softly could mean that the person has a strong hand. That is particularly true if the person usually throws his or her bets in. However, it is normal for some players to do this all the time. The same is true of players who normally look at you when they bet. Most players are bluffing, that's true. However, if the player is action-oriented he or she gets high on challenges and will stare you down with a good hand. Know your player. Some will place their bets in softly with garbage. Why? Because someone told them that soft bets meant that the player had a good hand. So, go figure context—not content of such tells (bluffs).

Learning to read goes beyond merely observing actions. It's learning to observe the difference among each person's action under different circumstances. Telling people apart includes the art of telling tells apart. A tell about a tell is what I've called a meta-tell. Going beyond bluffs and reading how different personality types will bluff is learning to be a bilingual reader.

I have demonstrated how The Boss, System Player, Loner, Party Hardy, High Roller, Hunch Player are quite different with each of their bluffs. For example, Mike Caro refers to "Law 7" as *"The friendlier a player is, the more apt he is to be bluffing."*[20] While this is usually an act for most styles, it is a way of life for Hunch Player. When this latter player is being friendly she is not bluffing. When she gets serious and stops smiling, Hunch Player is usually on a bluff.

The important skill in reading people is to take their past behaviors, compare them to their present actions, and if you find them to be inconsistent, they are speaking with a forked tongue. What the fifteen-year-old didn't notice was that his parents were much easier to deal with

20. Caro, M. *The Body Language of Poker.*

when they got respect. Yet, at school he didn't have this problem. He was able to read what would get him good grades at school but not at home. The good news is that everyone can learn to improve their reading skills—at home and at the poker table.

Surprise

The most valuable ability in poker is often the least discussed. The element of surprise is the sine qua non tool of a successful bluff. It's the ability to avoid telegraphing what you have, the talent of hiding in the bushes, the wisdom of letting others do your betting, and the finesse of setting successful traps for your opponents. In the end, he or she who surprises the most will usually leave with the most chips.

A lot has been written about tells and bluffing. Little, though, has been written about reading opponents and how to know when a person is setting up a surprise for you at showdown. Generally, the more surprised you are, the worse you are at reading your opponents. Similarly, the least surprised players are the best at playing hide-and-seek and figuring out what other players have before they attempt to surprise them.

Players good at surprising others will use telegraphing to their advantage. First of all, if they have a strong hand, this will get you to thinking that their hand is weaker than yours. They seldom telegraph their hands. Rather, they are telegraphing what they want you to think. In the way, they will use telegraphing to bluff or mislead you into thinking their hand is strong when it isn't. For example, in a no-limit game of Texas Hold 'Em, a player called a big bet with top pair and a small kicker (Kings and 7 unsuited). The original bettor had top pair and a strong kicker (Kings with a Queen unsuited). After the river, the bettor checked (concerned that the caller had two pair or a better kicker). The caller (with the weaker kicker) went all-in. The original bettor folded to this semi-stone-cold bluff. Although the "all-in" was not called, he showed his King/7 when the original bettor showed his folded King/ Queen. This was using telegraphing to surprise an opponent with the worst hand that won.

Hiding and letting others do your betting is another effective way to surprise opponents. For example, a player flops two medium pairs (7s and 9s). He slow-plays to see if anyone wants to bet the top pair (Kings). When there are no bets, this player checks again and this time gets a bet. The player "in the bushes" jumps out and raises the bet to trap the bettor who later is surprised to see two pairs to his one pair.

It's not possible to trap another player unless you have succeeded in first deceiving him or her about what you are holding. Trapping is where the art of surprising prevails. Usually, though, the surprise comes at the switch when the trapper comes over the top of the bettor. When a player bets after being checked to, the original checker is surprised. When he loses the hand or folds, he's not really surprised; but, it's too late.

Earlier, in Chapter 1, I discussed this type of "switching" using the Bluffing Formula. That is:

$$B + P = PD \longrightarrow T \longrightarrow Payoff$$

It takes a bluff (**B**) plus a pigeon (**P**) to have a pigeon drop (**PD**). The above drop was when a pigeon player bets into the bluffer's check. This led to the trap (**T**) accompanied by the pigeon's surprise. The resulting payoff (**P**) comes to the bluffer in the form of winning the pot and feeling superior. The surprised pigeon gets the payoff of feeling kicked and earns some whining rights.

So, perhaps poker is an adult form of childhood games of hide-and-seek, Kick the Can, or NIGYSOB (Now I've Got You, Surprised Old Buddy). In the final analysis, poker is a license to deceive, mislead, and surprise unsuspecting opponents. Those who are least surprised can tell who's telling the truth and who isn't. If you are often surprised, you are probably the table pigeon.

The Least Mistaken

The best players in baseball will work hard to get three or four hits out of ten. Those who have high batting averages are the players who make the least mistakes. The same is true in poker. Good players make fewer mistakes both with good hands as well as with bad cards (pitches). When they bluff, they have a higher average of successes.

If you make a lot of mistakes in a poker game, chances are that you will leave with fewer chips than you had when you started. It's safe to say that the player who makes fewer mistakes will have more chips at the end of the game. Knowing about areas of mistakes and avoiding them will definitely improve your game.

I began to research how many ways we can make mistakes. It turns out that poker mistakes are based on decisions we make about *betting, calling, checking, raising,* or *folding.*[21] When these areas are employed to bluff, mistakes can be made both in time (when we bluff) and in place (who and where we bluff). Bluffing is the art of inducing opponents to make mistakes, such as calling, checking, or folding. First, let's visit the areas of mistakes made.

1. *Checking instead of betting*—It's often a mistake to show weakness in poker unless that show is a bluff. Checking instead of betting can lose the chance that weaker hands will fold. Slow playing good hands has proven to usually be a mistake. It's asking to get outrun.

2. *Betting instead of checking*—At the same time, it could be a mistake to bet instead of check. If you have a marginally good hand that can only be beat if you are called, it's usually best to check and call. If you bet and you are called, chances are you lost.

3. *Calling instead of folding or raising*—One of the best skills in poker is the ability to lay a hand down when you think you are beaten. Calling instead of folding usually comes from chasing hands. It's often a good idea to raise rather than just call. Still it's often better to just fold. It's always best in early stages of a game to avoid chasing.

4. *Folding instead of calling or raising*—However, folding a winning hand can be a costly mistake. Folding, instead of calling or raising, often occurs before the flop by playing too tight and folding hands that would have flopped two pair or trips. That's where "no fold 'em hold 'em" has an advantage. However, getting other players to make mistakes is an art in poker. So, often raising instead of folding can invite others to make the mistake of folding.

5. *Raising instead of calling or raising*—Raising bets is usually designed to build a pot or to narrow the playing field by getting players to make the mistake of folding. The time for calling,

21. Note: If you would like a more detailed guide to avoiding such mistakes, look for David Sklansky's book *Getting the Best of It,* published by Two Plus Two Publishers in 1989.

instead of raising the bet, often means that you are doing someone else's betting. If your raise is a pure bluff, it's a mistake when players have hands good enough to call. It's best to simply call or fold.

Instead of counting the "outs" we have to make our hands in poker, perhaps we should also be counting how many ways we can be beaten with the cards we are playing. If you start paying attention to how you can be beaten, how would that affect how you bet, call, check, raise, or fold?

There are, of course, many ways to make mistakes not mentioned here such as playing too many hands. We also haven't mentioned mistakes related to lack of responsible gaming such as playing more than you can afford to lose or playing on-tilt.

Fight or Flight

"He knows no fear!" "He bets on anything and when he loses, he doesn't flinch or whine!" That's the kind of "over the table" gossip you can hear every day in a poker room. It brings up the question of whether people who play with no fear are better players or, quite frankly, what role fear and emotions have in the game of poker.

When we are strongly stressed there's an automatic response from our nervous system. It's referred to as "the fight or flight response." It's our body's primitive, automatic, and inborn response that is preparing our body to "fight" (call, raise) or "flee" (fold). This is based on a perceived attack, harm, or threat. Therein lies the rub. What one player would call an attack (like an all-in move), and what another player would call a trap (like soft-playing the nuts) often makes the difference between fighting and folding.

Some players never show emotion and may never even experience emotion. They are in a zone all their own. Emotions, like fear, hunches, and intuition, are a good player's arsenal. These players can "smell" a bluff that looks like an attack. You will, however, find players who interpret every loss as a threat to their survival. This is the case for players who know how to handle a short stack of chips. Notice any tournament and be aware of how often the lowest stack ends up winning the tournament. Is that because the player has no fear or is it because he or she listens to feelings and knows how to handle bad times as well as good ones?

Here's an interesting way to view this fight or flight response:

Notice that successful players determine to stay or fight based on odds and probability. Players who stay in, no matter what, are loose and don't do so well over time. Players who are tight as a bark on a tree may get out whenever the going gets rough.

Rate yourself on how much you flee when things get tough.

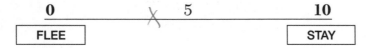

Now put an "x" on the horizontal line in the above scale. Folding a lot would rate close to "0" and calling a lot would be close to "10."

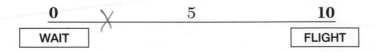

Now put an "x" on the horizontal line in the above scale. Folding a lot would rate close to "0" and calling or raising a lot would be close to "10."

Now you can put an "x" on the horizontal line (the first scale) in the working chart below. Next, put an "x" on the perpendicular line (the second scale) in the working chart below. Join the two "x's" to see which quadrant is your style of playing when things get stressful. Example:

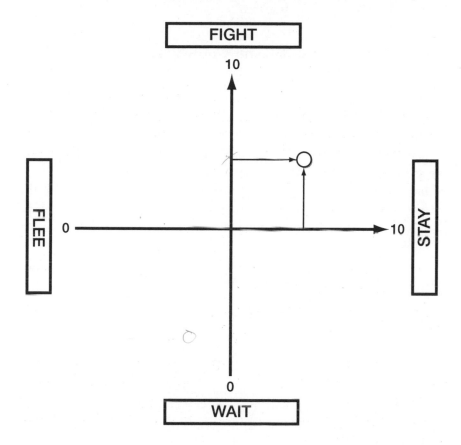

So, what's the verdict? Do you stay too long because you don't listen to your feelings or because you are just stubborn and let your feelings rule your game? Do you decide to fight or withdraw based more on how worth the risk it is for you? How do you determine this risk? By pot odds and the number of outs you have? Or, by the seat of your pants because you hate to be forced out of anything? Now, tell me about the guy who knows no fear and I'll show you a player who goes home mad or sad instead of scared.

I've had some fun grouping players in these four categories. Of course, it's just for fun and I am sure that you could add a bunch of your own ways of looking at calling, raising, bluffing, and folding. Remember, though, that better players don't fight every hand and will often lay down a good hand. That's because they know how to, "Fold today and live to play another day."

Best Hand Confusion

A lot of players, particularly new ones, will confuse themselves about what the best hand is in a poker game. If you look at a chart describing the ranking of hands (see appendix C), you will find the lowest hand is the hand with the highest card. After that it goes from one pair to two pairs through to a Royal Flush. Just because your cards have a high rank doesn't mean that you have the best hand. You may even have three of a kind (say Trip 10s) and your opponent only has one top pair (in this case, let's pretend it's an unsuited Ace and King). This still doesn't mean that you have the best hand—you have the best showdown hand and outrank your opponent. *The best hand is the hand that draws in the pot at the end of play.* Sure, with trips you may be very confident of your hand. However, a good player who knows how to handle bad hands may also be very confident that he can force you to fold this hand.

Let's test your mettle a little. Suppose that you still only have three of a kind and the board has four hearts on the river. You are now head to head with a player that you are pretty sure has been betting his top pair (Aces). You check your three 10s and he goes all-in, making the bet well over $400. That means that if you call and you win, you will make about $600. He's made it hard for you to call, since you will only get a $200 profit from your $400 investment. Then again, you could lose to a flush or to three Aces. What would you do?

The Not So Tender Trap

Trappers in poker wear sunglasses, cruising baseball caps, and like to snipe from behind bushes. They don't wear trapper's hats and are there to trap second-best hands. Some will be their own trappers.

Letting second-best hands do the betting and pretending to be a call station is a most common trapping technique. Although trapping is usually a heads-up between the best and the second-best hands, a good trapper will often get several callers before pulling the switch.

Another trap occurs often when a player with high cards is calling one or two bets and the flop doesn't come anywhere near to supporting his or her hold cards. Suppose that you are holding Ace♣, Jack♠, and the flop is 6♦, 7♦, and 10♥. Would you call with these two over-cards after two bets before you? The bettors could have two small pair, a flush, or straight draw, and, besides, a top pair still beats an Ace high. If you stayed with just Ace high and the turn comes out a 9, you now have a gut-shot for a straight. Who trapped you? Or, would you fold this since someone could be going for a higher gut-shot? If you don't fold, who's the trapper?

Self-trapping occurs when players have good cards and haven't learned to lay down a hand that has been beaten. How often have you stayed to the river with pocket Kings when an Ace is flopped and one or two players before you bet?

Often you will see a player flop two small pair and stay to the end. For example, the player comes in with suited 7 and 8. The flop is K, 8, 7. Wow! Probably the best hand. Yet, on the turn comes a Queen. Now someone who bet the King on the flop could have two higher pairs with a K and a Q, 8, or 7 for a kicker. This wouldn't slow down some players. Then, let's suppose that the river is a King. You are pretty sure that the King now has just tripled-up—if not made a full house. Would you lay down this hand? Some players are like a "dog with a bone" and refuse to let it go. Of course, the higher two pair, such as Kings and 8s, could have slow-played, checked, and waited for you to bet your two little pair. Then you'd have two trappers: your opponent and yourself.

There's sweet revenge in trapping the trapper. Show me a player who doesn't enjoy trapping the trapper and I'll show you a saint. Suppose that you have pocket Kings and your opponent has pocket Aces. The Aces have bet and you of course just call. The flop is King high. The Aces check and you check. The turn is no help, but made two pair for the Aces. You check to the Aces that bet and then you raise that bet. The Aces, who put you on a pair of Kings, tried to trap you by slow-playing the Aces. When he jumped out of the bushes with Aces over, you jumped from behind your bush with Trip Kings. Ah, how sweet it is!

While trapping and bluffing may be the same at times, both activities seek answers to two different questions. Namely, trappers will ask themselves the question, "How can I get people to stay in so I can make more money with this hand?" While, on the other hand, the bluffers think, *How can I get people to get out so I can win with this hand? Or, prevent anyone from outrunning me?*

These are just a few of many trapping techniques. Let me know your favorite or your worst (depending which end you are on). I enjoy the comradery of poker and as a writer I've also enjoyed your email feedback.

Worst Player Traps

There are intentional traps in poker and then there are traps that we set up for ourselves. The obvious self-trap is playing bad starting cards as in "no fold 'em hold 'em." Being trapped by the worst player at the table is another example of a self-made trap. If you can't identify the worst player at the table, it's probably you. If it's someone else, you can be trapped by playing different from the way you would with a better player. The trap being that the bad player may actually have the best hand or may make a hand from garbage.

Recently, in a no-limit Texas Hold 'Em game, the loosest player had lost and went back for more chips. While he was gone a few of the players said, "Good. He's coming back." I wasn't that optimistic. I've seen loose players do a lot of damage when they are beating the odds. The problem with what I call the worst player trap is that good players will call a lot of hands they shouldn't just because they don't believe the worst player has anything but a dream.

Often playing quality cards can be a trap in the wrong game. I saw a player with Queen, Ace (unsuited) get trapped with the best hand by the worst player. On the flop, a Queen, 6, and 7 (mixed suits) came. The player who had just returned with more chips bet. The Queen with the Ace kicker raised that bet. The rest of the players folded. The other player just called the re-raised bet. The turn drew an 8. The loose player went all-in. Here's the trap. The player with top pair and top kicker called the all-in and went all-in himself. When they turn over, the loose player has a 9, Jack (unsuited). It would be dramatic to say that the final (river) card was a 10. Well, it was. This is being trapped by holding quality cards by a player who would call a barking junkyard dog off a porch.

Another worst player trap is one where the player is much better than he appears. He appears to make mistakes and he is setting the table up to liberally call him. I've even seen this worse player trap performed by a player pretending to have too much to drink. Whenever you can invite someone to take advantage of a weakness (pretend or real), it's a trap that few poker players can resist.

Faking weakness is a trap meant to teach greedy players a lesson. For example, there may be an Ace, King on the flop and you have pocket Aces. To check once is not necessarily a trap but a way to "take temperatures" to see if someone has the other Ace or a King. However, when a player checks Trip Aces a second time, that's when a trap is being set. The first player to take advantage of such "weakness" will soon get the surprise that good poker is designed to produce.

Another way to feign weakness is to bet your top pair once and then check the next round when called. This is designed to pretend that you have the second high pair and that you are afraid of the one with the high pair. Or, if you've got the top pair with the top kicker (Ace), you pretend to have a weaker hand by checking. Not all checks show weakness. However, some player will interpret a check as weakness. Again, it's important to know your players.

Some new players who got their training watching poker on television shows will often win from pure luck. Forgetting that the professionals on TV are playing loosely because of already having thousands of dollars in action, these worst players will break all the rules by playing any two cards and often drawing out a winner on the river. Go figure!

Competitive Comradery

Comradery is a big part of playing poker for some. For others, it's also a part of bluffing. For still others it's an annoyance. However, for those who enjoy comradery, shooting from the lip is part of the game. That means that most of what is said is spoken in poker-ese and needs to be translated. For example, when a young lady entered into the game and was sitting down, several players said something like, "Uh-oh, we're in for it now!" Translated this meant, "You'll like this. She is loose and I can beat her!" Recently, a player shouted across the room at me and said, "Hey, Jim, there's an opening at this no-limit game!" What he was saying was, "I'd like some of your money!" because he thought he could beat me. On the same day I heard two other comments directed at other players. As one sat down, another said, "I bribed the floor to get you in this game." Of course, he was just kidding and he welcomed some easy money. At another table I heard, "Hey, Mike. Come on over. We've got ten players, but we'll make an exception for you and play with eleven."

Are these "put-downs" or do they really mean it? Often, such competitive comradery is designed to disarm another player. At times though, it becomes a war of put-downs. For example, a player might say, "I can't believe you stayed in with that garbage!" To which is replied, "I only played it because you were betting!" Or, when a player makes a hand on the river, he or she might hear, "Runner, runner!" And hear back, "You have to go to the river to catch the fish!"

Instead of comradery could this also be counter-phobic behavior? By that I mean, a player may actually be afraid of you and instead, places a bet and says, "Call that if you don't like money!" Usually, though, negative comments are the way people (mostly men) who like each other show it. You may occasionally hear, "Nice hand. Well played!" from someone not in the hand. This is usually sincere and needs no translation. However, you are more apt to hear, "Better buy a lottery ticket. This is your lucky day!" Often, though, "Nice hand!" coming from the loser means, "Nice hand, you °#$+."

Even when a player folds, there's the competitive zing of, "I'm folding this for your sake." Or, "I'll let you have it this time!" Loose calls will get comments such as, "I'll just call." Or, "You can't win!" Now why would a competitor try to talk you out of calling?

Beware of laments when a player is called, such as, "I'm in trouble now!" That's poker-eese for, "Please don't leave me when I bet again." Another frequent lament is, "I know I'm doing your betting for you." This can be translated into, "I hope I'm not betting for you." When a player folds by saying something like, "I didn't like the way you threw that bet in," it usually means they were going to fold anyway and didn't have much.

I mentioned earlier that comradery for some is an annoyance, particularly when it comes from someone you just beat. For example, instead of hearing, *"Wow, you made it and all those outs came through for you!"* you are more apt to hear, *"I can't believe you made that hand!"* When I made such a hand on the river and heard how lucky I was, an astute dealer said, *"Yeah, he only had thirteen outs and great pot odds!"*

Finally, when you leave the table you may hear, *"Tell 'em where you got it!"* This can mean, *"Send some other fish over here."* Still when you hear, *"Nice playing with you,"* you'd better check if it's coming from the one who won most of your chips or from someone who really enjoyed your company.

Have you ever said when you've gotten beat, *"I knew that!"*? So what does that mean?

8

Favorite Bluffing Styles

When it comes to being deceptive and misleading, each personality type comes to the table with predispositions to bluff in certain ways. This doesn't mean that they are "stuck" with such predispositions. It means that when they are not consciously recalling how they have been bluffing, they may return to a home-base style of bluffing that matches their personalities.

Favorite Bluffing Tendencies

Each style will have certain favorite bluffing predispositions. For example:

♦ *The Boss* will usually sit with head tilted up looking down on the cards, players, and the action. These players seem to be constantly judging and look like someone's mom or dad. In fact, when this player looks down and then peers up, he or she is likely bluffing. The Boss likes to look you in the eye when bluffing (with the head tilted down).

♦ *Party Hardy* will nervously move around a lot and stop when scared. Notice them wrapping, shuffling chips, or getting up and leaving the table a lot. They like to engage others in conversation when they are bluffing. When they are serious and uninvolved with others, reject their ploy—they deserve it.

♦ *High Roller* is flamboyant and wants to be noticed in good times as well as bad times. When things are good, they may tease. In bad times they will want to fight or throw cards. Once they're on tilt, their soul's not yours, but the pots are.

♦ *Hunch Player* gets friendlier and smiles directly in proportion to how bad things are. If things are good, the hunch player stops placating and being nice. Instead, they get quiet and hope things continue to go well before something bad happens. A forced smile would mean, "Sorry, this is really going to hurt." The absence of a smile means, "I sure hope that sword hanging over my head doesn't fall."[1]

♦ *Loner* will stay behind the bushes and prefers that someone else do the betting. Look for sighs or sounds of sadness at their more aggressive bluffs. Loner ordinarily will quietly tolerate bad cards. They seem almost tantalized by frustration—much like Tantalus in Greek mythology.[2]

♦ Finally, *System Player* will be trying hard to play the perfect game—usually playing very conservatively and being predictable to the aware player. For example, in seven-card stud, they will check to scope out if anyone has a pair and wait until they have two pair before betting or raising a bet. That's their system. They live their lives just as conservatively and cautiously as they bluff. Their bluffs are also predictable. That's also the system to use with System Player. Believe them most of the time.

Responsive Versus Assertive Bluffing

Players will bluff at different levels of assertiveness as well as in planned and impulsive ways. Bluffs can range from very passive to very aggressive bluffs. Also, in addition to assertiveness, there is the factor of whether a player responds to things more with their emotions or more with logic. Some players are very structured and so their bluffs are predetermined. As mentioned earlier, their bluffs can also be paradoxes. Others bring little or no structure to the table and will bluff only from

1. The Greek myth about Sword of Damocles describes how Hunch Player worries when things are going well. King Damocles ruled successfully until one day he noticed a sword held by a single horse hair was dangling over his head. After that, he couldn't do anything right.
2. Tantalus was condemned to an eternity of hunger and thirst, but not allowed to eat or drink.

their guts, their hunches, or their intuition. If we compare a player's aggressiveness and responsiveness,[3] we can also predict how they are likely to bluff. We can determine different bluffing styles that fit players' styles of play. This comparison will also produce another useful grid for assessing bluffs.

Just as players have different styles, so the same bluff can have different meanings when the factor of personality differences is added. Some players naturally bluff softly. For others, it's natural to aggressively bluff. Both are bluffing according to how responsive they are. It's important, then, not to assume that all soft bets are good hands and that all aggressive bets are bluffs. Some soft bets may not be bluffs—particularly if coming from a passive playing style.

Responsiveness in Bluffs

Players respond to the game with varied structure and logic versus hunches and intuition. Players normally vary how passively or aggressively they bet. Players react to cards and to life in different degrees of responsiveness to their surroundings. Many people respond in planned ways. If a player is very logical and structured, planning is their way of life. Such a player would score as "0" on the responsiveness scale. The other extreme would be people who are very emotional and impulsive. They usually fail to plan. Such players will usually bluff impulsively and be scored as "10" on a bluffing-responsiveness scale.

Figure 9. Gauging Planned and Unplanned Actions

0—1—2—3—4—5—6—7—8—9—10

Planned Actions   **Unplanned Actions**

Ask yourself, "When I am representing a hand I don't have, do I act in a planned way or in an impulsive way?" Then, rate yourself from 0 to 10 on the above scale to rank how you respond when bluffing.

3. For more information on this comparison of aggression and structure, see Jung, C. G. *The Collected Works of C. G. Jung.*

Also see communications styles discussed by Carlson, R. K. and Brehm, R. T. *Understanding Communication Style*, and Thayer, L. *Communication and Communication Systems*, listed in Suggested Readings.

Assertiveness in Bluffs

Some players approach the game very passively and let the cards play themselves. Others will be very active and play aggressively to influence play with betting. You will notice people who just play the cards and others who play the people. The professional will play both. You can also score yourself on how assertively you play with passive play being "0" and very active or aggressive play ranking "10."

Figure 10. Gauging the Power of Actions

0—1—2—3—4—5—6—7—8—9—10

Passive Play   **Aggressive Play**

How would you score yourself in the manner in which you tend to bluff? When representing a hand other than you actually have, do you bet softly or do you get aggressive? Ask yourself, "When I am bluffing, do I hide or do I attack?" Bluffing styles evolve from measuring the way players respond (planned vs. unplanned) with how assertively they apply their bluffing skills (passive or aggressive).

Bluffing Preferences

When both attributes are compared, the four basic styles will produce these bluffing preferences: (1) "sneak bluffing" (passive and planned), (2) "dare bluffing" (aggressive and planned), (3) "attack bluffing" (aggressive and unplanned), and (4) "dream bluffing" (passive and unplanned).

If a player is bluffing the way his personality dictates, then such bluffs are congruent. It's when the bluffs change characters that the next level of awareness is required to survive the deceptions of meta-tells. Conservative players can be expected to be "straight bluffers." This means that they will mostly semi-bluff[4] and will demonstrate the usual unconscious bluffs. When on a steal, however, such conservative bluffers may do the opposite as part of their strategy. On the other hand, loose players will

---

4. A semi-bluff occurs when a player has a good start, like one pair or four cards to a flush, with potential to improve.

do the unexpected and become "paradoxical bluffers." Their bluffs are impulsive and/or flamboyant. If a loose player is not overly impulsive, many bluffs are semi-bluffs. However, most of a loose player's bluffs are high-risk bluffs, involving low-odds chases and "on the come" bets. An assessing grid for bluffing then becomes apparent.

Assessing Grid for Bluffing Styles

The Assessing Grid for Bluffing Preferences will result in the following normal bluffing styles:

Chart 8. Assessing Grid of Bluffing Styles

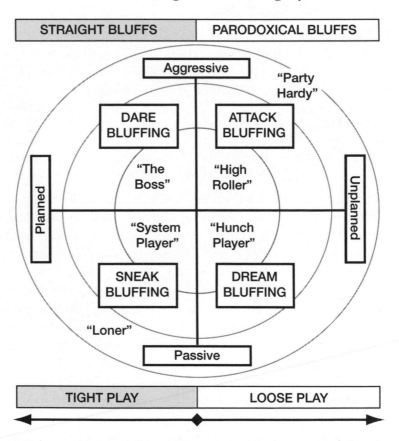

Dynamic Bluffing Styles

There's no such thing as a pure style. Also, at times a player will move to different quadrants—depending on a variety of factors. For instance, players will move around this grid, depending on their mood and how much money they've got. However, each of us has a favorite quadrant from which we generally approach life. We have a home-base quadrant and may often visit our relatives (other quadrants).

The extremes in each style are on the outer circles of the above quadrants. For example, Party Hardy is generally much more impulsive and aggressive than High Roller, who will be closer to the center. Similarly, Loner is much more passive and structured than System Players. System player is closer to the center and Loner is in the outer circle.

One final word about bluffing styles is important. There's really nothing new under the sun. When we discover something, it seems new to us at that point in time. With a user-friendly map to help guide the journey, one can quickly assess how differently people approach things like gaming conditions. We are actually already assessing others on a daily basis whether we realize it or not. What's perhaps a new discovery for most readers is that there is a logical frame of reference into which playing the cards of life can be categorized. Since we don't live or play in a vacuum, making sense of players' bluffs must be based on how players make sense of most things in their lives. Again, no *bluff-tell* fits all and all *bluff-tells* fit each player's personality.

The Surprise Factor

The ability to surprise other players is a skill of not revealing how good your hand is. Players who get surprised a lot are players who don't read others very well. Loners and System Players, as I will demonstrate in the next chapter, are very adept at surprising their opponents.

After the trap is sprung, what will follow are surprise and some confusion once the bluff is revealed. This is the trap in the Bluffing Formula.[5] There are a variety of traps to catch pigeons, animals, birds, fish, and poker players. There are general traps of nets that fishermen use to

---

5. In the Bluffing Formula, it takes a con and a pigeon (**B** + **P**) to get together to have a pigeon drop (**PD**). Anytime after that, the trap can be sprung.

catch a bunch and a variety of fish. Then, there are traps the prey enter into one at a time. There are speed traps that catch careless drivers. There are traps that unsuspecting prey, such as turtles and crawfish, walk into before they are trapped and surprised. All of these traps are referred to as live traps, since the prey give up their freedom—not their lives. Poker traps are aimed at freeing opponents of their chips.

The common denominator of traps, including poker traps, is the lure and the bait. Unsuspecting prey are lured into making mistakes that will cost them their chips. As mentioned earlier, much like the lure of the sirens in Greek mythology something has to get players to wreck their chips. A successful trap always results in the prey being surprised. These surprises lead to good and bad feelings (payoff) at the end of the process ($T{\rightarrow}P$). The payoff for the trapper is chip profit and the excitement of getting opponents (prey) to make mistakes. The payoff for the poker-prey is disappointment, surprise, and loss of chips.

To understand trapping in poker it's necessary to look at how the various styles of bluffing are likely to set traps. Some players aim their traps at a specific kind of opponent. Others are setting traps to catch a whole sea of fishes. Still, there are trappers who set themselves up and fall prey to the radar of speed traps. After integrating this information, you will have new radar to catch a variety of "poker speeders."

9

Pigeon Trappers

If you have the right trap and you systematically use it, you can catch a lot of pigeons. I'm talking about the players who become pigeons. System Players and Loners are left-brained players who like a lot of structure in the hands that they play. What they lack in aggressiveness, they make up in skill and the ability to set traps. Their favorite way to trap other players is to slow-play their hands until they get some action. They just let pigeons walk into their traps. For example, in a game of $2–$5 no-limit Texas Hold 'Em, all but three players limped in with the minimum bet of $2. When the flop came—

—three players checked and the fourth player just bet $10. Everyone folded except one. He called. The turn showed a blank (2♣). So, the first bettor just seemed to limp in with another $10 bet. The other player raised it to $50. Then the first bettor re-raised it to $250 and the second player folded. This is planned bluffing and being passive. The $10 bets were like bait and the pigeon knew when he got caught.

I call this kind of trapping "Sneak Bluffing" (passive and planned bluffers). Pigeons walk into them, baited by the lure of showing weakness. Whenever traps are used, trappers will need some kind of bait that lures the prey into the trap. For real pigeons, the bait is food. For this pigeon, the bait was pretending weakness. It occurs from the quadrant of bluffers who will likely be the Loner and the System Players. Both types of players focus on the cards and let the cards play themselves, preferring not to be flamboyant or to scare any pigeons away by being aggressive. These players prefer to play from "behind the bushes," will hide their hands and let others do their betting for them. So, if you have already determined that a player is a thinking-oriented, quiet person who plays systematically, then you can expect bluffing to be systematic, conservative, and yet unobtrusive. Look for System Player, though, to show more aggressiveness in bluffs than Loner. In photo 36, System Player (right) had the winning hand on the flop, yet he's "sweating" (acting cautious) and plans to check, then raise.

Photo 36. Passive/Planned: System Player "sweating" the "nuts"

Similarly, Loner (photo 37) is checking and waiting for others to act, even though he already has two pair.

These players may raise any bets if holding over-cards to what is showing in stud or hold 'em. Such a raise is their plan to narrow the field down to fewer players and to avoid missing the high cards he or she wants. Raising bets is seldom a bluff with Loner and System Player. Rather, the bluff is checking to get some action before coming in. A

Photo 37. Passive/Planned: Loner waiting for action

raise is more apt to be a semi-bluff. In other words, they hope to get control. They have something that could get better; but, they could improve their hand. The potential is there, it's a calculated risk, and it's usually a good conservative system.

Planning and structure are combined with slow-playing and predetermined moves. In blackjack, basic play will often be combined with a counting system for such players. For example, a system player will split 10s, but only if the count is very, very rich. That's what their system calls for.[1] Let's get back to poker.

These "sneaky" players will play the cards more than playing the people. However, if they have learned a system of bluffing, look for sys-

---

1. Stanley Roberts, the world's leading blackjack writer, gives ways to obtain instant advantage with basic strategy and a simple system to immediately know when the remaining cards favor the player. See his book, *The Beginner's Guide to Winning Blackjack*, in Suggested Readings.

tematic bluffs here. For example, such players will systematically slow-play good hands until someone else bets. The bluff here is that a player is representing that he or she doesn't have anything. Then, such passive, structured players are more likely to continue to let someone else do their betting. They frequently win. If the leading bettor gets better, this player will fold if re-raised. Why? Because it's the right thing to do, even if they think they are being bluffed. However, if there is enough money in the pot, their system may say they should call with two pairs or better. This is the person who will "wait in the bushes and bush-whack" others as soon as they know they have the nuts.

People in this quadrant are both thinking- and non-action-oriented. Routine and procedures are more reliable than people are. Order and being alone are important wants of such people. Poker is one of the few social events that such players can be a part of without being too involved. When under stress these players will overadapt by either trying harder to play a perfect game or getting more withdrawn and quiet.

In the real world, such people know more about their jobs than rela-tionships. Doing a good job is important and predictable—something they learned to do early by applying themselves to school and work. Outside the casino, Loner prides himself on his ability to change. Such players have a highly developed capacity to cope and not show pain. Their chameleon ability to blend in and not be too noticeable will also be evident in their homes and occupations. In his personal life, Loner stays uninvolved. Belief for these players is that, *Others can make me feel bad: but, they'll never know it.* Loner will play as if, *Nobody really cares, so why try?*

System Player believes that, *I can make others proud of me by doing better than my best.* They need to be needed and in the real world they make good caregivers. They are good givers, but seldom accept from others. They will overadapt when things go badly by trying to do every-thing themselves and failing to delegate. They live life from the point of view that, *I won't feel,* and *I can't depend on anyone else.*

Advantages of Passive Bluffing

Bluffing is an act of pretending to have something that you don't have. By being passive, a player is representing that he's a little scared and doesn't have much to play with. When they check and then just call, such players may still be passive. The advantage to such slow playing is that it misleads opponents into becoming more careless than they might. However, such carelessness is really foolishness when you are playing a left-brained player who ordinarily is quiet and doesn't draw much attention to him- or herself. Why this is foolish is because you can expect that if such players are bluffing that is how they will pre-dictably bluff. They won't be flamboyant, rowdy, or boisterous. They will quietly call until they have the nuts and then they will raise—but still in an unobtrusive manner.

Disadvantages of Passive Bluffing

Playing "behind the bushes" and letting others do your betting has the above advantages of surprise. It also has certain disadvantages. Often, when a player does this kind of slow playing it misses bets and fails to build pots. Unless a player is very aware of the players who are playing behind him or her, checking can result in giving free cards. If you are fairly certain that you will get a bet, then a check is a wise move. A lot of players don't even consider this when they decide to slow-play good hands. For example, suppose that you have a pair of Kings and the flop in hold 'em is a "rainbow"[2] with nothing higher than a Queen. A slow play would be to check or (in higher limit games) to bet small. This is only a good move if you are fairly certain that someone behind you will bet. Otherwise, it's giving free cards and inviting yourself to be outrun.

Another disadvantage to slow playing is that of reputation. If you are known as a player who likes to check to trap bettors, you will seldom be able to make this trap work. I saw this was the case with a tight, quiet player who let others do the betting. Once he tried to move up to higher limit games. Most of the players were familiar with his style from the lower limit games. Whenever he slow-played, they slow-played. Whenever he bet, they folded. He couldn't get a decent pot. So, he went back to the lower limit games where he got a little more action—not much.

---

2. Poker jargon for mixture of suits.

Advantages of Planned Bluffing

The advantage of bluffing in a planned fashion is that it forces players to consider who, what, and how to bluff various players. Remember, it's a mistake to bluff everyone in the same way. Different personalities demand different bluffing techniques. Also, to bluff effectively players must speak the language of the person that they are trying to bluff. Is the other player visual, auditory, or emotional? The answers to such questions will dictate the kind of bluffing that will work. If your goal is to aggravate or put someone on-tilt, you will need to mismatch their ways of representing things as discussed previously in Chapter 4.

Disadvantages of Planned Bluffing

When you plan your bluffs, you are teaching people that you are a structured player and that you are paying attention to what's going on. Ordinarily, this is a good thing. Yet, it has its liabilities. For one, it makes you a prime candidate to be bluffed by your opponents. That's because, as we mentioned earlier, it's not possible to bluff someone who's not paying attention. So, be careful what you are paying attention to. If it looks like someone is yanking your chain, he or she probably is. Here's an example that happened not too long ago. The tight player was playing her usual systematic style. Only coming into hands when she had at least two cards that added up to 20, two high-suited cards or above middle pairs (8s or better). Everyone who had played with her before knew this. When she was in the hand or called a bet, she wasn't chasing dumb—that's for sure. The highest card on the flop was a Jack, and no one had raised pre-flop. Everyone, including above System Player, checked. The player next to the button bet. Now everyone folded except the systematic player. She raised the bet. She only had a pair of 10s yet she was convinced that the bettor was trying to buy the pot since everyone checked to him. He was yanking her chain. She was right. The bettor was playing with an Ace high only. He folded. It wasn't a bad move on his part. He had the attention of a tight player and hoped she'd fold. It's just that she knew her players and knew that if he didn't make it three bets that he was semi-bluffing. If you are playing against Loner or System Player, you can expect to be bluffed in a planned yet passive manner. Often, I look around to determine what type of player I am playing and then I can pretty well guess what type of bluffing to expect. So, let's review what characteristics to look for in your opponents.

Characteristics of Passive/Planned Bluffers

The "Loner"

Loners are motivated into action by people or things. In this sense, they are not self-starters and can be expected to wait for others to lead things off. Their playing attitude is one of being decisive and determined. They are there to play cards and not to socialize. As players who are receptive and reserved,[3] their style of playing is to be analyzing.

Loner's strengths are that he is reflective, perceptive, and able to be directed. This also means that he has the patience to wait for hands and not play out of boredom. It's best to leave them be alone at the table. They require having private time and their own space. In fact, solitude charges their psychological batteries. The prefer being directed and as such are easy to lead into folding. It's best not to socialize with Loner— just play cards.

Loner dresses for the weather or for comfort—not to please others. Their color coordination or latest styles are not that important. The way they handle their chips is revealing. There is an absence of frills or ornaments. Their chips are usually in place (in trays) or neatly arranged. They usually will buy in at or around the minimum. Their time is spent withdrawn and arranging or shuffling chips. About 10 percent of the U.S. population are Loners (60 percent are females and 40 percent are males).[4]

The System Player

System Player is thinking-oriented. As such, these players think first and departmentalize and structure things and people into categories. They play every hand as if it has a time and place. There's the right way, their way, or no way to play poker. They too, like Loner, are reserved

---

3. See *Beyond Tells*, page 163.

4. These figures are the result of Taibi Kahler's research. See *The Mystery of Management* in Suggested Readings.

and receptive, making their approach to poker one of being analytical. Their strengths are that they are logical, punctual, responsible about tasks, and well organized. Their attributes serve them well in a game like poker where odds and probabilities are so important. System Player usually speaks in monotones with limited animation, keeping his head level, seldom cocked to either side—except when bluffing.

These players require time structure and recognition for their playing abilities. They think in terms of odds more than gambling. They can have conversations while playing and still know what's going on with the cards. Such players prefer one-on-one relationships to group situations. That's why they are more likely to be talking to one other player, rather than to the whole table. They dress functionally, for playing cards. Yet they are always neat, clean, tidy, and pressed.

They nest their chips in a systematic way: organized, functional, and orderly. Often, out of their need for order, they will upon arriving at a new table, ask that the dealer "square" the table. This is to ensure that their space is ample since they like "everything and everybody in its place." About 25 percent of the U.S population are thinking-oriented, like System Player. Of that, 25 percent can be expected to be females and 75 percent are males.

10

Fish Trappers

We've all heard some good fish stories. They are usually told by fisher-men who spend a lot of hours casting. Some days they catch a few, some days a lot of fish. Then, there are the times that they catch the big one. These fishermen are serious about their sport and go about catching fish in planned and aggressive ways. Aggressive and planned bluffers are full of a lot of "shoulds." In a game of Texas Hold 'Em, such play-ers will "should" all over other players.[1] They are highly opinionated and their bluffs are forceful and well planned. They will take others to task for bluffs that are not sophisticated in their opinion. Their bluffs are more like dares. You've heard, "Call that if you don't like money!" It probably was said by a planned-aggressive player. These are more likely to be the self-appointed "Boss" players. They usually have years of play-ing experience and will do what is needed to win once they decide to get into a hand. They are not likely to be in a hand unless they have live cards and over-cards to what's showing.

The Boss may bet heavily on just a pair of Aces—semi-bluffing that he has more than the aces showing in a game of seven-card stud. For that matter, such full bets are well planned to make people chasing with lesser hands pay a premium to stay in. In this case, the aggressive/ planned bluffer is semi-bluffing and making people who might be chas-ing them pay to outrun them. Another planned semi-bluff here is to bet/raise with a high pair to get people out. If working on filling in a

---

1. In Texas Hold 'Em, unlike seven-card stud, other players are more apt to see the cards you are playing since they are playing five of the same flop cards.

straight or a flush, such players might also bet softly and avoid scaring anyone out. This is because with such hands they prefer multiplayer action. More people in the pot will increase their chance to make a flush or straight.[2] For another type of player, slow-playing a possible flush may mean that he or she is disguising a full house. For example, an ordinarily aggressive, impulsive High Roller may suddenly start playing slow. In this case, you can rely on Caro's Law of Tells #20, "*A gentle bet usually means strength.*"[3] In photo 38, the Boss is raising in a hold 'em game with a high pair in the hole. He's hoping to improve his odds by getting some players to fold. That's because he knows the two little pair will beat him if he doesn't improve his Aces.

Photo 38. Aggressive/Planned: The Boss raising with high cards

The Boss (photo 39, left) checks in Texas Hold 'Em with a pair of Ace in the hole. In photo 39, when he trips his pair on the turn, he checks again. When someone finally bets, he then raises.

2. Sklansky, D., Malmuth, M., and Zee, R. *Seven-Card Stud for Advanced Players*. Las Vegas: Two Plus Two Publishing, 1994. Also, for more detailed information on betting strategies, see *Caro's Fundamental Secrets of Winning Poker*. New York: Cardoza Publishing, 1996.

3. Caro, M. *Body Language of Poker*. California: Gambling Times, 1984, pages 160, 282.

Photo 39. Aggressive/Planned: The Boss (*left*) checks with high cards.

In other games, such as blackjack, the structured/aggressive player will raise their bets when the count is rich. Others are raising their bets from hunches or simply because they haven't seen many 10s in a while. While that may be a "down and dirty" way to count, the Boss will require a more precise count to increase the amount of his betting units. This player is convictions oriented. He makes sense of the world by finding out what's proper and what's wrong. Things have to fit their value system to be accepted or understood. In their personal lives, the Boss is an overachiever. Publicly, they give a lot and take a lot. Privately, they don't ask for what they want. They have a low tolerance for errors in themselves and others. The Boss is more inclined to look for what's wrong, rather than what's right. At the same time, you will notice that they refuse to take negative feedback from others. When distressed they will push their beliefs. They hate to be wrong. When the Boss gets distressed, he or she is will even crusade long past the incident that was wrong in their judgment. So, in cards they play very tightly—although aggressively. The Boss believes that, *I can make others succeed, if they listen to me.* They tend to live life as if *I can't trust anyone except myself.*

Aggressive and Planned Bluffing

There are advantages and disadvantages in bluffing in an aggressive and planned manner. Some of the advantages are based on the player's judgments about other players. Many of the disadvantages are related to telegraphing what you have and inviting others to bluff when they have garbage. Let's look separately at both.

Advantages

Using planned and aggressive bluffs when you think that you have less than the best hand will give you the advantage of representing more than you have. This is particularly true if you are bluffing from an early position. Here's an example. A player is in middle position and everyone limped in before the flop. When the flop showed and Ace♣, Queen♠, and 7♦, everyone checks representing that no one has an Ace. When the turn comes with a blank, the middle player is the first to bet. He's representing that he's got middle pair. When everyone folds, his plan worked. That's what he will do aggressively when everyone checks top pair.

Other players have a plan to call all bets when the odds are favorable. The advantage to this is that on the average, you will be ahead. For example, suppose that you have middle pair (9s) and a flush draw. You have fifteen outs on the flop (thirteen suited cards and two of your pair) before the turn. This means that even though you have a pair of 9s and there is a possible pair of Jacks betting, you have a 60 percent chance of improving your hand. That's better than 1:2 chances. With a plan employing outs and odds, you have the advantage. Some players will make this call on a hunch. The same players will fold this hand with a hunch.

Disadvantages

Bluffing in aggressive/planned fashion is only as good as any player's abilities to figure odds and read what others may have. If you already have the best hand, bluffing is not necessary. It only invites people to lay down hands that you already have beaten. It makes the pot that you finally win a lot smaller. Another disadvantage to aggressive/planned bluffs is that it often reveals a poor planning. Some players plan to bet every time they have the top pair, regardless of the size of their kicker.[4] This is not a good plan. Why? Suppose you have a great kicker, like a King. You make top pair when an Ace comes on the flop. If you bet, you are inviting people to fold. So, even if another player has an Ace, you probably will win the "soccer game" with your big kicker. This is where having a plan that is inflexible will be a disadvantage. If it's your plan to slow-play when you have a good hand and then call or raise when you get some action, this can be a disadvantage. The first couple of times that you set this trap, it will be profitable. The disadvantage is "the hot stove" effect. Players are not likely to step into your trap when you check. They will avoid your trap and avoid being burned. Of course, you could use this as an advantage and check/raise garbage while your opponent's fear of being burned again still exists.

Another disadvantage to planned/aggressive bluffing is that it tells people that you know how to play chess. In other words, you are a systematic player who only plays good cards and when you bet, they may fold at times that you'd wish they stayed in.

Characteristics of Aggressive/Planned Bluffers

Conviction-Oriented Players

Conviction-oriented players like the Boss will judge people and things first. They bring preconceived opinions to the table. They even have opinions about whom and how everyone should bluff—if they are going to bluff in a proper manner.

As reserved/assertive players, their style is to be controlling. Their strengths are that they are disciplined players. As such they are pragmatic about cards and people. They will persistently play only hands with good odds.

Look for furrows between their eyes which are usually intense. They present a stern look when betting or calling, as if to say, *Call that if you don't care about losing.* Their pychological needs are to have their convictions and beliefs recognized. Statements such as, "I admire your approach to bluffing"—"I value your opinion"—"What do you believe I

---

4. This is poker jargon for the size of the second-best card in your holes cards. For example, 6 might be the kicker, if your hole cards are Jack and 6.

should've done?" are all ways to pace a conviction-oriented player. Such players prefer one-on-one conversations to talking to the whole table. They dress for what's proper—usually conservatively. When they are talking to another player, they prefer to be discussing such topics as how proper the previous playing was.

Their chip nests are functionally arranged—similar to a System Player. They also will want the table "squared," only with an attitude of what's proper. In the U.S. population, 10 percent are conviction-oriented, like the Boss, with 25 percent being females and 75 percent being males.[5]

Advantages and Disadvantages of Fish Trapping

Believe it or not, there are smart fish. Players know a lot about who's likely to be bluffing and who's got a real hand. Players who like to trap unsuspecting players know a lot about the game and other players know it. When we discussed reputation we mentioned how very conservative and structured players can bluff with garbage. If they bet enough to make a call costly, they know it. However, when a "fish trapper" attempts to build a pot by slow-playing or raising, most players (potential fish) will fold in order, "like trained pigs," as a friend of mine is fond of saying. That's the disadvantage of planned/aggressive bluffing. These players won't bluff a lot and when they do, the fish seem to disappear.

Such players, though, are hard to bluff. These experts of the art of trapping other fish in systematic and aggressive ways will also excel in reading the bluffs of others. In other words, they not only are smart fish trappers; they also are smart fishes themselves.

5. See Kahler's research, *The Mystery of Management*, Suggested Readings.

11

Speed Trapping

In the game of Cops and Robbers, it's often hard to tell which is which. That's because there may be some truth in the saying that, "It takes a thief to catch a thief." Have you ever wondered how some cops know where to hide their radar speed traps, while others don't catch as many? Some players are better at trapping and others are prime targets to be trapped. Bluffing can be a sudden impulse designed to act strong when holding a weak hand. These styles of impulsive, aggressive bluffs will reveal the Party Hardy and the High Roller bluffing preferences. Both like to be aggressive in their bluffs and usually will engage their bets before their minds. Often you will see such bluffing occur aggressively, with flare, and the bettor hasn't even looked to see what he or she is betting into. When they get in trouble, there's a useful way to tell High Roller from Party Hardys. When Party Hardy is in distress she will blame everyone else but the cards in a whining fashion. High Roller will get strong and combative, will also blame others—but more in a parental tone.

When placing his bet softly, as in photo 40, on page 208, this High Roller is on a steal. If he had a good hand, he'd be more flamboyant in how he bets.

High Roller will take risks more liberally, will bet into over-cards, and can be a threat to the most seasoned of players—particularly if the loose player is catching good hands. Their loose play is a tell in itself—both expensive and profitable. Because High Roller is playing more out of impulse and seeking excitement, he will chase and gloat when he makes his hand. Unfortunately, for the professional player this happens often

Photo 40. Aggressive/Unplanned: High Roller (*right*)
gently betting (on a steal)

enough to throw away good hands that would end up costing too much
if High Roller is on a lucky streak. At the same time, veteran players like
a High Roller who is on a bad streak. They will give the action and stay
in longer than they should. This can be profitable for the other players
who get their excitement more from reaching out and saying, "Send the
Money!"

However, High Roller deserves a word of caution. They are closer
to the center of responsiveness/aggressiveness and can modify impulsive
bluffs and become more structured when needed. This is different for
Party Hardy who will stay with the impulsive bluff to the end.

Party Hardy is there to gamble and contact her surroundings. These
players are playful and are enjoying the people more than they enjoy
the cards. When they bluff they are more likely to say, "Let's gamble!"
while raising the bet. They are looking at other players a lot, but don't
be fooled into thinking they are observing tells as the Winner is. They
are making contact with others. That's primarily what they're there to
do. Playing cards is seldom a way to make a living for Party Hardy. In

fact, another sign is that they will usually play until they run out of money. It's almost as if some Party Hardies can't leave with any money. They are more apt to leave if the people at the table are boring.

Photo 41. Aggressive/Unplanned: Party Hardy (*left*) sweats and is on a bluff.

For the serious player, both Party Hardy and High Roller present a paradox. There are usual tells for other players that are *not* the same for these impulsive, aggressive players. Party Hardy will often look away from the action—whether she has a good hand or not. In fact, these players may even stare at an opponent when they have a good hand. The reason they are doing the opposite of what Caro describes as acting tells[1] is because Party Hardy is not even aware of the other cards. When they stare at others or the action (photo 41) they are making contact. They very well may have the best hand and want to see your face when you make the mistake to call their raise. Whether or not he has a good hand, High Roller (on the other side of the table) is splashing the pot and aggressively throwing in chips. This player is there to risk and get high on the game.

This is where looking for congruency in body language is most important. If a High Roller is playing a good hand flamboyantly, it's not to throw you off (as in the case of a System Player). It's because they approach life in the fast lane and so their bluffs will be more in the order of a sudden change in this trait. For example, if High Roller sud-

---

1. Caro, *Body Language*. Mike Caro observes that a person looking away is appearing nonchalant because they have a good hand. Also, he notes that a player staring at the action or another player is usually pretending to have a good hand.

denly gets quiet and starts playing passively, he is now bluffing. It's not their nature to be so calm and thoughtful. When High Roller slows down or gets passive, he usually is on a steal and doesn't have the hand he is representing.

Party Hardy may not be looking at the cards because this player is having fun. At times, such players are as stubborn as a Missouri mule. They refuse to give up their hand. Since they like to bluff a lot, they may be convinced the other players like themselves are bluffing. So, it doesn't matter that their opponent has scare cards. Win or lose, Party Hardy has made contact and gets a payoff either way. If this player wins, the thrill of victory is to see the opponent frown. If they lose, they can whine and get some "poor babies."

These same patterns follow a High Roller and a Party Hardy into their personal lives. High Roller will have lots of excitement at home and on the job—even if created alone.[2]

Party Hardy believes that *Others are responsible for what I do.* High Roller, on the other hand, believes that *People or things make me feel good or bad.* High Roller will live life like, *I have to fend for myself, and so does everyone else.* Whereas, in reverse, Party Hardy approaches life as, *If you don't love me as is, you don't love me.*

Characteristics of Aggressive/Unplanned Players

Both High Roller and Party Hardy will use aggressive/unplanned bluffs. They both are bluffing for the sport. Each is searching for excitement. High Roller likes to create incidents and Party Hardy wants contact with the environment. There are some differences worth noting.

High Roller

These players are action-oriented and their bluffing is more like, *Ready, fire, aim!* They present a flippant attitude and draw a lot of attention by their usual flamboyant mannerisms. As assertive/responsive players their playing style is advocating. As such, they make good salespersons.

---

2. For more information on the personal lives of each of these styles and how people will substitute crises for excitement, you can read my more clinical book, *Permission Not Granted: How People Who Were Raised in Crisis-Oriented Families Carry Their Childhood Don'ts into Adulthood.* St. Louis: Emily Publications, 1991.

These players are enthusiastic, personable, and expressive. They will build large pots and liven up the table. You'll often notice they have a ruddy complexion, a sign of being outdoors a lot. They dress with a "rich" look, since they like to impress with expensive clothing and jewelry. Their need for action may result in their frequently moving around the room in between hands. Their psychological needs require incidents—a great deal of excitement in a short period of time. They avoid boredom and need activity to curb their impatience. If bored, they often create crises to get some excitement generated.

They have the ability to be firm and direct. They seldom check or miss a chance to bet. As such, expect these players to play nearly all hands and chase hands a lot. As far as others, High Roller prefers detached involvement with groups. They like to be admired for boldness and will draw a lot of attention. Their playing motto is, "If you've got it, flaunt it." Rather than fold, they will call to stay in the action. That's because they think most bets are just bluffs. In their homes and offices, they like elegance (such as thick carpets, stuffed chairs). In their chip nests, they will arrange chips as if they are trophies. Their color preferences are blacks and reds. This means that they will play with large stacks of red chips ($5) and black chips ($100). Five percent of the U.S. population are action oriented, like High Roller (40 percent are females, 60 percent are males).

Party Hardy

Party Hardy is there to make contact with people. These players react to people and things with likes and dislikes. When they get a hand, they will impulsively either like it or not. If they like it, they will play aggressively. Figuring out their standards of liking or disliking will help to read this kind of player.

They also come with an attitude of, *Ready, fire, aim!* The difference from High Roller's playing is that this "firing" is designed to relate to others. Their attitude is *Let the chips fall where they may.* This unplanned/aggressive player bluffs impulsively more for stimulation. The strengths they bring to play are that they are imaginative, creative, and spontaneous. Their willing risks can pay off in rushes of good luck. Over time, though, their rushes are more with people than with pots.

The body language of Party Hardy will reveal smile lines around the eyes and mouth. There's usually a twinkle in their eyes and they dress unfashionably with clashing colors or in mismatched ways—all designed to establish contact (earrings, tattoos, messy hair styles). On a psychological level, these impulsive players require being contacted playfully by others. They avoid serious discussions. They are looking more for small talk and fun. Gaming is a way to contact others more than to study cards. They have the ability to play and enjoy the present. Although they are people oriented, they prefer being on the fringe of groups rather than any close relationships. You can often identify such players by the way they dress. Their dressing is for attention—often unique and/or unusual.

Party Hardy keeps a messy chip nest. Their stacks are full of stimulation and lacking order. Their chips may be in piles rather than stacked neatly. If stacked, the stacks are messy and mixed. They may even have little toys or trinkets to adorn their play space. In the general population of the United States, reaction-oriented players, such as Party Hardys, comprise 20 percent of the population (60 percent are females, 40 percent are males).

Advantages and Disadvantages of Speed Trapping

High Rollers and Party Hardies are *not* good candidates to bluff. Why? Because they are too busy racing their cards and are seldom paying attention to the warning signs. If they are having an unusually lucky day they will outrun good players and cost a lot of money. As far as being trappers, they do this more from their psychological needs for making contact and creating incidents. In this sense, they accidentally trap other players who have good hands and get outrun by these looser players. However, when a player has the best hand, these players are the first to step into a bluffing trap. If you check, they are sure to attack your show of weakness. When you bet, they will more often call. Some speeders will try to outrun a cop. In poker, you will often see them re-raise your check/raise, not so much for the value of their hand as for the excitement and the thrill of being chased with the fastest car.

12

Net Trapping

When a fisherman (or woman) is gambling and just wants to see what's in the water, he or she may just cast a net. Many players do this in the way they bluff. Their bluffs are on the come, even though they are betting as if they already have their hand. This style of bluffing will belong mostly to Hunch Player. These players will do little to influence play and pretty much let the cards play themselves. Their bluffs can also present a paradox to the belief that "weak is strong and strong is weak." The reason, though, is more because they are bluffing as if they are strong because they actually believe that they are going to win the hand. They are dreaming of the hand they are going to get. The difference is that often a Hunch Player will bet like he or she already has the hand. It can't even be called semi-bluffing, because they are bluffing on their dreams. They also don't want to scare anyone away. They will bet more on the come and play as if they already have the hand. This is because Hunch Player is playing more from emotions while being passive. They want to be accepted for who they are and will seldom get negative or show any aggression (like raise) for fear of getting someone angry with them. Where being friendly may mean for some players that they are bluffing, for a Hunch Player being friendly is all he or she knows. They are more likely to get their feelings hurt than to get angry or bet in anger.

Betting softly is also more a way of life for Hunch Player. So, if a bet if placed slowly into the pot by a Hunch Player, does this means they are bluffing—pretending to not have much? Maybe, but usually it's more to not upset anyone by splashing the pot. On the other hand, a

213

Photo 42. Passive/Unplanned: Hunch Player throwing chips (stealing)

Hunch Player may place a bet aggressively. This is not their nature. So, look for Hunch Player to be bluffing and not have the hand she is representing when she suddenly gets aggressive. The exception to this might be if they are trying to please a friend (or spouse) by betting the right way. Then, the forceful bet might be to please a spouse, who says, "Bet 'em like you've got 'em."

Photo 43. Passive/Unplanned: Hunch Player smiling and
placing chips has a strong hand.

In their personal lives, Hunch Players rarely say "no" to others. They handle negative situations by trying to please people. They will require a lot of validation from the other people in their lives. They won't show anger or disagree openly. They will make mistakes and feel rejected in their personal lives as well as at the gaming tables. Hunch Player believes, *I can make people feel good*. They will approach casino play and their lives as, *I can never be disagreeable or I'll be rejected*.

Characteristics of Passive/Unplanned Bluffers

Net fishing is a passive way to catch fish. Bait is seldom used. The net is cast and what is gathered is more accidental than planned. Hunch Player bluffs in passive/unplanned fashion. What determines whether they will bluff will be their hunches. They may have a hunch about someone who is bluffing, so they will over-bluff. They may have a hunch that certain cards are coming, so they will bet as if they are sure to show up. It's hard to read their bluffs because they don't subjectively act like they're being misleading. They actually think that they have the hand that they are dreaming about. Even their eyes might be up and to the left, seeing the hand as a memory rather that as a constructed image.[1]

Hunch Players' Nets

Often, when casting a net, these players are using their intuition to determine where and when to net-trap. Such players feel things first, including the way they play poker. That means that Hunch Player will cast her nets (bet, raise, and fold) by her feelings and intuition. The attitude of these players is one of optimism. Hoping for hands to come based on their intuitions or hunches that they will. When using their intuition to chase hands they will do poorly. However, when their intuitions are focused on players, they will be uncannily accurate.

As passive/unplanned bluffers, they tend to use a facilitating style. When they bluff, their biggest fear is that people will dislike them. For this reason, they will seldom check/raise and when it happens to them, they feel attacked. When they win a hand, you will often hear them say,

---

1. See "Eye-Leading Systems" in chapter 5.

"I'm sorry." They are really saying "Don't dislike me." This same sensitivity can intuitively read people well when not distressed.

Hunch Player has eyes that are expressive. Her eyebrows will even rise to soak in the world. The way these players dress and their appearance are very important. That's because they require being noticed and not ignored while playing; They would rather hear, "I've missed you, where have you been?" rather than comment on how well they play cards. They perform best in a playing environment that's stimulating to the senses (perfumes, flowers, soft furniture). Trash talk is likely to devastate such players. As far as putting a player on tilt, disapproval will interfere with their intuitive play.

Their ability to nurture, give to others, and be empathetic makes them good at being with people and being congenial. They prefer groups and social events and are playing poker more to socialize than to make a lot of money. Hunch Player dresses to please others and has a well put-together look, well groomed. They prefer "nesty" and warm surroundings. They will also keep their chips neatly stacked or in chip tray, making sure not to crowd anyone else at the table. They may even make designs with their chips (stacking in circles, symmetrically arranged, etc.).

There are a lot of these emotionally oriented players in the U.S. population. With the arrival of more women to the poker world, these percentages are misleading. In the general population we can expect to find 30 percent are emotionally oriented (75 percent are females, 25 percent are males). However, poker attracts women who are more thinking oriented. Still, if they are Hunch Players, look for the telltale signs that will guide how they bluff. As mentioned earlier, these players will bluff as if they have the nuts. Even though a Hunch Player is on the come, in their own mind they play as if they already have the hand.

Advantages and Disadvantages of Net Trapping

Net trapping is a loose way to see who's got something to fold or to bluff with a raise. When I do this kind of search for fishes, I call it taking the table's temperature. The move is not toward a particular person. It also violates the rule not to attempt a bluff with more than two or three players. At this point, it's not a bluff. It's more a loose bet to see what others might have. However, when Hunch Player is casting a net, she is applying intuition and is attuned to responses to such moves. In this sense, intuition and hunches are more valuable than knowing the odds and just playing cards. Hunch Players are playing people and that gives them an edge over some "left-brainers."

The disadvantage to this style of bluffing is that often the net will get what the trapper doesn't want. The movie *Jaws* is a shining example. When they were fishing for sharks and they saw the monster shark, they exclaimed, "We're going to need a bigger boat!" When casting a net and betting on the come, passive/unplanned bluffers will often catch a big shark in their net. Their intuition, though, often has such a strong hold on such players that they fail to let the trap go. Bluffing with too many players active is a loose bluff. When you choose to do some loose bluffing, be prepared to throw the trap away if you get something too big for your hand to handle. That's the time to stop betting on the come and to fold on the heart beat.

From Traps to Tilts

Filling in the gap between how the same bluff can work with some and not on others led me to wonder, *How can I know what type of bluff will work?* With some players, check/raising to trap a second-best hand just won't work. For that matter, how can a player know what predisposition they bring to the table? That's when I developed a questionnaire to fill in this gap between self-awareness and actions. In *Beyond Tells*, I introduced the Gambler's Awareness Profile (GAP).[1] I now think that we could use a "Bluffer's Profile." However, before we go there let's discuss going on tilt. Nothing seems to put a player on tilt more than being bluffed or trapped. So, I also devised a way to profile a player's distress.[2]

Tilting Players

When you abuse a pinball machine it will go on "tilt" and stop playing. The same thing will happen with many poker players. If they feel abused, they will go "on tilt" and stop playing their best game. They proceed to getting angry, overadapting, or playing loose and foolishly. Instead of taking a walk and cooling off, they will stay in their seats and go into a distress pattern.

Some players like to get others on tilt. I call them the "tilters." A part of their strategy is to get control of another player. Others (the "tiltees")

1. McKenna, J. *Beyond Tells*, pages 67–69.
2. See appendix A, for "Your Tilting Profile" and what your score means.

are prone to go on-tilt. There are few players who never go on tilt. Most good players have techniques to manage such stressors as being beat on the river by a "river runner"[3] who stayed in with garbage and won.

Everyone gets upset about things some of the time. It usually is not what happens to us that makes the difference. Success or failure is the result of how we handle bad times. This skill can hinder or improve our game. Most of us can handle good times. Sometimes the cards just play themselves, if we don't get in their way. When we go on tilt, it's a mistake to minimize or ignore negative feelings. When a player stuffs such negative feelings, it's just a matter of time how it will interfere with his or her best game. Profiling categorizes such traits as personality types and playing styles. Profiling also will help to understand how going on-tilt can affect a player's game. If you would like to check out how going on tilt is affecting your game, I have put together a list of twenty typical behaviors that put people on-tilt. You can rate yourself or prioritize the list to see how you are dealing with poker stress.[4] Some of these behaviors are just a part of the game of poker. Since poker is a game of domination, getting a player to go on tilt is just as valuable a tool as bluffing to get people to fold or build a pot. However, players bring their assets and their disabilities. Poker can be the stressor that can send a player into his or her worst game. As the saying goes, "Anyone can play good cards." Everyone can't play well when invited to go on tilt.

Here are conditions (sometimes contrived and often just bad luck) that lend themselves to putting players on tilt:

♦ When another player bets, checks, or raises out of turn, this can annoy players with good hands that want people to call. Such actions out of turn could lose some bets, since players with marginal hands may have called a single bet.

♦ More often than one would expect, a dealer will burn and turn too soon. This can ruin a hand since often the correction is to put the premature board card back into the deck and flop a different card. Suppose you had a pocket pair of Queens and the dealer burned and turned another Queen before a player acted. That would be enough to put even a veteran player on tilt.

---

3. Poker jargon for someone who needs two cards in a row to make their hand.
4. See appendix A for more information on profiling tilts and rate yourself.

♦ When players are beaten on the river by a hand that should have folded or even should not have been played in the first place, they can be annoyed to say the least. True, over time such calls will bring the money back to better players. However, it's still not unusual to see players upset by such chasing. When a player goes on tilt after such bad beats, other players will seize the opportunity to play by putting more pressure on the player gone tilt.

♦ Often a player with the nuts will slow-roll after another player thinks he or she has won. This is like pouring salt on some players' wounds. It's frowned upon and it's a way to annoy and put others on tilt.

♦ Even though checking and then raising a bet is a legitimate poker move, it still annoys some. Particularly players, who are there more to socialize, will take offense at such check/raises. If you do this and put a player on tilt, why not make another move that would get them to fold later on—like check/raising garbage?

♦ If a player thinks that you are being sneaky by slow-playing and waiting for someone else to do the betting, he or she might go on tilt—especially, if he or she was the player who stepped into your trap.

♦ Frequently, a player will hide his or her hole cards, resulting in action behind that player. Although this is often just a bad habit that a dealer missed, it's also done on purpose by players who want to know what players behind them will do. This action will put a lot of players on tilt, particularly if they were the one who acted out of turn because they thought the player didn't have any cards.

♦ Whenever a new player comes into the game and immediately asks players to move and make some room, this can annoy some players. Although "squaring-up" the table is a legitimate request, I once heard a player ask for more room. He seemed to have ample room. Later, when another player left the table for a few minutes, he said, "I only did that because I know it gets under Lou's skin."

♦ Getting caught bluffing (speeding) can ruffle a player for a little while. When caught trying to steal a pot, it's a good time to take a short break to recover your composure.

♦ When a player folds and the winning player shows that his hand was garbage, the player who folded the best hand will often go on tilt. Often, this move is done on purpose to not only put a player on tilt, but to set up a bluff when that player has the nuts.

♦ Loose players will chase hands that have slim odds. Often, though, they make their hand on the river. When this type of runner-runner makes her hand, she may be met with a lot of trash talk. Loose players love to hear it because a lot of them are searching for excitement—even though it might be negative.

♦ A player or dealer who is not paying attention ("looking out the window") can slow down the game. This will put some players on-tilt. Some players will feign being distracted as their way to bluff. If it puts others on tilt it gives them all the more advantage.

♦ Long pauses or "sweating" calls can aggravate some players. Players who orchestrate these long pauses are often attempting to intimidate opponents before they call, raise, or fold. I previously referred to this move as "hocus-focus."

♦ Some players will put themselves on tilt. For example, a player does everything "perfectly" and still loses the hand. If such outcomes put you on tilt, you best re-look at how you are managing stress. Some "Rumpelstiltskin players" will turn this kind of stress into golden opportunities to practice patience. Others will turn this stressor into distress.

♦ Similarly, players who chase hands with good pot odds and fail to make their hands will be understandably disappointed. It's nothing to go on tilt about. It's the "3" in a 3-to-1 shot.

♦ There are players who chase with total garbage hands and make it. Pure luck is part of the game and without such play good poker would not be as profitable. A veteran player will not seize this as an opportunity to go on tilt. Some will. Others realize that this kind of playing will eventually, in time, come back in profits.

♦ A lot of mistakes, like hiding cards, holding up the game with cell phone calls, or acting out of turn, can be aggravating. When a dealer fails to control the table, this can put some players on tilt.

♦ A player who's more aggressive than you are and able to gain some control over you can be unnerving. Again, it's possible to go on tilt. It's also an opportunity to avoid making such stress a distress. Use it to get the other player to do your betting for you when you have the better hand.

♦ There's some common, unwritten table etiquette, such as chopping the blinds whenever other players have folded. I once did this when I had a good starting hand (unsuited big slick).[5] The very next time I was in the blinds with this player, she refused to chop. She had good cards. That infuriated me enough to say, "I will never chop with you again!" and I haven't. It's just common courtesy to either always chop or never chop—at least, that's what most players I know will say.

♦ Openly criticizing how an opponent played his or her hand is usually from a sore loser. It's also trash talk that is often designed to put another player on tilt.

Avoiding Tilts During Poker

When a player turns stress into distress and goes on-tilt, he or she is playing more out of a Life Script.[6] Scripts are unconscious agendas that only show when a person is distressed. They don't unfold in good times, only bad ones. However, through the work of Taibi Kahler and Hedges Capers,[7] we have a handy guide to predict certain kinds of distress patterns[8] a person will have. When things don't go right, people who go into first-degree distress will display what Capers and Kahler describe as "driver behaviors." These are telltale behaviors that reveal both the kind of player and their distress pattern. First-degree distress behaviors are socially prevalent actions that a person will get into to defend against their stress. These drivers are conditional okay-ness. In other words, "I can be okay if I . . ." there are these five drivers: Each completing the sentence, "I can be okay, if I or you . . ." *be perfect, please, be strong, hurry up,* or *try hard.*

5. Poker jargon for Ace and King.

6. McKenna, J. *Beyond Tells.* For a complete listing of the kinds of Life Scripts players have, see chapter 3 of this book. Also, see the works of Eric Berne, and Claude Steiner in Suggested Readings.

7. Kahler, T., and Capers, H. "The Miniscript." *Transactional Analysis Journal*, Vol. 4, No. 1 (1974): 26–29.

8. For more information on distress sequences see, Kahler, T. *The Mystery of Management* Little Rock, AR: Process Communications Management, 1989.

Tilt Drivers

Any of these drivers can orginate from various script positions. For instance, a person may be blaming others and expect them to "be perfect." This is usually the case with the Boss. Similarly, a person may expect themselves to be perfect. This is true of System Player when he is distressed. The "please" driver usually shows up when Hunch Player gets distressed. They will overadapt and try to please. High Roller, on the other hand, will expect others to "be strong" for him. The be strong driver may originate as an endurance contest for Loner. When Party Hardy is distressed, expect her to get into "trying harder."

If these driver behaviors don't help to quell the distress, players will go into second- and third-degree distress actions. Some will start making more mistakes, like Hunch Player. Others will attempt to over-control the table with raises and re-raises (such as System Player). In second-degree distress, actions are serious and either the player becomes more down on themselves or others become more the blame for what's happening. Some will just passively wait, as in the case of a distressed Loner. Others will handle distress at this stage as a Party Hardy and blame others. In second-degree distress, the Boss will push his beliefs. High Roller likes the negative excitement. In second-degree distress, though, High Roller will become more manipulative and lead a game of "Let You and Him Fight."

When distress goes into the third degree, there is usually "tissue damage." That means that the person will get more disturbed, may hurt themselves, or will hurt others. This stage is seldom seen in a public poker game. However, I have included the behaviors. They are the "script payoffs" and are included here for the leaders. Figure 11 (on p. 224) will summarize this sequence as it applies to different styles of playing.

Looking at the various playing styles (the *Boss, System Player, Hunch Player, Loner, Party Hardy*, and *High Roller*),[9] it's possible to predict how they will behave when they go on tilt. When players go on tilt, if they stay and play, you can expect the following distress reactions.

Figure 11. Distress Sequence of Players On-Tilt

Playing Style	First-Degree Distress (Conditional Okayness)	Second-Degree Distress (It's you or me)	Third-Degree Distress (Script Payoff)
Hunch Players	*Please*	Make mistakes	Guilt, sad, depressed
System Players	*Be perfect (for you)*	Over-control	Grief, fear, worry
Loners	*Be strong*	Passively wait	Anger, frustration
Bosses	*Be perfect (for me)*	Push beliefs	Distrust
Party Hardies	*Try hard*	Blame	Confused, unloved
High Rollers	*Be strong*	Manipulate	Righteous

Be Strong (for Me)

When the Boss is distressed, he will take a position that he's better than you. He may sound a bit condescending when he says things like, "How does it feel to be lucky?" He won't show much emotion, will talk in a monotone fashion, and is stone-cold serious. His face will reveal few eye blinks and it's clear that he's upset. The first defense against a person in this blatant discount is to refuse the invitation to over-adapt. Sometimes humor will ensure that you are not being perfect for such a player. A response such as, "It feels soooo GOOD! Try it, you'll like it."

The Boss style of player is by makeup an opinionated type of poker player. When he or she is on tilt you can expect them to take a righteous position. Their driver then is a be perfect (for me) type. When distressed, they will expect others to be perfect in how they play and may even trash-talk opponents who beat them. While doing this they will often use big words or ask complicated questions, like "That was an opportunistic, if not a foolish move, even though it could only have happened once in eleven tries!"

9. See appendix C for summaries of each playing style.

Be Strong (for You)

Often you can expect System Player to start explaining his mistakes. He will say things like, "It occurred to me that you might have an over-pair; but, since you just checked, I thought it was my turn." When a person is in this driver, he will substitute the word "it" for "I."

System Players, like the "Boss," will also expect perfection when they are distressed. However, it's a be perfect (for you) driver that they assume and expect themselves to do better. They like recognition and will overdo to make up for mistakes. They also will use big words when they go on tilt and tend to over explain their mistakes. You can expect them to make statements that seem to over qualify things, like *That was a stupid chase on my part. I deserved to lose that one. Oh, well, sometimes I'm the dog. That time, I was the fire hydrant."*

Be Strong (for Me)

While System Player reacts to distress by toughing it out and over-adapting to other players, Loner will "be strong" in a different way. He or she can't trust or rely on others. Their *be strong* is to patiently wait and endure and not expect any understanding from other players. Since they are not self-starters and react to what is happening more than starting anything, they will suffer in silence and just wait things out. They are being silently strong and their emotions will get them to play carelessly.

Try Hard

When some players get distressed, they will try all the harder to make things right. They get into a *"try hard"* driver. This will render them playing desperately with little regard to thinking or planning. They just plug away pushing those "Sisyphus boulders" (cards) up the table. Their anger will be taken out on their chips. In short stacked, they may go "all in" out of frustration—not because they have figured out whether it was a good move.

Party Hardies will get flustered when they go on tilt. Their driver is a *"try hard"* one. That's why if you ask them, "What were you thinking?" they will not answer you directly; rather, they may stutter and say, "Huh? Oh, uh!" They will become somewhat helpless and expect others of do for them.

Please (Me)

When a player gets a little bossy, yet they are more of a Hunch Player, they will handle distress by wanting you to please. *"I want you to get out of my pot!"* This is usually said in jest and it is designed to invite you to be pleasant and fold. You'll know that you are being conned by a patronizing tone and eyebrows that are slightly raised. It's best to ignore such invitations and to find something that you like about this distressed player. A statement like, *"Well, you're one of my favorite people—I guess I'll just call instead of raise."* That will recognize the person and may get such a player out of his or her driver—if that's what you want to do.

Please (You)

When a Hunch Player is over-adapting, he or she is trying to please others. They will talk tentatively and with little aggression. This player will be indirect when distressed and be using words like *"maybe," "you know,"* or *"kinda."* They will also have a whine about what just happened. They say things like, *"I kinda out-ran you. I thought you were chasing, too. Sorry."*

Again, you may want the player to stay distressed. If not, say something kind like, *"Well, it was your turn. Don't worry about it."* When Hunch Player is distressed, initially she will try to smile and get even more into her *please* (you) driver. They become over-adaptive and may say things like, *"Oh, that's all right. It was your turn anyhow!"* You can expect them to go on making mistakes as when they are distressed they seem to continue to be rattled.

Weaknesses That Lead to Tilts

Our weakness will show up at times of stress. Our strengths will also be apparent when we are stressed. When we turn stress into distress we will go into tilt when playing poker. Our tilts may be slight (first-degree) or strong enough to have to leave the table (second-degree). Third-degree distress involves tissue damage where we are hurting ourselves or others in a physical way. We won't even go there in this book. Although, once I heard about a fistfight that broke out on an Omaha Hi-Lo game. I was playing blackjack at the time and a dealer said,

"They had a fistfight in the poker room this morning." I said, "It must have been the Omaha table." He said, "Right! How did you know?" There's something(s) about that game that seems to result in a greater amount of conflicts. I'm still trying to figure it out. At any rate, first- and second-degree tilts will be our focus.

There are four main areas where a player will demonstrate strengths and weaknesses. By observing these areas, you can learn a lot about what areas need improvement and where a player's assets lie. You can also learn where you need to focus if you are going on-tilt and it's hurting your game. These areas are your *betting,* how you *manage* your cards and money, how much you are *thinking,* and your ability to *quit* a hand or table.

First, let's take a look at each of these factors and discover how different frames of references that players have will affect tilts (distress patterns).

Betting Weakness

1.Betting—First of all, ask yourself, "How do I bet my money?" In other words, how do you spend money?
Many players will bet on hunches only. Others will be very structured and their bets are based on odds. How one invests their money can tell a lot about a player. Having guidelines to determine when you will bet, raise, or fold are attributes of good players. Playing your hunches without regard to what is possible will identify the poor player. There are visual, auditory, and kinesthetic ways to place a bet. Each of these frames of reference will have different tilting outcomes.

Figure 11A

Frame of Reference	Things to Notice When on Tilt
Visual bettors	*Will splash the pot, throw chips and cards.* Eyes will move up and to the right when they are bluffing. When they are looking to their left, play your cards for value.They will place their bets for you to notice. Softly means beware, splashing usually means bluffing if it's normal way to bet.

| Auditory bettors | *Will trash talk and slam bets down. Sighs and whines.* Will be looking down and to their left or at their chips. Usually will place bets with verbal comments. They have the gift of gab and use it as their betting style. |
| Kinesthetic bettors | *Hunch betting mistakes under stress.* These bettors are playing mostly with their hunches. Their bluffs are hard to read, since they actually believe that the hands that are coming are the hand they are betting. Their hunches loose accuracy when they are on tilt. |

Managing Weakness

2. Managing—Next, ask yourself, "How well do I manage my stake?"

This is one area where most players can improve. Money management is one of the essential keys to survival in any casino. Some players will use stakes that they can't afford to lose. Often, a player may play with what is called "stolen money." Money taken from household or business budgets to gamble is always a mistake. Chasing your luck and getting more and more into debt is not the way to manage your money. However, these mistakes will increase for many when they go on-tilt. Winners know when to invest their stakes and when to wait. The ways that players think will influence their choice of managing. Their nature will determine how they go about managing their stakes. Each of these frames of reference will have different tilting outcomes.

Figure 11B

Frame of Reference	Things to Notice When on Tilt
Visual managing	*Will fail to pay attention to size of their stack and the odds of calling.* These players usually pay attention to whether they are short-stacked or not. When managing their chips looser, they will nest lower value chips. They usually pay

attention to how their chips are arranged. When they are on tilt they will fail to first look at their chips and will bet more aggressively.

Structured managing
Will depart from usual predictable plays. These bettors will abandon their win/loss formula to guide their betting and will stay longer than they ordinarily would—chasing their luck.

Auditory managing
Become noticeably quiet. Will be looking down and to their left or at their chips. Usually will place bets without usual verbal comments. Their comments usually will refer to how poorly or well they are doing.

Impulsive managing
Will either get more reckless or will be super careful. Will pay very little attention to how many chips they have. They will bet until they are broke, as long as they are getting action. When ahead, they stay until they have to leave—without chips.

Kinesthetic bettors
Start making mistakes. These bettors are playing mostly with their hunches. They manage their funds often in the same manner. If they are feeling lucky, they'll stay and re-buy. If they are feeling unlucky, they will call it a day, take their losses, and leave.

Thinking Weakness

3. Thinking—Another important question is, "How much am I thinking during play?"

Playing styles can range from passive to aggressive and from structured to impulsive. Somewhere in the middle of these traits is ideal. Good players know how to mix hunches with the odds of making wise bets. Betting with no regard to the odds of making a hand is the same as not thinking at the tables or driving blindfolded. Casinos love non-thinking play and may even encourage you by providing complimentary liquor. There are differences in how aggressive and loose players are thinking. Also, their frame of references may influence how they think about their money. Each of these frames of references will have different tilting outcomes.

Figure 11C

Frame of Reference	Things to Notice When on Tilt
Visual thinkers	*Will start constructing hand that they wish to have rather than have.* These bettors think in pictures and will start visualizing themselves as losers. If they are good at constructing images, they will start a doom and gloom that will influence their play. Some will see themselves leaving broke.
Structured thinkers	*Get more boisterous and over-detail to explain their mistakes.* These bettors usually bet with the odds in their favor. If there is enough money to justify the risk, they will bet. When they are on tilt, look for them to bet slim odds and chase hands that they ordinarily would not. They will abandon, temporarily, their win/loss formula and stay longer until they recover from their tilt.
Auditory thinkers	*Eyes down with internal dialogue. So distracted, they miss what's happening. They stay stuck in the past.* They do a lot of self-talk, advising themselves on whether to stay, play, or fold. Unfortunately for them, they will not listen to reason.
Impulsive Thinkers	*Noticeably nonverbal or acting out feelings.* Will pay very little attention to planning and seem to not be thinking much. They are more inclined to make negative contact or to create negative excitement.
Kinesthetic Thinkers	*Pay more attention to negative feelings.* These players use their hunches. They will escalate feelings over thinking. Their thoughts are dominated by how they are feeling.

Quitting Weakness

4. Quitting—Finally, ask yourself, "How much control do I have?" In other words, do you stay too long, bet too much, and never quit when you are ahead?

I've asked players, "Do you have a win/loss rule?" Many didn't know what I meant. Quitting is an important skill in gaming. Some players will get ahead and stay too long. These players often only give back their winnings, but lose their original stake. Knowing when to leave ahead is as important to casino survival as leaving before you are busted. Have a guide like leaving when you lose 70 percent of that day's stake. Also, learn to leave ahead of the game. Some will leave when they have doubled their stake. Others, in limit games, will leave when they have won twenty to thirty times the big bet allowed. Frames of reference don't seem to have as much influence on this factor when players go on-tilt. The more structured players, whether auditory or visual, seem to recover from tilts and will quit before they are ruined. The more impulsive players will ignore their feelings and self-talk and end up staying longer than they should after going on tilt. Frame of reference doesn't seem to have any influence on a player's ability to quit and say no to herself.

Trapping Awareness

Earlier in this chapter, I mentioned creating the Gambler's Awareness Profiles (GAP). I wondered if a Trapping Awareness Profile (TAP) would be useful. After forty years of gaming and observing players, I noticed that some never bluff and some only bluff. The range of personalities playing poker led me to develop an inventory that I have called the Gambler's Awareness Profile (GAP). It is based on the Behavioral Exchange Inventory (BEI), which was validated by the University of Miami over a ten-year period. The report that it generates will give gamblers feedback on the four essential elements to successful gaming.[10] I am currently developing an inventory that will reveal what kind of bluffing a player will employ. It can be used by yourself and/or to assess

10. For more information on the Gambler's Awareness Profile (GAP), go to my website at www.JimMcKenna-PhD.com.

how your opponents are likely to bluff. With my fondness for acronyms, I decided to call this new profile the Trapper's Awareness Profile (TAP). It will require more time than my current deadline for this book will allow. You can be sure that you will be hearing more about TAP.

Meta-Bluffs

A meta-bluff is a bluff that is used to bluff. It's a bluff about a bluff. These are bluffs that are used mostly by veteran players who know their opponents. Most experienced players realize that other veteran players are tuned in to bluffs. That's when they will use a bluff, hoping that their opponents think that their bluff is a bluff. Or, they will not bluff and hope that their slow play is taken for a bluff. It would be a mistake to use meta-bluffs against inexperienced players—straight bluffs would be enough. Here are some examples seen at more advanced tables.

Types of Betting Meta-Bluffs

Betting as mentioned earlier in chapter 2 is a way to bluff. A bet is usually saying before the flop in Texas Hold 'Em, "I've got cards good enough to call the big blind bet." Actually, it's really not betting—it's calling. Often, after everyone has checked the flop, an early player will bet with garbage, pretending to have second pair. This is a bluff that often works. With more experienced players, it won't work. So, an experienced player with the nuts may do the same thing in early position to pretend that he or she is bluffing. This action is meant to induce calls. Sure, a check is also intended to do the same thing. However, experienced players know that it's also a way to set a trap. So, to bet the nut becomes a meta-bluff—a way to pretend to be bluffing (with the best hand).

A bet after the flop can be saying that *I've got some of that*. If it is coming from an early position, it usually means that the bettor has top pair. However, this bet from a later position could be a bluff, if not a semi-bluff. A player with middle pair may be on a semi-bluff, hoping others will fold or that he or she will improve on the turn. It could be a stone-cold bluff, particularly if the bet is in near last position after several checks. When betting after the flop is used as a meta-bluff, it is designed to mislead the more experienced players. As such, it will not work at a loose table. So, don't attempt this if you have several loose players to your left. It works best when you are head-to-head with an experienced player and that player is to your right. That means that you have a positional advantage over him or her. If you have a good hand, you would ordinarily check to get some action or to set a trap. Since you have a position advantage, a bet might be seen as a semi-bluff. So you bet and hope your opponent thinks you are bluffing and raises you. Then the bet that seemed a bluff becomes a meta-bluff when you re-raise.

The important thing to distinguish bets that are meta-bluffs is the appearance of bluffing to a player who knows something about bluffs. It won't work on a naïve player. So, if you think that a player will think that you are bluffing, only bluff if you are pretty sure your hand is better. If not, a bluff will get the intended call and you will lose. Similarly, if you think that a player is putting you on a bluff and you have a good hand, bluff a good player but not a bad one.

Types of Meta-Bluff Calls

Calling, instead of raising, is a way to slow-play and makes a profitable bluff. It keeps players in who might fold to a raise. When you are head-to-head with an experienced player, that player might be thinking that you are slow-playing when you just call. That's what you want him to think if you think he has a better hand than you do. If you had the second-best hand and got the best hand to fold, it probably was by using a meta-bluff. Here's an example:

Everyone folded on the turn. Your opponent with pocket Aces checks to you hoping that you bet a pair of Kings (high card on the board). You check to pretend that you are betting Trip Kings and that you are slow-playing. Actually, all you have is position, with nothing near a good hand. You know your player, who finally bets his Aces on the river. Then you re-raise—his biggest fear is realized (he thinks), and he folds. This worked because you were playing a good player who read you as having Trips or two pair. It won't work with a poor player who can't seem to read other players.

Loners are players who seldom raise. They may appear to be "calling stations," but, they are not. It's their way to bluff, hang back in the bushes, and let others do their betting. Occasionally, when the opportunity arises, their call acts as a meta-bluff. They know that you know that they will seldom raise, even when they have the best hand. So, when they don't have much, they may call pretending to have more than they do. Then, when an over-card, like an Ace, comes on the river, they may bet into your check. That's their meta-bluff, thinking that you are thinking they have a good hand because earlier he or she was just calling.

Types of Meta-Bluff Raises

Raising, as mentioned, can be a desperation move. Good players will seldom employ a stone-cold bluff. Their raising bluffs are more than likely semi-bluffs. This means that they don't have the best hand, that they have something that could get people to fold by representing that they have more than they do. They also know that an experienced player will see a raise as a possible semi-bluff. So, when playing a more experienced player, a meta-bluff would be raising so much that the opponent would have to have the nuts to call you. An all-in raise is such a meta-bluff. It's a bluff that looks like it's a bluff; however, it would cost too much to call. So, it's a bluff to create a bluff.

Types of Meta-Bluff Checks and Folds

Checking is a bluff when it is pretending weakness to get action to a player's left. The usual checking bluff is to raise when action is gotten. However, some players will check to keep players calling and don't want to draw attention to their good hand. That's when it becomes a meta-bluff. The first check was a simple bluff. The second check is a bluff that's a bluff. Don't expect this meta-bluff to work twice at the same table.

Folding can be a useful bluff, but, only if your opponents know what you folded. That's where showing your folds is likely to be a setup for a later bluff. These players, however, will show when they have garbage, but not flash their hole cards when they have a strong pair. When the opportunity to bluff comes they will pretend to be bluffing with the best hand. Their earlier move was to induce calls if they tried to bluff again. They know this and they know that you will call. So, their bluff (with the best hand) is a meta-bluff. Suppose that the next time this player bets, and had little strength in her hand, she'd know that you would call because that's what she was leading you to do by flashing her bad hand previously. Now, with bad cards, that same player may pretend to be slow-playing a good hand. She's already established distrust in her opponents' minds. A meta-bluff here would be to *not* raise, but to check, or to just call. That call could slow down an opponent. Then when a card comes that's higher than the opponent has, a check/raise might get the pot. That's a meta-bluff check that began with a fold.

The Ultimate Meta-Bluff

It's a good idea to call whenever a player is on-tilt. This includes raising when you've got a good hand, expecting the player on-tilt to make a bad call. Occasionally, though, a solid player may be pretending to be on-tilt. That's when calling or raising a player who's on-tilt is a mistake. This is using the phenomenon of tilts as an avenue of bluffing. Remember, a good player has the discipline to avoid tilts. Yet, a good player knows that people are greedy and will take advantage of players when they become distressed. This is when the victim becomes the persecutor.

Here's a story that happens often among good players who are playing less experienced ones.

A solid player, who's got some table respect, gets beat on the river by a runner-runner. He acts angry, throws his discards into the muck, and seems to be on-tilt. This is highly unusual behavior for this player, yet, some of the newer players at the table don't know this. The very next hand, the player who just got beat is dealt a suited big slick (Ace, King). The flop gives him the two top pair. His task now is to get the most value out of his hand. He continues the act of being on tilt and says something like, "Check! Let's see who else has an Ace!" He knows that the other players know that strength means weakness, so he's acting strong to appear weak. When everyone checks, he still pretends to be fuming. The turn brings a blank and he bets. He is called and someone even raises it to two bets, figuring that he's on-tilt and was bluffing about having an Ace. Guess what the player who was supposed to be on-tilt did? Yep. He re-raised and he got a lot more in value for this hand. In the end, because he pretended to be angry, a looser than usual player who was still on-tilt, he succeeded in trapping players who like to take advantage of others when they are down.

The bottom line is to know when an action is the usual behavior for a player. If not, if you take a deep breath, you can smell a bluff.

14

Tools in the Playing Shed

I admit that I am not the sharpest tool in the shed. In fact, I have often amused players who were part of my research by saying, "I am a poker player, trapped in a writer's body!" That's not humility, it's just a fact. I've played with players who are poker players and yet they would have trouble writing about what they know. What I know a lot about is people and I have taken that knowledge and applied it to my poker research. What I have attempted to do, in this book and in *Beyond Tells*, has been to apply that knowledge about people to sharpen the tools of poker players. The bottom line in this integration of knowledge is to help players be better able to respond to gaming. This response-ability will sharpen tools and hopefully build character. There are no stupid players—just players who are doing the best they can with the circumstances that they bring to the tables. The goal of these books is not so much to improve your poker abilities as to improve how you live your life. The focus of this book has been dealing with stress to turn such stress into solutions. When players turn stress into distress, they are blunting their tools. Bluffing is a source of profit in poker. It's also a source of stress. Whether you are bluffing others or you are being bluffed, your reaction to stress will give you an advantage or put you on tilt. When you succeed in bluffing an opponent, you can expect a negative reaction. That's their tilt. How you handle such reactions may result in your tilt. I've seen this. A player who was bluffing by slow-playing raised when the river gave her the best hand. This put a player on tilt.[1] She then got upset, apologized, and proceeded to go on tilt herself.

Some players confuse bluffing with being untrustworthy. In basketball, a player with the ball may start to move to the left and suddenly go right. Such "faking out" is part of the game. It's not the same as lying. The same is true of prizefighters when they fake a right cross and surprise the opponent with a left jab. The ability to surprise other players in poker means that you are hard for other players to read. In sports and in cards, faking out is part of the game. You have learned about pacing and leading as skills needed to successfully bluff. Such pacing and then switching is part of poker. Actually, I've heard it said that honesty becomes a bluff in poker. A player may say, "I'll check my two pair." Then a player to his left bets. He then raises and says, "I told you I had two pair. If you just got one pair, you are in trouble now." Even with this, the other player calls. Why? He was sure that his opponent was lying. He actually wasn't and his two pair beat the top pair. So, honesty is often a bluff in poker.

Sharpening Betting Tools

How you bet can get full value out of your hand. It can also get more than the hand is worth. The use of betting can be a valuable tool to bluff, to invest in certain hands, or to simply call and let the cards do their job. Betting can be a problem for those players who don't manage their stakes too well and stay too long to bet. To repeat what I said earlier, betting can also be a problem when a player bets with "stolen money"—money that the player is stealing from their household to play with money they can't afford to lose. Betting can be a problem when it seems that you have second-best hands and are betting *for* the best hand.

Problems come from betting too soon or too often. Early bets will telegraph your hand and invite some players to fold. Betting too often will lose respect and find players calling or even raising when you bet. Similar problems arise when a player raises too soon or too often. Rais-

---

1. Actually, he put himself on tilt. As Eleanor Roosevelt was famous for saying, "No one can demean you without your consent."

ing too soon can cost money from the players to your left who would have called one bet. When players are raising too often, other players will put you on playing too loose, trying to build pots, or just plain recklessness. They know that one player is not likely to have so many raising hands in a row.

Here's a story about a player that I know who seemed to have nearly all of these betting problems.

Carl is a friend of mine who had to stumble into improving his betting problems. (I like this story because it demonstrates how he overcame his betting problems and it shows that even this bad a player can improve his or her game.) The problem Carl had was that when he was betting too loosely or too often, he couldn't keep his mouth shut. He is an engaging player who likes to tease other players. He would call or raise and say things like, "I'm going to bet so much, it won't be poker to call me!" It seemed that everyone at the table knew, except Carl, that when he was gabbing, he didn't have that much—just a probing tongue. He'd get called a lot and most players would call if they had anything other than total garbage. I noticed another pattern with Carl that when he was not teasing or verbally making jokes, he would have a real hand. In fact, when he got quiet, I would fold in a heartbeat. Carl, however, never seemed to notice this. These were his betting tells and nobody was about to tell him—including me (it was saving me money).

One day, his wife came to visit him while he and I were playing. The same pattern prevailed. About a week following his wife's visit, I noticed a strange thing had begun to happen. Carl became quiet and would cease his verbal onslaughts. In fact, his playing improved and although his bets still got more calls and raises than would be usually expected, he also won many more pots. Pretty soon, other players began to slow down on their calls. They called it, "Getting out of the way of your rush . . ." It seemed that his wife's coming that day had helped his play. Either that or someone spilled the beans and let him know about his betting problems.

Since Carl was a friend of mine, I could tease him a little. One day I said in jest, "Boy! Ever since Eileen watched you play you have changed." He quietly nodded his head to affirm this. Later, he confided in me that Eileen had said to him, "I bet you couldn't play poker with your head instead of your mouth!" That's when Carl realized that his joking and teasing was interfering with his game. He said, "I decided to take her challenge and play a game without socializing at all. I was going to prove to her that I could play without talking." Instead of his usual wisecracks, Carl told me that he was thinking of his bets more as investments than as "cattle probes." What I thought to myself was that it also got Carl to think more when he bet, and that improved his game. Even though Carl is a good friend, I will still call or raise him when he's kidding around. When he's quiet, I'm gone—unless I'm sure I've got him beat.

Another betting tool is the ability to fold and not bet, even with good cards. It's been wisely said that a good player has the ability to lay down a good hand when he reads that another player has him beat. Some players are like a dog with a bone and will refuse to lay down a hand until it is proven that they are beat. It's recklessly referred to as, "keeping you honest."

So, sharpening your betting tools begins with an honest assessment of what you are doing wrong. If too many people are calling your bets, that could be a red flag. If you are getting raised a lot, take a closer look. If you are staying too long and your calling is building pots for your opponents, ask yourself what stops you from laying down second-best hands. Sharp betting tools will bring less work and dig deeper holes for your opponents.

Sharpening Managing Tools

How you manage your money and your playing habits may need a little or a lot of sharpening. Having dull management tools will be revealed in loss of profit and playing more out of need than out of want. The need to catch up and chasing your luck are signs that your management tools need sharpening. Let's look at typical management problems encountered in poker. These problems have to do with how players manage their stakes and how they manage the ways they play, such as bluffing.

If you don't have a win/loss formula, it's way overdue. No one, not even the best of players, can win time after time. There are bad days and good ones. Like I said before, *"Sometimes I'm the dog and sometimes I'm the tree."* A win/loss formula means that you have predetermined when to invest and when to leave that market. You know what types of stocks to spend your money on and you've got a handle on the kinds of investments to avoid. You know when to stay and when to leave. You make sure that when you leave that you are leaving with more money than you came in with.

The one paramount gambling issue is related to players not knowing when to leave—whether behind or ahead. When Eric Berne, who was an avid poker player himself, was treating a compulsive gambler, he discovered this underlying problem. The patient said to him, "If only I had permission to lose, I could beat this thing." A lot of compulsiveness in gaming is that players keep trying to make up their losses, instead of taking a loss and coming back another day to invest again. On the other end of things, players will often get ahead and then stay too long until they have lost what they won and then some. Having predetermined win/loss goals will prevent these kinds of impulsive mistakes. Some players who use a win/loss guide will call it a day if they lose 60 to 70 percent of their daily limit (that's what they can invest in any one day). When you are having a bad day, it takes skill and character to take losses in stride and to quit for a while. Similarly, when players get so far ahead they will leave and enjoy their profit for that day. I know players who play limit games and when they have won thirty times the big bet they will stop pushing the envelope. For example, in a $10–$20 game, when this player got ahead by about $600 he would start thinking about leaving. He says that if he starts to lose a couple of pots, he will leave before he gives any more back.

Here's a true story about a couple who learned to manage their family. I have disguised their identities; but their story is one that improved their family relations.

The Adams family was busy and packed with problems. Mike and Alice had eight children about three years apart. The oldest was Harold (twenty-nine) who was single and still living at home. The youngest was Annette (eight). The four younger children were all still in school. The older kids, including Harold, had dropped out of school and had trouble holding jobs. Now Mike and Alice both worked to make ends meet and they thought of themselves as good parents. They had done what they could, had spoiled more than they needed to, and had lost control of their children for many years.

Discipline was frustrating. Whenever either Alice or Mike expected the children to do their share of household duties, they were met with defiance. They tried to intimidate them, threatening them with being grounded, and losing privileges. However, nothing seemed to work. The children continued to defy them. They were about to throw in the towel and just let the kids go without consequence.

One day, Alice heard a TV psychologist talking to a family that sounded a lot like hers. The kids were out of control and the parents had turned to national television to get some help. If this psychologist could help this family, maybe there was some hope for them.

Mike said that he pretty much had approached the kids in the same way. He had no favorites and what he expected from one was expected from all. Yet, he agreed with Alice, nothing seemed to get through. Even Harold, their firstborn, who had trouble with his bosses and got fired from several jobs, was hard to talk to. Alice heard the doctor on the TV program say something about finding out what each child valued most and begin negotiatiing such things as rewards for listening and doing what was expected. She discussed this with Mike, who agreed that they needed to treat each child a bit differently. When they would get severe and start to enforce their rules, they began to do it differently with each of their children. They discovered that Bobby (fourteen) seemed to pay more attention to things that they said after being reassured of how important his birth was to them and how much they had been looking forward to having him. This kind of talk, though, didn't get anywhere with Hank (seventeen) who paid more attention to how they looked at him than what they said to him. In fact, he liked video games, and when they negotiated with him they agreed to finance new games if he began to do his part. When he resisted, Mike got more action from Hank when he'd bring out a picture of the game Hank wanted and remind him, "No tickee, no washee."

Things began to improve because they started to approach each of their children differently. They also began to speak differently to each other. Mike liked to show Alice his love by doing things for her around the house. Alice, though, told him that she would rather hear him say, "I love you" more. This was hard for Mike. He said that all the things that he did were saying that. That she wasn't listening. She got his attention when she said, "I don't listen with my eyes!" She said, "Just as we have learned to treat each of the children in their ways, not ours—so too we need to treat each other the way we prefer. I do a lot of things for you and you appreciate them. I know. It's just that what I want is for you to tell me how much you care with words, not actions."

Alice and Mike not only sharpened their management tools with their family, they also managed their relationship with each other in a better way. As outlined earlier in this book, by approaching each player in a manner that fits his or her style of playing and their frame of references, players can improve their game. To bluff everyone in the same fashion is like disciplining all the childen with the same rewards. Players respond to different bluffs. Some pay attention more to what they seen than to what they hear. So, using verbal bluffs on a visual opponent won't work as well.

Sharpening our management tools requires us to pay attention to the tools that conserve energy and helps us to effectively use the tools that fit the job. You wouldn't bring a knife to a gunfight. Why bring a hammer to dig a ditch? Finding the right tool is often as important as honing your tools. This includes bluffing the right player at the right time and not "over-bluffing."

Sharpening Thinking Tools

It's possible to "fly by the seat of your pants" and do well in poker—for a while. However, over time, impulsive players will lose more than they win. Think about that. The laws of average will dictate outcomes more than luck in the long run. That's the reason when a loose player comes to the table and does well with careless moves, experienced players just hope that they stay a while. In the short run, they can hit and run. Over time they will crash and burn. The thinking tools of good play are learning about probabilities and figuring odds. If you are playing poker with no regard to playing hands guided by odds of probability and figuring pot odds, you need to add these tools in your shed. There are many resources to learning these mathematic skills. The Internet is rich in how to figure odds. I have included some of these in Suggested Readings.

Sharpening your thinking tools is important. Yet, some of the complicated formulas for calculating odds would require bringing a calculator to the table for many. There's the expression of "keep it simple" that likewise applies to the game of poker and calculating odds. For example, in appendix B, I have calculated odds, using complicated formulas that I learned on the Internet. Yet, it's not always practical to bring such a list to the table or to memorize such tables. So, here's how I have simplified figuring odds in a game of Texas Hold 'Em. It only requires the ability to figure "outs" and then multiply those outs by 4 or 2. On the flop, if you have eight outs to improve your hand, multiply 8 times 4 and that will give you a 32 percent chance that the next card (the turn) will improve your hand. As my chart shows, that comes out as a better than 2-to-1 chance of improving your hand. Next, figuring pot odds can become simple. If you must bet $20 to take that risk, ask yourself this: "Is the pot bigger than 2 times $20 or at least $40?" If it is go for it. If you still haven't improved your hand at the turn, your chances go down to 8 times 2 or a 16 percent chance that the river will improve your hand. So, you don't need a calculator to count your outs and either multiply them by four (4) on the flop and two (2) on the turn. That should sharpen your thinking.

You can check on how much you are thinking by observing yourself. Ask yourself if you are playing selectively and when you do if you are being aggressive. Thinking players avoid taking risks with hands that have little potential in a showdown. When they do play they have thought ahead, anticipated those who are still calling, and will play their good cards aggressively. Unless they think they have the best hand. Then, they might check and let someone catch up—that's still thinking, though.

You can sharpen your thinking tools by being a positive player who is fun to play with. The adage that you can catch more flies with sugar is true. You can also keep people at the table longer if you eliminate trash talk and criticizing other players.

Players who are not in the hand are thinking when they are using this time to observe how other players in the hand are behaving. Some of my best information about opponents comes at such times. When I am in the hand, I can easily miss important tells and actions when opponents are bluffing.

When you do play, develop some starting standards. It's true that you can win with any two cards in the hole. Yet, to play the whole game like that reveals that you are not thinking. Using your impulses to decide or only playing hands that *feel right* to you may work for a while. In the end, you will have to develop your left, more logical, brain to balance your creativity.

This reminds me about the time when I was working with a young woman who seemed to only be attracted to men that would end up abusing her.

Sandra came into counseling because she was tired of failing to find a relationship that was rewarding. She preferred to date men who were rough and liked a good time. So, she didn't have a problem enjoying herself—when she was on a date. In the long run, however, when later she'd decide to live with a guy and get more serious she started having problems. She would give and give and end up wondering, "When is somebody going to take care of me?" She knew that she was picking out "cowboys" who were a lot of fun, loved to ride hard, and only knew how to take care of their horses—not women. They were little boys who looked like men. She knew this but would say, "The other kind of man is just not attractive to me!" She knew what kind of man wouldn't have to be taken care of and could provide some of her deeper needs. The men that she was attracted to could only meet her need for excitement, wild play, cheers, and laughs. So, that was her dilemma. She wanted a mature man to spend her life with; yet, she was only attracted to immature men who refused to settle down into everyday living.

Sandra was living in her right, impulse-ridden brain when it came to men. In counseling her, I knew that she needed to listen to her left brain that was telling her that the less attractive, somewhat boring men were better for where she wanted to go.

She mentioned that there was a guy in the building where she was employed who was making some moves on her. She wasn't interested in him. He didn't turn her on. He seemed to be a nice and solid enough guy, but she was not interested. She would ignore him when he came around.

So, here's what she agreed to do. As an experiment, she would change her dating pattern and would encourage this boring guy and start dating him. She even groaned at the thought. Yet, she did assign this task to her left brain. Her right brain was totally nonplussed.

Sandra stayed with this man and ended up getting married to him. Several years later, I learned that she was still happily married, being respected by her man, loved, and cared for. After the initial dates, she discovered that he was also a lot of fun. She learned to change her dating habits and was able to reach her goals of improving her relationships with men. She even confided to me that she was having better results with her male bosses and supervisors.

What's this story got to do with playing poker? A lot! Just as Sandra was attracted to men who would end up abusing her, a lot of poker players will be attracted to playing cards that will in the end abuse them. These players even know when they are playing for thrills and not paying attention to themselves, that they are setting themselves up. Yet, they continue to play cards mostly with their right brain. They have fun, some rushes, and yet when things get serious they end up with short stacks. Sharpening your thinking tools may require you to put some tools away for a while (as Sandra agreed to do) and start playing (dating) cards (people) that show some promise in the long run. By selecting your hands (dates) and then playing them aggressively (getting serious), you will play more hands (relationships) that will not end up abusing you.

Sharpening Quitting Tools

You will hear a lot about players staying too long and not quitting when they are ahead. Yet, the ability to quit goes further. It includes refusing to play with cards that have slim odds of winning. It includes knowing when to give up a bluff that is not working. Finally, when a person knows when to quit, it includes the ability to lay down a hand when you know your opponent is not bluffing.

Laying down good cards is the most difficult skill there is in poker. New players will seldom do this. They will play their "good" cards to showdown and then complain that the day has been full of "second-best" hands for them. Veteran players know that even if they are laying down the best hand, the discipline of quitting when you are sure that you have been beaten will pay off in the long run. Not betting and not calling bets is money saved when you have the best hand and can be more aggressive. Quitting when the risk is not worth it will make more money. Suppose that you have figured out that the odds of improving your hand is one chance in five (1:5). You are in a $5–$10 hold 'em game and it's two bets to you. That means that someone bet and another player after you raised the bet. The flop looks like this:

With this flop, you have only the middle pair. One person has bet and another player behind you has made it to two bets to you. The blinds fold and the original bettor calls. Your call would cost you $10 with the implied threat that betting will go to $10 a bet after the turn. And, the original bettor could re-raise. The size of the pot at this point amounts to $42. One time in five tries you could make another Jack or get two pair. Would you call or would you quit?[2]

Here's another true tale that at first doesn't seem related to poker. However, it very much is *and* you may remember it when it comes time to quit a hand.

Bill and Patti were a typical couple who were married for more than forty years. They were married when long courtships were the rule and the divorce rate was much more a rarity.

Although they had a long marriage, their relationship was not as lasting. They both had little patience with each other. They actually did very little together, except share the same roof. Each had their own set of friends and together they seemed to have no friends. So, as far as entertaining, that was a seldom occasion and it was usually his or her relatives.

They finally came into counseling because Patti had met a man at work, was infatuated, and got to thinking that maybe with so many

2. If you would fold, you already have sharp quitting tools. Pot odds say with a 1-in-5 shot that you should fold. Betting $10 to gain $40 would make sense only if you had a 1:4 chance. It would mean that you'd only have to catch once in four calls like this to break even. Your chance was 1 in 5.

divorces prevalent, just maybe it was time to quit her long marriage to Bill.

After an initial evaluation of the problems that needed to be addressed, I brought them together to set some goals. They both wanted to work things out and Patti knew that the man at work was a passing thing. One of the things that both of them said when I saw them individually was that they were confused about what the problem was. They seldom, if ever, argued. In fact, they had very little to say to each other. They both had been faithful and although Patti was tempted to go astray, that was what brought them into counseling. Bill admitted that he'd been tempted but that was not enough to ring any exit bells for him. They kept saying how they have been married for over forty years.

I began the goal-setting session with the statement: "There's a difference between forty years of marriage and being married for one year forty times over and over." This startled both of them. And, it was my way of getting their attention. I knew they were going to bring up how long they were married.

So, I described how they were continually making the same mistakes with each other.

They both ended up getting somewhat close to each other and never any closer. They actually had very little in common except their religion, their children, and their house. They had no mutual friends. Their work around the house was done separately—not together. They were living each day like Bill Murray in *Groundhog Day* where each day was a repeat of the day before. They knew what they'd like the other to change; yet, neither of them spent much time looking at what they had to change.

We ended up setting some specific goals that each of them could work on to improve the relationship. They started to change and developed a life together. When they celebrated their fiftieth wedding anniversary, I received a thank-you note from Patti. It said, "I no longer claim to be married for fifty years. I think of the first year of my marriage as lasting for forty years and the last ten years have been terrific. I now tell close friends that I've actually been married for ten years. Thanks again, and God bless."

During my research of observing poker players, I have noticed that a lot of players are like Bill and Patti. They have been playing for years and they have been making the same mistakes over and over. They never seem to learn. These are players that can't be labeled as "losers" or "winners." I refer to them in a previous book as "nonwinners."[3] They end up breaking even and seldom get much ahead. Yet, they are proud that they have lasted so many years without being close to getting busted. They still have money, but not much more than they started with. They have learned to quit in time and they seldom quit very far ahead. If anything, their quitting tools are *too* sharp. They need to learn to risk more. These players seldom, maybe never, bluff. They need to learn to bluff, rather than quit, sometimes.

You will need to sharpen your quitting tools in your playing shed if you are playing too many "second-best" hands. Your quitting tools also need sharpening if too often your bluffs are not working. This often means that you are attempting a bluff with too many people in the hand. With more than two other callers, multi-way pots are hardest to bluff. You can put a big edge on your bluffs just by deciding never to bluff unless you have only two opponents. Another way to sharpen your bluffs is to quit attempting to bluff loose players. The better the player, the more likely a bluff will work. Along this line, don't even attempt a bluff if an opponent is paying little or no attention to the game. For a bluff to work other players have to be paying attention and have to be able to think about what you are representing. A loose player is there more for thrills and won't be doing that kind of thinking. So, quit annoying yourself with bluffing hopeless hands against players whose hands are equally as hopeless and who are playing for adrenaline rushes.

Taking Inventory

Any time is a good time to take inventory of how you are playing with the tools you have and how others are using their tools. A good way to take such inventories is to look at how you and others are handling playing tools.

Betting habits can help you or they can render you broke. How you spend your money and invest your estate will show up at the tables. How you manage your chips will also reveal the kind of player you are.

---

3. In *Beyond Tells* I go into detail about these "Over and Over Players." See pages 48–50.

Whether you are thinking or playing by the seat of your pants, your betting style will also reveal how sharp you keep your thinking and folding tools. These are all revealed in the manner in which you manage your money.

Money Talks

There are many currencies that are used to play out a losing or nonwinning script. Some people use drugs and alcohol. Others turn to conflicts and sexual behaviors as a currency around which to play games. In the gambling arenas, the common denominator of money issues will show up and tell a lot. People bring a wide range of issues around money to the gaming tables. It's much like the bell curve where the average or majority of people use money in appropriate ways. In the center of the curve, most players spend and manage their stakes well. They plan what they can invest and stop when they reach their limits. They're willing to risk. However, similar to investing in the stock market, they don't bet funds needed for other necessities in life. They bring an attitude of harmony[4] between themselves and their money to the table. The players at the low and high ends of the bell curve will create money games. They are also the minority of players. Money issues will cluster around four main extremes.

1. How people *spend* their money. The range of betting habits will go from very tight to very loose. This includes how wisely they invest their money in bluffing.
2. How people *manage* their money. They range from those who are very methodical and plan every bet to those who just bet on hunches. This can be seen also in methodical, planned bluffs, and unplanned hunch bluffs.
3. How people use money as a *drug*. The thrill seekers vary from those who avoid and withdraw from any stimulation to those high rollers that are reckless and use risking as their drug of choice. A careful analysis will also reveal how some players use bluffing as their *drug of choice*.
4. How people use their *moral attitudes*. One extreme of money attitudes is treating money as sacred and worshipping at the "Temple

4. See Mellan, O, *Money Harmony*, Washington, DC: Walker, 1994.

of Chips." The other is seeing money as something that ruins
people and the belief that money is the root of all evil. Such attitudes can limit a player's bluffing approaches due to prohibitions
about dishonesty. The other extreme comes in players who define
success as pulling off the biggest bluff with rags.

Nesting Chips Speak

Often, how one keeps their nest[5] will tell a lot about a person. Notice
here how different personality types manage their chips. In photo 44, a
systematic player's chips are arranged both in order and for function. It's
easy to check on how good or bad she's doing at a glance. It's also
arranged in piles ready to bet or fold. An arm around the stake to protect what is hers is not insignificant. She's there to the make money,
play the odds, and not so much to socialize. She's a closed system.

Photo 44. Guarded attitude about money

Compare photo 44 to the more spontaneous player (photo 45, opposite) and her unorganized pile of chips. The chips are just there, probably the most insignificant part of what the player is there for. She's there
to make contact with people. If she starts to make contact with the chips,
it might be to build a semi-organized pile (see photo 46, opposite).

5. For an interesting article on how people spend their money, see "The Psychology
of Money," by M. Rowland. *Modern Maturity*, Vol. 39, No. 2., March–April (1996)
50–54.

Photo 45. Loose attitude about money

Photo 46. Party Hardy with semi-organized piles

Notice in photo 47 (p. 252) how some players use chips to decorate their nest. Chips are things to play with and to show in some stylish arrangement. She's there to be noticed and if her chips can help that happen, then so be it. Also, since this is her buy-in, more whites ($1 chips) may mean she will be betting looser today.

Photo 47. Nesting: Hunch Players

Tight Versus Loose Bettors

Some people will guard their chips and only bet on sure hands. They don't like to risk and when they bet, most other players will fold. They've already revealed that they only spend their money when there's almost a guaranteed return. Such people will save for a rainy day (which never comes). They're savers who tuck their money away in very safe accounts. At the tables, they generally will play all day and night and may be a little ahead. They don't lose much and they don't usually win much. For that matter, they seldom bluff.

The counterpart player is the "compulsively loose bettor." Such players never saw a hand they wouldn't like to bet.[6] They also can't stand to see a pile of chips in front of them without betting. Their bets are usu-

---

6. Veteran players have labeled such players as "Will Rogers" players.

ally on impossible odds. Or, they'll raise a little pot to the maximum just to make the pot look bigger. Most often, though, they're building a pot for someone other than themselves. One loose bettor I heard about would practically diet on crackers and water to save money to play. Then, when he'd bet the money, he would all but throw his money away. These players like to bluff with their money and are the hardest to bluff—also because they don't like money.

In their private lives, these same loose bettors love to run credit cards to the limit. Based on Rowland's study, they're likely to give little thought to how much they're charging. In fact, spending money is a way to feel better.

Informed Versus Intuitive Play

The way people manage money in their lives is also reflected in how they manage their playing stakes. On one extreme, players will over-manage and seldom enjoy the game. They're too busy fretting over losing any money. They are easy to bluff because their scared money seldom calls a bluff. They're more obsessed with money than playing cards. Such players will only play if the cost to their stakes and the risks are low. They come to the table with a plan and religiously follow it. There's no room for changing betting habits. As a consequence, most other players might often forget that these players are present, since they'll play few, if any, hands. When players want to get them out, they will often just bet or raise.

The opposite of such micro-managing of funds is the player who lacks any plan for betting. These players spend their money on hunches. They'll procrastinate until the feeling moves them. Then they'll bet. They have no system for betting other than their intuition. Like luck, this way of managing money will sometimes bring a windfall. In the long run, though, such players generally end up losing all their money. For this reason, they are hard to bluff. If they don't have a hand, they are apt to call a bluff—not because they don't believe you. Rather, their call is on a hunch that they will outrun you. They often do. So, it's best not to attempt to bluff these players and to play them aggressively when you have good cards.

In their personal lives, such players will fail to balance their checking accounts and are late in paying their bills and taxes. They think that the word *budget* is some kind of a flower that has yet to bloom. They'll skip buying insurance, convinced that life will remain a bundle of roses.

Low- Versus High-Risk Players

Besides betting and managing playing stakes, there are some people who avoid and others who search for stimulation in money. The low-risk player will avoid any kind of stimulation. For this reason they are easier to bluff. This player will avoid confrontations unless he or she is the one with the gun showing up to a knife fight. They're there to play cards, to concentrate, and not to socialize. In fact, if others are enjoying and talking too much, one might hear them complain, "Are we here to play cards, or what?" If they're enjoying playing, they need to notify their face and body for anyone else to know it. Everything about them is designed to stay uninvolved. Their money is precious and they have to be serious about how they're betting. Mostly, they're afraid to fail or lose their money. They avoid not only being social, they avoid all risks. In their personal lives, they won't change jobs and seldom, if ever, move. Change is something that involves too much risk and stimulation for such low-keyed players.

The other extreme from the above introversive player is the extrovert who gets high on risks. This player is there for the excitement. Attempting to bluff this player is just adding fuel to his or her excitement needs. They don't actually care if they win or lose. They enjoy the rush of risking. In fact, I've heard such players say how they just had to raise even though they thought they were beat. It's that one chance in a thousand that they might win that excites them. Then, when they do win, often such players will say, "Is that all there was to it?" These are probably the most superstitious of gamblers. They believe in pure luck aided by rituals. They will wear lucky clothes, get up and walk around the table to ward off bad vibes, and never play without their lucky hats or charms.

Righteous Versus Tainted Funds

Moral attitudes about money are probably the most revealing and the most contradictory. One of the extremes is people who worship their chips. These are the "High and Mighty." They're usually regular players who play a great game. If you ever doubt how good they are, just ask them. They're proud and ready to show it. They also will take pride in the fact that they will lay down a good hand. This makes them fair game for players who are good at bluffing. They like someone to give them a reason to fold and show how good they are by not playing "second best" hands. It's never a good idea let them know when they are bluffed to fold. Why ruin a good thing?

Some will build towers in front of them with their chips. At first it appears that they won all those chips. This is not necessarily so. They'll buy in with a large stake and then display their stockpiles as trophies. Once, I heard such a player say he had to buy more chips when he began losing. He explained, "I just like to have a lot in front of me. It makes me feel like I am ahead." That was actually his "con." He was looking for young pigeons that might want to take a shot at him. So, a large display of chips may act as trophies and may actually be "come-ons" to entice the unsuspecting novice.

These high and mighty players usually do pretty well. However, their worship of money makes losing a very stressful event. When they lose a hand they'll talk for quite some time about how unavoidable the loss was. They don't like to spend money. They like to display it. They believe that money is for the necessities in life. They are not playing cards for recreation. They're there to make more money so they can show how successful they are. Being frugal is their virtue and spending or betting foolishly is a sin. When seeing others betting in anything but a solid way, these players become quite self-righteous about it. They may even get angry if someone bets when they shouldn't have and wins. Such "keepers of the chip towers" are the "parents" at the gaming tables. You'll hear them scolding and moralizing on how others are handling their money.

Then, there are players who seem ashamed to win. They usually have little stakes and will sometimes apologize when they win a pot. Their attitude toward gaming is that they shouldn't be spending any money and they seem ashamed of themselves. "Money is the root of all evil" paraphrases their attitude. They'll bet very cautiously and agonize over losing even a little bit. Yet, they'll come back for more. It's as if gaming is a way for them to feel bad about going out and having a good time. It's much like some people who love to dance, yet feel guilty every time they do. They don't lose much. Yet, they will *not* feel great whether they win or lose. They often have more money than they need and could probably afford more stakes than anyone else playing does. In short, they use betting money to feel tainted. In their private lives they'll be very miserly with money. Having money is their source of safety, and spending seems to deplete their sense of power.

In the final analysis, attitudes about money will influence how a player will bet and manage his or her chips as well as reveal how they think and how willing they are to fold. Some players refuse to ever lay a hand down. These are the players that you must avoid attempting to bluff. "Calling stations" are good when you want to fill up. Just be sure that you have a hand that will be the best at showdown when playing such an opponent. Other than that, don't play rags against them—they may be luckier than you.

Maintenance of Tools

I have seen many players be what my mom referred to as "street angels and house devils." That's an Irish expression that means a person who looks good to others and actually isn't as good as he or she appears. In other words, a devil dressed up like an angel. In poker, though, you will find various disguises. Some players are angels dressed up like devils. Others are devils disguised as angels. Bluffing lends itself to such disguises. So, my dear mom, who never played a game of poker in her life, could spot a person pretending to be better than he or she actually was. She had a blind spot, though, when it came to one of her eight children. I never heard her say anything about, "street devils and house angels." Does that mean that the good kid (the angel) at home could be a devil when Mom's not looking? You bet. That happens a lot in homes and at the poker table.

The ways these things happen in poker are how people are *betting, managing, thinking,* and *folding.* In order to maintain your tools and keep them sharp, it's important to play and get some table time. I know a professional player who handles "dry spells" by playing more rather than less. When he is having a run of bad luck and bad cards, he won't stop playing. Instead, he will go to lower limit games to continue playing—only risking less money during his bad spell. He reasons that it's just a matter of time and by playing lower limit games he can exhaust that time until the bad luck is over. You've heard of chasing your luck. Well, I guess this is more like keeping active while you're waiting for your luck to return.

Others will practice using the Internet and risking no money at all at the "play money" tables. The important thing is maintenance through practice.

Above and Beyond

In going beyond bluffs, we learned the secrets of master communicators. We learned the mysteries of how they tell the ways that people are thinking and making sense of the world around them. We have translated this knowledge, previously reserved for mental health professionals and educators, into something poker players can use. By going beyond bluffs, poker players, who are master communicators in their own right, will now have sharpened the tools in their poker toolsheds.

A poker player is only as good as he is at any point in time. Anyone can beat anyone else at the poker table. That's what makes poker a game that will last. Poker is not a fad, despite the surge of popularity with Texas Hold 'Em because of TV. It was here long before and unfortunately hold 'em has given great games like seven-card stud and draw poker the backseat—for now. Whatever your preference is, poker is played with people. So, whether you are in a game of hold 'em, stud, Omaha, or draw poker, you can use your newfound people skills.

My previous work and research integrated the mental health information about people with their predispositions and life scripts. I demonstrated how people play poker the way they live the rest of their lives. Some are losers, some winners, and some break even and are nonwinners. At the time, poker being such a psychological game, I wondered why there had not been more books about the psychology of poker. The closest was discussing the body language of players. So, I decided to go *Beyond Tells* and described the real power of poker—understanding the players and their various styles of play. From what I have heard, you too have seen yourselves in that book and have learned to understand your opponents better. That book was aimed at players understanding themselves better. True, in studying people, you also learned about your opponents. However, more was needed to be researched about opponents. So, this book gives birth to not only how to improve your poker but how to read your opponents.

I would be surprised to hear that one read would give you all the skills that you will need to read your opponents. To tell when a person is bluffing and when he or she has a real hand. I have written this so that the reader can go back and re-read and practice until those skills are second nature. That's why in this work you will find an index, to facilitate going back and practicing such things as eye movements and what they reveal. How different personality types can be expected to bluff will also be an invaluable tool and will pay for the cost of this book many times. Expect profit from this knowledge. Psychologists have been making money in the form of fees for years on their knowledge of people. Why not poker players who build their people knowledge?

As I said earlier in this book, I am glad that I resolved my dilemma about whether to share some of the mental health secrets of hypnotherapy and Neuro-Linguistic Programing (NLP). That has allowed me to write this book and share with you proven techniques in understanding people. A word of caution is important. Don't go out now and think that you can read minds. These tools will help you to know *how* a person is thinking, not *what* they are thinking. Another caution, associated with this last one. Because you have noticed that a person has looked up to his or her right may let you know they they are contructing pictures they haven't seen yet. It doesn't tell you what they are constructing. They could be imagining the hand they wished they had and are representing to bluff you. They also could be constructing a picture of how you are calling and they are dragging in the pot with their unbeatable hand (the nuts). So, just because you have learned a tool to read whether a person is remembering or creating pictures in their head, be humble enough to realize that you won't know exactly what they are thinking until showdown—if that ever comes. Another final word is that you may have learned about how to pace and then lead other players to improve your bluffs. Just remember this. Be sure that you are leading and that your opponent is not pacing and leading you. After all, your opponents are probably going *beyond bluffs*.

That information is enough to sharpen your game . . . or is it?

I haven't told you the rest of what I know and this book is long enough. Look for the sequel to *Beyond Bluffs*. You have sharpened your tools and even added some new tools to your poker shed of poker skills. We have focused mostly on your opponents this time. Next, we will delve deeper in to what you bring to the table, what you can change, and what you'll have to accept as your God-given gifts.

Now, I invite you to test what you have learned. Go back to the stories in the Prologue and before you read the answers, see if you can figure out who's lying and who's being truthful. The stories have all the information that you need, now that you have sharpened some of your poker tools. Knowing what you now know will also help you with the people in your life—including other poker players, fellow workers, family, and friends.

Epilogue

A Player's Story

There once lived a player who knew a lot
About poker, people and odds.
He knew when to bet, call, and fold; but,
He still could not win a decent pot.

He'd read books and talked to good players
Who knew how to leave with money
Ahead.
He had played for years, and seemed only
Able to draw dead.
The thought of losing again became his
Constant dread.

Sometimes when he'd bet, other players
Would fold.
When he'd get good cards was the only
Times that he would get bold.

When he had a bad hand, he either wouldn't
Play or he'd start to whine about the bad
Cards that he'd been dealt.
He tried the things he read and he imitated
People whose playing he knew was svelte.

Still his game did not improve while others
He knew were getting better and better.
One day he wore a favorite sweater and
He began to think that it was his sweater

That made him play better.
Instead, he was more himself when he wore
His favorite sweater.

His luck didn't last long, even with his
Favorite sweater, he returned to his old
Ways of proper poker play.
He went back to playing like the books said;
He even got good at imitating players
Whose styles brought many pot-pays.

One day, he threw away all his poker books,
And in desperation just sat down and
Began to play like his own person who
Successfully built five corporations.
He paid attention to other people—his
employees and customers, to trends,
And waited for opportunities to invest in
Whatever opportunities were available for
Computation.

He knew how to influence the market, so he
Brought those skills to his poker game.
He was a winner in real life and now by
Being himself at the poker table, he could
Do the same.

He learned to play the game his way and
That led to his opponents having to pay.

—Jim McKenna

Final Lesson . . . This Time

A lot of players will imitate what they read in books or what they see works for other successful players. Poker is the kind of activity that reflects and imitates how players live the rest of their lives. By trying to be somebody you are not, you lose the advantage of being who you are.

As a wise observer once said, "No matter where you go, there you are!" Each player comes with his or her own unique personality and ways to make sense of things. Some are aggressive or passive by nature. At the same time, there are players who by nature are more structured in their approach to the game. Their counterparts are players who are impulsive, prefer long shots, and live on the edge. Many *see* opportunities; others *listen* or have the *gift of gab.* Still there are those whose intuition and *feelings* guide their success. Trying to be a visual thinker when you do your best work with sounds will limit the strengths that you have to be a winner in the game of poker and of life. It's best to discover three things and then build on them to get the most out of your game.

First, respond to the game your way. If you tend to be more structured in your play, it would hurt your game to play like you are a very impulsive or creative player. Just play using your left brain to its fullest. If you are a creative, intuitive person who likes to live a bit on the edge, go for it. That's your way. You have moves that players who rely on their left brains haven't even thought of. Use your creative right brain to its fullest. Of course, it doesn't hurt to exercise the muscles that you haven't developed much. Do it, though, your way.

Second, as we all make sense of the world differently, discover how you organize your thoughts. Do you think about things (including cards) in pictures? Or, are you more intuitive and can read people pretty well? These are strengths that will help your game more than reading how some left-brained player, who retired from playing to write books, plays.

The third weapon that you bring to the table is your ability to figure out how others play and the ways other players think. This knowledge will help you in developing marketing plans to sell your bluffs. It also helps to know when others are trying to sell you junk. If you are imitating the way that others make sense of things, that's pacing and using good communication skills. It's a lot different from trying to be other players. Being a good communicator is a major source of success with people—both in poker and in life.

Appendix A
YOUR TILTING PROFILE

Here are some typical tilt makers. Rate yourself and see how vulnerable you might be to going on tilt and compromising your best game

How much do these things upset you when you are playing in a game like Texas Hold 'Em? Rate each behavior from 1 to 5 as it applies to you.

5—NEVER   4—SELDOM   3—OFTEN   2—FREQUENTLY   1—ALWAYS

1. Another player betting/checking out of turn. — 1. ____
2. A dealer "burning and turning" too soon. — 2. ____
3. Being beat on the river by a hand that should have folded or not been played in the first place. — 3. ____
4. A player with the nuts slow-rolls after you think you've won. — 4. ____
5. Players checking and then raising your bet. — 5. ____
6. Slow-playing and waiting for someone else to do the betting. — 6. ____
7. A player hiding his or her hold cards, resulting in action behind the player. — 7. ____
8. A new player asking players to move and make some room (squaring-up the table). — 8. ____
9. Getting caught bluffing (speeding). — 9. ____
10. Folding and learning you got beat by a player who had garbage for a hand. — 10. ____
11. Runner-Runners (players with weak hands chasing hands with poor odds) who are making their hands. — 11. ____
12. Player/dealer not paying attention ("looking out the window") and slowing down the game. — 12. ____
13. Players who orchestrate long pauses designed to intimidate other players and then call or fold. — 13. ____
14. Playing your hand "perfectly" and still losing the hand. — 14. ____
15. Chasing with good pot odds and not making your hand. — 15. ____
16. Players chasing with total garbage hands and making it. — 16. ____

(continued)

---

17. Dealer failing to control the table.   17. ____
18. Being controlled by a player who's more aggressive
    than you are.   18. ____
19. Plays against common table etiquette, such as
    sometimes chopping the blinds and sometimes refusing
    to when he or she has good cards.   19. ____
20. Another player openly criticizing how you played
    your hand.   20. ____

Add ratings for all behaviors—Total: _____

What your tilting score means

    80–100 You are an excellent player and you handle everyday stress.
    60–80   You can be somewhat controlled and may need to get up
              and take a walk more often when "stuff happens."
    40–60   Don't quit your day job.
    20–40   You are probably the table pigeon and a tilter's delight.
     1–20   Seriously consider getting some anger management help.

Another way to use the profile is to rank-order from 1 to 20 your tilt makers. "1" meaning most often to "20" meaning your least often tilts.

Appendix B
POKER ODDS

For those interested in the poker odds, I have compiled this information from various experts on the Internet. Their websites are included for your reference.

The way to figure odds is taught on: www.texasholdem-poker.com/odds.php. Using this website's method. I calculated the odds of making certain hands on the flop in Texas Hold 'Em. Example 1 is calculating from what you have on the flop. Example 2 speculates on odds of making hands starting with pre-flop odds.

Example 1. Calculating Probability and Pot Odds in Texas Hold 'Em

PROBABILITY AND POT ODDS									
	Two Chances After the Flop			One Chance on the River		POT SIZE NEEDED FOR ONE BET			
After the flop you are chasing:	Outs	% Chance	Odds	% Chance	Odds	$3/6	$6/12	$10/20	$15/30
Open Ended Straight and Flush Draw	15	54	1:2	33	2:1	$12	$40	$40	$60
Trips for a Full House or Quads (River Draw)	10	38	2:1	22	4:1	$24	$48	$80	$120
Flush Draw	9	35	2:1	20	4:1	$24	$48	$80	$120
Open-Ended Straight Draw	8	32	2:1	17	4:1	$30	$60	$100	$160
Trips for a Full House or Quads (Turn Draw)	7	15	6:1	—	—	$36	$72	$120	$180
At Two Over-cards for an Over-Pair	6	24	3:1	13	7:1	$41	$84	$140	$210
At Two Pair for a Full House or Inside Straight Draw	4	17	5:1	9	11:1	$66	$132	$220	$330
At One Over-card for an Over-Pair	3	13	7:1	7	14:1	$84	$168	$280	$420
At a Pair for Trips	2	8	11:1	4	22:1	$132	$264	$440	$660

Appendix C
RANKING HANDS

Ranking Poker Hands

Poker is based on obtaining five cards and having hands that will beat
your opponents. Here are those hands in rank order of the best to the
worst combinations.

- **Straight Flush** (10-9-8-7-6 of the same suit. If the Ace is the highest
  card in the straight then it is called a Royal Flush and is the highest hand
  possible)
- **4 of a Kind** (9-9-9-9-K)
- **Full House** (a 3-of-a-kind with a pair—, 7-7-7-J-J)
- **Flush** (any 5 cards of the same suit—, 3-5-8-10-Q all in hearts)
- **Straight** (any 5 unsuited cards in sequence—, 9-8-7-6-5 unsuited)
- **3 of a kind** (5-5-5-7-Q)
- **Two pair** (3-3-J-J-A)
- **Pair** (K-K-7-9-J)
- **Single high card** (3-7-4-9-A of differing suits.)

Frequency of hand combinations

In a single deck of fifty-two cards there are these possible hands. The
fewer the number of hands, the more difficult it is to get.

Rank of Hand	Number of Hands
Royal straight flush	4
Straight flush	36
Four of a kind	624
Full house	3,744
Flush	5,108
Straight	10,200
Three of a kind	54,912
Two pair	123,552
Pair	1,098,240
No pair	1,302,540
Total number of hands	2,598,960

Check the website: www.freewebs.com/jokerpoker/poker_rank.html for
this and other useful poker information.

Appendix D
PLAYER CHARACTERISTICS SUMMARY

Style	Perception	Quadrant	Use/Avoid	Approach	Notice When . . .	Then . . .
Hunch Player	Emotions	Receptive/ responsive	Benevolent/ autocratic	With caring	Placating others	Reassure and notice person
High Roller	Actions	Aggressive/ responsive	Autocratic/ democratic	Directly	Provoking others	Be direct and excited too
Party Hardy	Reactions	Aggressive/ responsive	Laissez-faire/ autocratic	Playfully	Trying hard and being confused	Be playful and fool around
Loner	Nonactions	Reserved/ receptive	Autocratic/ laissez-faire	Directly	Being strong and quietly suffering	Be direct and suggest time out
System Player	Thoughts	Reserved/ receptive	Democratic/ autocratic	Asking information	Trying to be perfect and overcontrolling	Be logical and clear—tell what's coming next
The Boss	Beliefs	Reserved/ aggressive	Democratic/ autocratic	Asking opinions	Criticizing others' plays	Ask questions and opinions

SUGGESTED READINGS

Alvarez, A. *Poker: Bets, Bluffs and Bad Beats*. San Francisco: Chronicle Books, 2001.

Assagioli, R. *Psychosynthesis*. New York: Penquin Books.

Bandler, Richard, and John Grinder. *The Structure of Magic*. 2 vols. Palo Alto, GA. Science and Behavior, 1975–76.

———. *Patterns of the Hypnotic Techniques of Milton H. Erickson, M.D., volumes 1 & 2*. Cupertino, CA: Meta Publications, 1975 and 1977.

Berne, Eric. *Games People Play*. New York: Ballantine Books, 1964.

———. *Sex in Human Loving*. New York: Simon and Schuster, 1970.

———. *What Do You Say After You Say Hello?* New York: Grove Press, 1972.

———. *Say Yes to Life: Continuing Care Program*. Long Beach, CA: 1998.

Booth, Leo. *When God Becomes a Drug*. Long Beach, CA: SCP Limited, 1998.

Carlson, R. K., and R. T. Brehm. *Understanding Communication Style*. Dallas, TX: Sales Development Associates,

Caro, Mike. *The Body Language of Poker*. Hollywood, CA: Gambling Times, 1984.

———. *Caro's Fundamental Secrets of Winning Poker*. New York: Cardoza, 1996.

Covey, Stephen R. *Seven Habits of Highly Effective People*. Thorndike: G. E. Hall & Company, 1989.

Crossman, Patricia. "Permission and Protection." *Transactional Analysis Bulletin* 5, no. 19 (1966): 152–154.

Custer, R. and H. Milt. *When Luck Runs Out*. New York: Facts on File, 1985.

Ernst, F. H., Jr. "The O.K. Corral: the Grid for Getting-on-With." *Transactional Analysis Journal* 1, no. 4 (1971): 33–42.

Gordon, David. *Therapeutic Metaphors*. Cupertino, CA: Meta Publications, 1978.

Goulding, R. L. "Decisions in Script Formation." *Transactional Analysis Journal* 2, no. 2 (1972): 62–63.

Harris, Amy. "Good Guys and Sweethearts." *Transactional Analysis Journal* 2, no. 1 (1972): 13–18.

Harris, Thomas A. *I'm OK—You're OK: A Practical Guide to Transactional Analysis*. New York: Harper & Row, 1967.

Hill, Ed. "Spread-Limit Seven-Card Stud: Playing on Third Street." *Poker World* 1, no. 2 (1996): 33–34.

James, Muriel. *It's Never Too Late to Be Happy*. Reading, MA: Addison-Wesley, 1985.

James, Muriel and Dorothy Jongeward. *Born to Win*. Reading, MA: Addison-Wesley, 1971.

Jung, C. G. *Psychological Types: The Collected Works of C. G. Jung*. Vol. 6. Princeton, NJ: Princeton University Press, 1971.

Kahler, Taibi. *The Mystery of Management*. Little Rock, AR: Process Communications Management, 1989.

Kahler, Taibi, and Hedges Capers. "The Miniscript." *Transactional Analysis Journal* 4, no. 1 (1974): 26–29.

Lessinger, Matt. *The Book of Bluffs*. New York: Warner Books, 2005.

McKenna, James A. "Stroking Profile: Application to Script Analysis." *Transactional Analysis Journal* 4, no. 4 (1974): 20–24.

———. *I Feel More Like I Do Now Than When I First Came In*. St. Louis, MO: Emily Publications, 1975.

———. *Us: Married, living together, family, friends*. St. Louis, MO: Emily Publications, 1978.

———. "Relationship Obstacles." *Relationships PACT Newsletter* 1, no. 1 (1986): 1–2.

———. *Permission Not Granted: How People Who Were Raised In Crisis-Oriented Families Carry Their Childhood Don'ts into Adulthood*. St. Louis, MO: Emily Publications, 1991.

———. *Beyond Tells: Power Poker Psychology*. New York: Citadel, 2005.

Mellan, O. *Money Harmony*. Washington, DC: Walker, 1994.

Palmer, G. "Script Currencies." *Transactional Analysis Journal* 7, no. 1 (1977): 20–23.

Roberts, S. *The Beginner's Guide to Winning Blackjack*. Van Nuys, CA: Gambling Times, 1984.

Rowland, M. "The Psychology of Money." *Modern Maturity* March–April (1996): 50–54.

Schoonmaker, A. *The Psychology of Poker*. Las Vegas, NV: Two Plus Two Publishing, 2000.

Shiff, Jackie, et al. "Passivity." *Transactional Analysis Journal* 1, no. 1 (1971).

Sklansky, David. *The Theory of Poker*. Las Vegas, NV: Two Plus Two Publishing, 1994.

———. *Hold 'em Poker for Advanced Players*. Las Vegas, NV: Two Plus Two Publishing, 1991.

Sklansky, D., M. Malmuth, and R. Zee. *Seven-Card Stud for Advanced Players*. Las Vegas, NV: Two Plus Two Publishing, 1994.

———. *How to Make $100,000 a Year Gambling for a Living*. Henderson, NV: Two Plus Two Publishing, 1997.

Spitz, R. A. "Hospitalism: An Inquiry into the Genesis of Psychiatric Conditions in Early Childhood." *The Psychoanalytic Study of the Child* 1 (1945): 53–74.

Springer, Sally P., and Georg Deutsch. *Left Brain, Right Brain* (revised edition). New York: W.H. Freeman and Company, 1985.

Steiner, Claude. "The Stroke Economy." *Transactional Analysis Journal* 1 (1971): 9–15.

Thayer, L. *Communication and Communication Systems*. Homewood: Richard D. Irwin, 1968.

Thorp, E. O. *Beat the Dealer*. New York: Vintage Books, 1966.

———. *The Mathematics of Gambling*. Hollywood, CA: Gambling Times, 1984.

Uston, K. *Million Dollar Blackjack*. Van Nuys, CA: Gambling Times, 1993.

Useful Websites

www.JimMcKenna-PhD.com
www.championshipdvd.com
www.freewebs.com/jokerpoker/poker_rank.html
www.texasholdem-poker.com/odds.php
www.gamblingtimes.com/poker_player

INDEX

275